There is a good reason why we have titled this
book *UFO Odyssey*, for an odyssey is an account of
an epic journey that takes the hero from his home
and follows him through a series of extraordinary
adventures, until he returns to his place of origin a
much wiser and nobler person. It seems to us that
the UFO mystery is somehow deeply entwined
with the equally enthralling enigma of what it is
to be human, and we believe that to seek out the
answer to either demanding riddle is to become a
much wiser and more enlightened individual. By
the time we reach our conclusions, we will have
undergone an odyssey of mystery and adventure
that will take us back to our origins as a species,
project us far into the future, and return us to the
present with a much greater appreciation of what
it is to be a human being standing on the edge of
tomorrow.

—BRAD STEIGER AND SHERRY HANSEN STEIGER

By Brad Steiger

IN MY SOUL I AM FREE
KAHUNA MAGIC
ASTRAL PROJECTION
TRUE GHOST STORIES
BRAD STEIGER PREDICTS THE FUTURE
INDIAN MEDICINE POWER
YOU WILL LIVE AGAIN
MYSTERIES OF TIME AND SPACE
ANGELS OVER THEIR SHOULDERS (with Sherry Hansen Steiger)
AMERICAN INDIAN MAGIC: Sacred Pow Wows and Hopi Prophecies
ANGELS AROUND THE WORLD (with Sherry Hansen Steiger)
THE STAR PEOPLE (with Francis Steiger)
THORPE'S GOLD (with Charlotte Thorpe)
ALIEN MEETINGS
FLYING SAUCER INVASION—TARGET EARTH
FLYING SAUCERS ARE HOSTILE
GODS OF AQUARIUS
REVELATION: THE DIVINE FIRE
STRANGERS FROM THE SKIES
THE FELLOWSHIP
THE FLYING SAUCER MENACE
THE NEW UFO BREAKTHROUGH
THE RAINBOW CONSPIRACY (with Sherry Hansen Steiger)
THE UFO ABDUCTORS
WORLDS BEFORE OUR OWN
UFO ODYSSEY (with Sherry Hansen Steiger)*

Edited by Brad Steiger

PROJECT BLUEBOOK**

By Sherry Hansen Steiger

POWER OF PRAYER TO HEAL AND TRANSFORM YOUR LIFE
SEASONS OF THE SOUL

*Published by Ballantine Books
**Published by Ivy Books

UFO ODYSSEY

Brad Steiger and
Sherry Hansen Steiger

BALLANTINE BOOKS • NEW YORK

A Ballantine Book
Published by The Ballantine Publishing Group
Copyright © 1999 by Brad Steiger and Sherry Hansen Steiger

www.randomhouse.com/BB/

Library of Congress Catalog Card Number: 98-093279

ISBN-0-345-42127-2

Manufactured in the United States of America

First Ballantine Books Edition: February 1999

10   9   8   7   6   5   4   3   2   1

Contents

1. Charting the UFO Odyssey   1
2. Earth under Attack   16
3. The Case for Extraterrestrial Invaders   58
4. The Sorcerers' Triumph   92
5. UFO Mysteries Undersea and Underground   116
6. Merry Pranksters from the Magic Theater   137
7. From Heaven Above to Earth Below   169
8. Superscientists from the Stars   189
9. Travelers through Time and Space   206
10. UFO Energy and Our Planet's Mysterious X-Force   230
11. The UFO Experience as Initiation to Higher Consciousness   245
12. Encountering Phantoms between Past and Future   256
     References and Resources   281

1

Charting the UFO Odyssey

As established authors and lecturers in the fields of the paranormal and UFO research, we receive mail each week that brings alleged eyewitness accounts of extraterrestrial beings working side by side with human scientists in advancing our space program. And, we are told very matter-of-factly, not only have our scientists incorporated alien technology into our most advanced cutting-edge aircraft and spacecraft, the extraterrestrial technical wizards themselves continue to work with their human counterparts to see that they get it right.

Many of our informants provide what appear to be authentic credentials and résumés and claim to be personally familiar with the extraterrestrials working at the National Aeronautics and Space Administration (NASA) and other secret underground government facilities. Some of the aliens, we are told, are tall and blond, very human in appearance; they are nicknamed "the Nordics." Others, small with big bug eyes, oversized skulls, and grayish skin, are referred to as "the Grays." And then there are those who look as though they are basically reptilian, a species of highly intelligent serpents.

Such interstellar cooperation is said to have been going on since soon after the UFO crash at Roswell, New Mexico, in 1947. Our scientists would never have been able to get astronauts to the Moon by 1969 if it hadn't been for the technological assistance of the extraterrestrials who were working among them at NASA. And the benefits of alien technology have gradually trickled down to hundreds of civilian applications, from transistors to computers.

Such claims as those made by our many confidential informants go down easy among many UFO researchers and with increasingly large numbers of the general public. But how true are they?

A number of highly respected and serious-minded investigators have made a compelling case for alien involvement in our earth sciences and swear that the proof of their allegations is haunting the skies in the very real embodiment of such formerly top secret aircraft as the Stealth bomber and the ultra top secret TR-3B. The U.S. Air Force may have washed its hands of "flying saucers" when it officially terminated Project Bluebook in 1967, but the enigma that is the UFO has continued to grow in degrees completely unforeseen by its early investigators and debunkers.

Discussions about alien abductions, cattle mutilations, missing time experienced by UFO percipients, the crash site of the alien spaceship near Roswell, and hybrid, mutant children have become staples of late-night radio talk shows throughout the United States, Canada, and Australia. Major and minor television talk shows have all presented their share of sincere men and women displaying mysterious scars that they believe were left on their persons after undergoing bizarre medical examinations conducted by alien doctors.

The ubiquitous oversized skull and black, staring, almond-shaped bug eyes of the Gray has become the Kilroy of the '90s. The artistic representations of the alien Gray adorn not only covers of bestselling books, but T-shirts, bumper stickers, night-lights, Frisbees, necklaces, earrings, candles, jogging socks, ad infinitum. As we write this, there must be at least six television commercials for major national advertisers that employ UFO or alien themes to lure potential customers.

In the summer of 1997, when we were interviewed by a crew from *Inside Edition* for a segment about celebrities who have claimed UFO encounters, we suggested that the UFO itself has become a celebrity, recognizable all over the world—which led us to recall that some years ago, a member of a United Nations survey team with an interest in the UFO mystery claimed that the flying saucer was the single most recognized symbol in the world. In an earlier work, we suggested that the UFO has provided contemporary humankind with a vital, living mythological symbol that communicates directly to the essential self within each person, thus bypassing the brain, evading acculturation, and manipulating historical conditioning. The UFO, then, could well serve humankind as a transformative symbol that has the potential to unite our entire species as one spiritual organism.

MAJORITY BELIEVES THE GOVERNMENT HIDES THE TRUTH ABOUT UFOS

A December 1996 poll conducted by *George*, a magazine of politics and contemporary issues, found that 55 percent of Americans believe that life exists on other planets; 79 percent maintain that extraterrestrials have visited Earth in the last hundred years; and 70 percent are convinced that the government is covering up the truth about UFOs.

In July 1997, in honor of the fiftieth anniversary of the alleged UFO crash at Roswell, New Mexico, CNN/*Time* magazine took a poll that indicated that 80 percent of Americans think the government is hiding knowledge about the UFO mystery. Other interesting data included the assertions that 54 percent believe that life exists outside of Earth; 35 percent expect aliens to appear "somewhat" human; and 64 percent believe that alien life-forms have made contact with humans. Of that 64 percent, 37 percent said the ETs have abducted humans, and 37 percent are certain that they have contacted representatives of the U.S. government.

On June 10, 1998, a followup CNN/*Time* poll revealed that 27 percent of all Americans believe that space aliens have visited Earth and 80 percent believe that the U.S. government is conducting a cover-up of the alien presence.

Texas Monthly (October 1997) reported that when the grandchildren of former president George Bush found out that he had once been head of the CIA, the first thing they asked him was, "Gampy, what did you do with the people from outer space?"

IS OUR KNOWN HISTORY A MANUFACTURED LIE?

Since the majority of Americans learn their history through the dramatic presentations provided by motion pictures and television, it is rapidly becoming generally accepted "history" that a secret branch of the government has conducted a massive cover-up of fifty years' duration so that our human scientists could work unhindered to employ knowledge gained through alien technology to accelerate the pace of human scientific accomplishments. The fact that two separate and independent polls found that as much as 70 percent to 80 percent of the U.S. public believes that there has been an organized government conspiracy to cover up the truth about UFOs demonstrates that such long-held and oft-repeated accusations by thousands of UFOlogists have grown deep roots in the mass consciousness.

The theme of *Dark Skies*, the lead television series in NBC's 1996 Saturday night "thrillogy," was that history as the viewers learned it in school was a lie. One of the "truths" that the series revealed was that in 1947 President Harry S. Truman ordered an extraterrestrial spacecraft shot down over Roswell, after an alien ambassador had demanded the unconditional surrender of the United States. Subsequently, whatever resources could be recovered from the scraps of the demolished alien craft were doled out to various giants of American industry to be freely incorporated into our own technology—and a sinister and ubiquitous supersecret government agency known as Majestic 12 was created to keep an eye on any undue alien interference in our political and social structures.

Before the series progressed toward its early cancellation, regular viewers learned that the aliens had the ability to possess human bodies with their larvae, thus allowing them to pass undetected and to accomplish an incredible number of foul deeds—from the assassination of John F. Kennedy to the conflict in Vietnam, from the murder of certain celebrities to the abuse of recreational drugs. As one satirical wit had it, we might soon have been able to blame those nasty aliens for high cholesterol.

At the 1996 Golden Globe Awards, the categories for Best Television Drama, Best Actor in a Television Drama, and Best Actress in a Television Drama were all won by

The X-Files, in which Agents Mulder and Scully regularly pursue UFOs and declare to an ever-growing audience that "the truth is out there," but it is being covered up by an ultrasecret and exceedingly ruthless government agency.

On June 19, 1998, the *X-Files* motion picture, *Fight the Future*, was released, thus allowing its small-screen paranoia to spread to big-screen multiplexes across the nation. The film became Number One the first week of its release, grossing $31 million. By July 1, *Fight the Future* had grossed $55 million, thus ensuring FBI Agents Mulder and Scully at least one more big-screen adventure to follow.

The millions of movie fans who saw *Independence Day* were thrilled by aliens blowing up half of the nation, and by the world being saved by the skills of the two heroes who managed to pilot the spaceship that a clandestine branch of the government had been hiding in a secret underground base since the Roswell crash in 1947.

The Rock, a recent very popular Hollywood action thriller, lists forbidden knowledge about the Roswell UFO crash among the reasons why the character played by superstar Sean Connery had been unjustly imprisoned for so long without a trial.

In 1997, the hit motion picture *Men in Black* took one of the most sinister aspects of UFO research—the alleged strong-arm tactics performed on UFO witnesses by mysterious terrorists—and transformed it into a special-effects comedy with Tommy Lee Jones and Will Smith portraying agents of a secret government branch that keeps the illegal extraterrestrial aliens who walk among us under surveillance. In the film—as suggested by real-life alleged victims of the Men in Black—any ordinary citizen who might happen to stumble on the truth about the government cover-up has all memory of the experience wiped out by a special brainwashing device.

Sadly, one reason why so many U.S. citizens are convinced that their government is hiding the truth about extraterrestrial contact is that so few of us continue to trust the government after decades of cover-ups and scandals that were eventually exposed. According to a survey conducted by Princeton Survey Research Associates for Pew Research and published in *USA Today* on September 12, 1997, only 6 percent of adults in the United States expressed trust in the federal government.

YOU AREN'T CRAZY IF YOU'VE SEEN A UFO

Another recent study proclaims that people who think that they have seen a UFO or a space alien may be just as intelligent and psychologically healthy as other folks. According to psychologists at Carleton University of Ottawa, Canada, writing in the November 1993 issue of the *Journal of Abnormal Psychology*, "Our findings clearly contradict the previously held notions that people who seemingly had bizarre experiences, such as missing time and communicating with aliens, have wild imaginations and are easily swayed into believing the unbelievable."

Dr. Nicholas P. Spanos, who led the study and administered a battery of psychological tests to a large number of people who claimed to have had UFO experiences, said that such people were not at all "off the wall." On the contrary, he affirmed, "They tend to be white-collar, relatively well-educated representatives of the middle class."

The informed opinion of open-minded psychologists

that an individual may experience a UFO encounter and not be considered crazy will come as no small comfort to those who have suddenly found themselves enmeshed in a maelstrom of bizarre and unexplainable occurrences.

"The thrust of UFO research is into the metaphysical, where things are not always as they seem," researcher John W. White said in a recent issue of a UFO newsletter.

While the public opinion polls tell us that the majority of Americans agree with the *X-Files* mantra "the truth is *out there*" when it comes to naming a place of origin for UFOs, our research has convinced us that a large portion of the "truth" about the UFO mystery is also *within* us and somehow has a great deal to do with who we are as a species.

ARE THE UFONAUTS FRIENDS OR FOES?

Since 1967, we have been distributing various versions of the *Steiger Questionnaire of Paranormal, Mystical, and UFO Experiences* to readers of our books and audiences of our lectures and seminars. We now have the personal reports of more than 22,000 UFO experiences—the good, the bad, and the ugly.

Whoever or whatever our alien visitors may be, it would appear that some of them may be motivated by visions and values consistent with our own most transcendent insights and sacred wisdom. Others seem more concerned with tormenting us and may be the same intelligences who were characterized in ancient scriptures and sacred traditions as diabolic, hostile to our very existence, and intent upon dominating us totally—physically, mentally, spiritually. We are reminded that in Ephesians 6:12 St. Paul spoke of humanity having to struggle not only against enemies of flesh and blood, ". . . but also against the angels, against powers, against the rulers of the world of darkness, and against the evil spirits under the heavens."

According to Roman Catholic scholar Matthew Fox, the number one cosmological question in the Mediterranean area in the first century A.D. was whether or not the angels who were being so frequently reported were friends or foes. With today's maddening mélange of accounts of UFO beings that on the one hand share their advanced alien technology, perform miraculous healings, and offer benevolent guidance and, on the other, conduct cruel abductions, institute sinister genetic experiments, and work to bring about our planet's destruction or enslavement, UFO researchers must ask a similar question in the 1990s: Are the UFO beings friends or foes?

Quite frankly, we consider UFO research to be among the most important work being conducted today, for as we perceive the mystery, it touches all aspects of human endeavor on the planet. And because the global phenomenon that we label "UFO" is so multilayered, so all-encompassing, and so complex, it is also quite likely the most confusing research being conducted today.

A number of years ago, when we were asked by a national publication to name our "favorite theory of UFOs," we listed *seventeen* possible solutions to the UFO enigma:

1. **They Come from Outer Space.** The unidentified objects in our skies are piloted by beings who come from one or more extraterrestrial civilizations. While it seems likely that the space beings have had Earth under surveillance for centuries, the visitors have most often chosen to conduct their activities in secret, perhaps even misleading humankind and deliberately

confusing us for some undetermined reason, such as one of the following:

- They are benign entities that follow a policy of noninterference in our planet's evolutionary development.
- They are indifferent to us as a species, and follow a policy of noninterference because they are dispassionately observing and studying our planet's evolutionary struggles. If Earth should be destroyed for whatever reason, they will probably record the cataclysmic event as an object lesson in self-programmed species obsolescence.
- The extraterrestrial visitors' intentions are basically hostile, and they are in the final stages of conducting important tests that will determine whether they will destroy Earth, exploit it ruthlessly, or totally enslave it. It is they who conduct human abductions and who have made secret deals with certain levels of Earth's governments—agreements that they will soon break with extreme prejudice.

2. **Military Secret Hypothesis.** The entire concept of extraterrestrial spaceships, "invaders from Mars," was created by military intelligence to mask highly classified research being conducted at such bases as Area 51.

- The UFO occupants are actually our own military pilots conducting secret maneuvers with highly classified aerial vehicles based on captured Nazi technology and the work of German scientists brought to the United States immediately after World War II.
- The UFO crew members are terrestrial astronauts conducting secret military maneuvers with classified aerial vehicles based on alien technology re-

covered in the crash of an extraterrestrial spaceship near Roswell, New Mexico, in 1947.

3. **UFOs Are Products of a Secret Society.** Centuries ago, a secret society of alchemists/scientists developed an advanced technology, which they managed to keep hidden in underground or undersea cities.

   - The Secret Ones have been subtly guiding Earth's more intelligent members throughout history, providing "outsiders" with scientific breakthroughs when they deemed human society at large was ready for certain advances.
   - The mighty secret society of alchemists only awaits the appropriate moment to conquer the outside world and to enslave it.

4. **Denizens of the Hollow Earth.** Ancient traditions and folklore have been revitalized to popularize the idea of an underground empire inside our planet, ruled by unpleasant entities who throughout human history have been responsible for an awesome number of our woes—and more recently, for the appearance of UFOs.

5. **Programmed Deceit and Delusion Hypothesis.** A secret branch of our government—perhaps allied with its counterparts in foreign nations—has created the UFO myth for its own nefarious purpose in bringing about a New World Order. The UFOs and their alleged occupants are actually something similar to holographic projections or elaborate special effects. Abductions, impregnations, and mysterious disappearances are all the sinister handiwork of this secret branch of the government—which may be assisted toward its goal by extraterrestrials or by members of an ancient secret society.

6. **UFOs Are Unknown Terrestrial Life-Forms.** The UFOs are previously unrecognized and unidentified life-forms indigenous to the upper reaches of Earth's atmosphere. They may be plasmic, electrical, nearly pure energy forms that have the ability to assume a variety of forms and guises.

7. **The UFOnauts Are Astronauts from Atlantis.** Today's UFOnauts are really the descendants of an ancient civilization on Earth that developed space flight and set about colonizing other worlds at the time when their terrestrial empire was being destroyed by cataclysmic forces. From time to time, the contemporary Atlanteans return to visit the old home planet.

8. **The UFOnauts Are Time Travelers.** The occupants of the UFOs are really our descendants from the future, studying the true destiny of humankind by using the past—our present—as a living museum. They cannot land and openly declare themselves for fear of upsetting the linear flow of history and thus altering the future—their present.

9. **UFOs Come from Other Dimensions.** The UFO entities come not from a physical planet in our solar system or any other, but from an adjacent space-time continuum, actually coexisting here on Earth with us, but on another vibrational level.

10. **Earth Is Haunted by a Planetary Poltergeist.** The UFO phenomenon is the result of some as yet unknown physical law that can at times activate (or be activated by) the unconscious human mind. This law—or energy—might not itself be intelligent, but it would be able to absorb, reflect, or imitate human intelligence.

11. **Projections of Human Beliefs.** The UFOs are a phenomenon of the collective human psyche that changes

to reflect the belief structures of the time. The UFO constitutes a paraphysical phenomenon that is related to the psychological state of the observer.

12. **UFOs Answer a Psychic Need.** Certain of humankind's basic psychic needs tap into psychokinetic and other paranormal energies and fashion images of fairies, holy figures, and UFO beings. The forms that these manifestations assume have been intrinsic elements in the human psyche since ancient times, but they appear modern in that humans perceive them in the context of ideas that the conscious mind has acquired through acculturation.

13. **UFOs Are Archetypes.** UFOs and their occupants are quasi-real objects created by the human collective unconscious. Jungian archetypes surface as the result of energetic thought fields that are accessible to humans through dreams, meditations, and other states of altered consciousness. These archetypes may, in certain instances, be directed by highly evolved entities who seek to influence and guide human affairs.

14. **Actors from the Magic Theater.** UFO manifestations are the result of the "magical" machinations of elves, devas, fairies, and other paraphysical entities who have coexisted with humankind as companion species and appear to participate somehow with us in an evolutionary design.

15. **The Supernatural Hypothesis.** The UFO intelligences are the same entities who are described in the scriptures of so many world religions as angels—both the messengers of God and the Fallen Ones. The entire UFO mystery is actually the continuation of the struggle between the two warring factions of angels

for the souls of humankind. The "signs in the skies" have accelerated as we approach an Armageddon, a great battle between these beings—with the fate of our species in the balance.

16. **We Are Property.** The UFO intelligences express so much concern over this planet because they are literally the lords, the creators of the human species. These superscientists from "somewhere out there" created the major life-forms on Earth and continually hover over it, shepherding their ongoing field project.

17. **We Are Playing the Reality Game.** The UFOnauts are playing a teaching game with humankind in which our concept of reality is being gradually changed. In the teasing fashion of a Zen or a Sufi joke, we are being provoked into a higher consciousness.

There is a good reason why we have titled this book *UFO Odyssey*, for an odyssey is an account of an epic journey that takes the hero from his home and follows him through a series of extraordinary adventures, until he returns to his place of origin a much wiser and nobler person. It seems to us that the UFO mystery is somehow deeply entwined with the equally enthralling enigma of what it is to be human, and we believe that to seek out the answer to either demanding riddle is to become a much wiser and more enlightened individual. By the time we reach our conclusions, we will have undergone an odyssey of mystery and adventure that will take us back to our origins as a species, project us far into the future, and return us to the present with a much greater appreciation of what it is to be a human being standing on the edge of tomorrow.

In our next chapter, we explore the grim reality that

someone or something appears to have placed our planet under attack and that our most paranoid fears about alien invaders have come to pass.

2

Earth under Attack

Although there were scores of encounters with mysterious, unidentified aerial vehicles long before Kenneth Arnold saw "flying saucers" near Mt. Rainier on June 24, 1947, many researchers find it convenient to say that the modern era of UFOs begins with that well-known sighting. However, the date that marks the beginning of the "war of the worlds," the day when Earth first came under attack by alien beings, may be February 25, 1942, when an air raid was conducted over Los Angeles by what many believe to have been a large extraterrestrial craft.

If the alien crew had the capability of monitoring Earth radio transmissions, they should not have been surprised that their presence was greeted with fire from antiaircraft guns. It was, after all, just two months after the sneak attack on Pearl Harbor, and the entire West Coast of the United States was prepared for the likelihood of Japanese bombing raids.

Newspaper articles from that time tell how the Army's Western Defense Command ordered an immediate blackout of the city from 2:25 to 7:21 A.M. Twelve thousand air raid wardens dutifully reported to their posts, and powerful searchlights swept the sky while antiaircraft bat-

teries dotted the heavens with orange bursts of shrapnel—
firing a total of two thousand rounds of twelve-pound
high-explosive shells.

A news photograph depicted a large, round, white object in the center of nine searchlight beams. The unidentified aerial object did not look like any conventional aircraft,
and it was surrounded by bursts of gunfire. Some eyewitnesses described the aircraft as being large enough to
dwarf an apartment house.

Although the U.S. Army steadfastly denied that any
fighter planes were dispatched to counterattack the UFO,
popular radio host Jeff Rense recently spoke to an eyewitness of the Los Angeles air raid who remembered military
aircraft being set on the mysterious craft. Katie, a highly
successful interior decorator and artist, who lived on the
west side of the city, watched groups of fighter planes
strafing the UFO.

"They were shooting at it, but it didn't seem to matter,"
she told Rense. "It was like the Fourth of July, but much
louder. [The fighter planes] were firing like crazy, but they
couldn't touch it." Katie estimated the aerial dogfight
lasted for about half an hour, before the UFO, completely
unscathed, leisurely moved out of sight.[1]

While some UFOlogists have argued that the unidentified aerial craft that visited Los Angeles that night was an
immense Japanese Fugo balloon bomb, the object remained
untouched by intense antiaircraft fire and no bombs fell on
the city. Six people did die as a result of the raid, however,
as shell fragments rained down on homes, streets, and
buildings throughout the Los Angeles area.

U.S. Navy Secretary Frank Knox officially stated that
no aircraft, enemy or otherwise, had been sighted, and he

characterized the Los Angeles raid as a false alarm caused by war nerves. In spite of the official disclaimer, the Western Defense Command at the time insisted that an unidentified aircraft had been sighted and they had not been firing at any mass delusion caused by collective "war nerves." The huge aerial object above Los Angeles had been very real.

The Japanese Fugo balloons were also very real. According to records in Japan examined after the Japanese surrender, Operation Fugo launched more than ten thousand bomb-carrying balloons during the winter of 1944–45. The balloons, constructed of rice paper and assembled by Japanese schoolgirls, were directed into the jet stream that flows from Japan to America's northwest. Almost four hundred balloons exploded in Alaska, California, Texas, New Mexico, and Colorado, causing minimal damage, but killing at least six civilians.

However, no records could be found among Japanese documents of any account of a gigantic Fugo balloon attacking Los Angeles on February 25, 1942. It would also seem beyond comprehension that two thousand rounds of twelve-pound high-explosive shells and several fighter planes could not bring down a floating craft made of rice paper as it moved slowly across the city.

THE "FOO FIGHTERS" OF WORLD WAR II

Throughout World War II, Allied pilots reported being harassed by mysterious round balls of fiery white light that paced their aircraft. These episodes seemed to happen most frequently over the German-French border, and the greatest period of "attack" by these unidentified flying objects occurred from April 1944 to August 1945. Airmen termed these eerie phenomena "Foo Fighters" ("foo" being a corruption of *feu*, the French word for fire), and they reported that the glowing disks seemed to be controlled in an intelligent fashion and appeared to be engaged in missions of reconnaissance rather than warfare.

One B-17 pilot, a veteran of more than fifty missions, remembered encountering the Foo Fighters on many occasions:

> Suddenly they'd be on our wing, six or eight of them, flying perfect formation. You turn and bank; they turn and bank; you climb; they climb; you dive; they dive. You just couldn't shake them. Little, dirty grey aluminum things, ten or twelve feet in diameter, shaped just like saucers; no cockpits, no windows, no sign of life.[2]

When asked if the saucer-shaped mystery craft had ever tried to shoot down any of the Allied airplanes, the pilot replied that, as far as he knew, "when the things finally got sick of the game they would just take off into space and disappear, flying at the most incredible speeds, five thousand miles an hour or more."

Numerous servicemen served as eyewitnesses to the wingless, cigar-shaped mystery aircraft that was attracted to the explosive violence of the invasion of Europe on June 6, 1944. While Normandy Beach erupted in bloody carnage, the Foo Fighter seemed to observe the progress of the invasion for about three minutes before it continued its flight toward the horizon.

A general consensus among Allied airmen concerning the identity of the flying saucers ranged from "more of Hitler's V-weapons" to "something from outer space because they maneuver so uncannily and fly at such incredible speeds."

A former war correspondent claimed that an intelligence officer with the Supreme Headquarters, Allied Expeditionary Force G2 in Paris told him that SHAEF knew about the flying saucers. "They were considered so secret," the officer said, "that they were in the 'eyes only' file. That means you couldn't make a copy of the papers. You want to know something else? Those flying saucers were reported in the closing days of the war over Tokyo as well as Berlin."[3]

BRITISH WORLD WAR II HERO CLAIMS AN ENCOUNTER WITH AN EXTRATERRESTRIAL

Air Marshal Sir Peter Horsley flew Mosquitoes against the Nazis and was decorated for his bravery during the Normandy invasion. He joined the Royal Household in 1949 as a squadron leader and became an intimate adviser to Queen Elizabeth and Prince Philip. In 1973, he rose to the crucial post of deputy commander in chief of RAF Strike Command.

In the autumn of 1997, the seventy-six-year-old British war hero decided to reveal a secret that he had kept for forty-three years. In 1954, he met an alien, a visitor from another galaxy.

According to Sir Peter, he met the mysterious "Mr. Janus" in a London flat, and they spoke for hours about traveling in space and time. When he returned to the flat sometime later, it was empty.

Sir Peter is adamant that the experience was genuine, but other high-ranking British officers think it unfortunate that the public will learn that the man who had his finger on the button at Strike Command was speaking with little green men from outer space.

ROSWELL, NEW MEXICO, JULY 1947:
GENESIS OF THE GOVERNMENT COVER-UP OF UFOS

As with nearly every major case file in the annals of UFOlogy, there are differences of opinion about how, when, where, or why an event occurred, but a tentative consensus has it that on the night of July 2, 1947, a UFO developed mechanical problems—or, in some scenarios, was shot down by U.S. fighter pilots—and crashed on ranchland about sixty miles north of Roswell, New Mexico. Headlines immediately blared that a flying saucer had crashed and that the Air Force had recovered the wreckage; they were just as rapidly transformed into an account that the supposed UFO had actually been a fallen weather balloon.

And thus was born the seed of nearly every UFO-government conspiracy theory that still thrives today. As this rolling stone of alleged deceit and cover-up progressed, it soon picked up the moss of alien bodies hidden away and autopsied by agents of a secret government. From the very moment those initial headlines of a crashed flying saucer were carried around the planet, millions of people have remained convinced that we are being visited and/or invaded by aliens from outer space.

In many ways, 1947 provided the ideal soil for such theories to germinate. It had been almost exactly two years since the Japanese had surrendered and the terrible days of World War II had at last come to a close amid the fire and destruction of the atomic bombs that devastated Hiroshima and Nagasaki. Nuclear power frightened the great majority of Americans, and many doomsayers were finding newly attentive audiences for their grim message that the world was about to come to a fiery end.

General George Marshall's plan to implement a program of recovery for a Europe badly ravaged by war seemed to be in place—and that was good. But the so-called Iron Curtain had dropped, and the free nations of the world had to start worrying about the Communist threat before they had really had time to recover from the Nazi threat—and that was bad. It kept alive the fears that nurture paranoia. Perhaps that was the main impetus for the Central Intelligence Agency (CIA) coming into existence in 1947, supplanting the Office of Strategic Services (OSS) of World War II.

Were those flying saucers that people were seeing in the skies over the United States a last-ditch stand by diehard Nazis hidden away in South America with an arsenal of secret weapons? Or were the bizarre circular craft new weapons created by German scientists who had been kidnapped by the Soviets during the last days of the war? While some laughed at the notion of spaceships, others who seemed to be "in the know" made convincing arguments for an invasion from an extraterrestrial source.

The year 1947 also saw a strange series of balancing acts between ancient days and the space age. The Dead Sea Scrolls were discovered in Wadi Qumran, Thor Heyerdahl sailed on a raft from Peru to Polynesia to prove his theory of prehistoric migration, and Francis Steele reconstructed the laws of Hammurabi from the excavations at Nippur.

As if to prove that our own technologies were soon to be equal to the test of extraterrestrial interlopers, in 1947 a U.S. airplane flew for the first time at supersonic speeds, British race car driver John Cobb established a world ground speed record of 394.196 miles per hour, and Bell Laboratories scientists were perfecting the transistor.

We Earthlings needed such technological accomplishments in 1947 to shore up our confidence in our own intellectual and material resources, for it did, indeed, appear as though our world was under attack by an unknown someone who didn't particularly seem to like us.

THE FIRST OFFICIAL FATALITY IN
THE FLYING SAUCER WAR

According to the majority of UFO historians, who give little credence to the six civilian deaths caused by the Los Angeles UFO raid on February 25, 1942, the first official fatality in the extraterrestrial attack on our planet occurred on January 7, 1948, when Captain Thomas Mantell was killed while in pursuit of a UFO. A combat veteran of World War II, Captain Mantell had participated in the Normandy invasion and had won the Distinguished Flying Cross among other decorations. He was an experienced airman unlikely to be deceived by natural phenomena.

It all began that day when the Kentucky highway patrol called the control tower at Godman Field Air Base to ask if they had anything strange flying over Marysville that might be confusing the residents and causing them to call in reports of unidentified flying objects about 250 to 300 feet in diameter. The control tower replied in the negative, and then a few minutes later, they sighted an object that they were certain was not a familiar aircraft or a weather balloon. At the same time, four P-51s were sighted approaching Godman Field from the south, and the tower radioed a request to flight leader Mantell to take a closer look at the object and attempt to identify it.

Captain Mantell's last words as he was still climbing at 10,000 feet—"It looks metallic, and it's tremendous in size. It's above me and I'm gaining on it. I'm going to 20,000 feet . . ."—set off a controversy that has never abated.

Witnesses said that they saw the P-51 explode in midair. While some could discern no reason for the explosion, others stated that the UFO had disintegrated Mantell's aircraft.

There were rumors of a closed-casket funeral because of mysterious wounds on Captain Mantell's body; there were startling claims that no remains could be found in the wreckage of the P-51. Whatever the truth of the matter, the Air Force found itself dramatically involved in the enigma of the UFO.[4]

UFO RECONNAISSANCE OF OUR MILITARY MIGHT

According to some researchers, UFOs have always exhibited a frank interest in the military aspects of life on Earth. Since the early 1940s, they have been reported buzzing military airplanes in flight, swooping down on naval vessels in midocean, hovering above military bases and rocket installations. Over the five decades since we began paying attention to them, the UFOs have remained consistently curious about Earth's military potential, its nuclear armaments, the space program, and its experiments with new and advanced avionics.

What has changed, according to many students of the mystery, is the attitude on the part of the UFO beings. The curious Foo Fighters that seemed content merely to observe our budding technology from a respectful distance have been replaced by much more hostile and aggressive UFO crews that seem determined to invade our planet.

Zapped by a UFO in Korea

A man who served in the Korean conflict as a private first class in the Army infantry described a chilling encounter when he was with "Easy" Company in what was known on the military maps as the Iron Triangle, near Chorwon. On a spring night in 1951, he and others of his company spotted an aerial object emitting an orange glow coming down across the mountain toward a village. Its passage provoked a burst of artillery fire that didn't seem to affect it.

After about forty-five minutes, the object changed from an orangish glow to a brilliant, pulsating blue-green light and began to approach the infantrymen, who commenced to fire at it with their M-1 rifles. The men were firing armor-piercing bullets, and they could tell by the metallic pings that they were hitting the mysterious aerial object.

Although the bullets apparently did the object no harm,

the craft suddenly became extremely erratic in its movements and its light began to blink off and on.

And then the UFO returned fire, aiming directly at the men a ray that was emitted in pulses or in waves that they could see coming toward them. Later, those who were struck by the ray described a burning, tingling sensation all over their bodies, as though something were actually penetrating their flesh.

The company commander ordered the men into their bunkers, underground dugouts with peepholes. From that safer vantage point, the soldiers watched the UFO light up the entire area—then it shot off at a forty-five-degree angle and quickly disappeared.

Three days later the entire company of men had to be evacuated by ambulance. Many were too weak to walk, most had dysentery, and they all had an extremely high white-blood-cell count which the doctors could not explain.[5]

General Douglas MacArthur Predicts an Interplanetary War

Was that grand old soldier General Douglas MacArthur aware that the citizens of Earth were about to participate in a war of the worlds? And did he attempt to warn the public that a secret government was already engaged in the initial skirmishes with a deadly alien enemy?

As quoted in *The New York Times* (October 9, 1955), MacArthur expressed his sincere concern that the nations of Earth must soon "make a common front against attack by people from other planets." The next war, he warned, would be an interplanetary one.

While addressing the 1962 graduating class at West Point, he stated: "We deal now not with things of this world alone. We deal now with the ultimate conflict between a united human race and the sinister forces of some other planetary galaxy."

Dr. von Braun Warns of "Powers Far Stronger Than We"

Late in 1958, after the peculiar malfunction of the United States' *Juno II* rocket, Dr. Wernher von Braun, the brilliant German-born rocket scientist, was quoted in West German newspapers that the rocket had gone off course as if it had been "deflected." He went on to comment to the press that "we find ourselves faced by powers that are far stronger than we had hitherto assumed, and whose base of operations is at present unknown to us . . . We are now engaged in entering into closer contact with these powers and [soon] it may be possible to speak with more precision in the matter."[6]

Such a statement by Dr. von Braun would lead some researchers to believe that, like General Douglas MacArthur, he was fully aware of the "alien invasion" and that he wished to maintain hope for some peaceful purpose to come from a "closer contact" with the powers that were "far stronger" than the military and scientific experts had assumed.

KEEPING WATCHFUL ALIEN EYES
ON OUR SPACE PROGRAM

Ever since the tragic launchpad fire that claimed the lives of astronauts Virgil (Gus) Grissom, Edward White, and Roger Chaffee inside their capsule in 1967, UFO buffs have accused aliens of causing such disasters to keep Earthlings from moving into their territory. According to those UFO researchers who believe that extraterrestrial beings oppose our intrusions in space, the aliens have also sabotaged the Russian space program. For a vivid example of such interference, they point to the pressure-valve malfunction that killed three cosmonauts in their reentry capsule as they tried to return to Earth after spending a record twenty-three days in space working on the *Salyut 1* space station in 1971.

A Strange Language Interrupts
Astronaut Cooper's Transmissions

During his fourth pass over Hawaii on May 15, 1963, astronaut L. Gordon Cooper's transmissions to Ground Control were abruptly interrupted by a voice speaking in an unintelligible language. NASA officials were both furious and baffled by the unidentified "someone" who had the technology to cut in on the VHF channel reserved for space missions. Linguists who were called in to identify the language of the unwelcome participant in the mission were unable to categorize the speech pattern into any known dialect or to derive any sense from the babble that the NASA technicians had recorded.

It was on that same mission that astronaut Cooper sighted a glowing, greenish disk with a red tail closing in on his space capsule. He was passing over Australia at the time, and personnel at the Muchea Tracking Station rushed outside to take a look at the object for themselves. Over two hundred technicians and scientists clearly saw the UFO, which appeared much larger than Cooper's space capsule.

Although his description of the unknown object was broadcast live worldwide, Cooper refused to discuss the matter further once he was on the ground. In a later interview, however, he did comment that as far as he was concerned, there have been far too many unexplained UFO sightings around the world for anyone to rule out the possibilities of some form of life existing somewhere beyond our own planet.

A NASA Physicist Declares the Skies Are Full of UFOs

On June 7, 1968, when we talked with Lee Katchen, an atmospheric physicist with NASA, he stated that he believed, on the basis of the seven thousand reports that he had examined, that UFOs were extraterrestrial probes.

Careful to emphasize that he was speaking as a private citizen, not as a spokesperson for NASA, Katchen said at that time that UFO sightings were so common that the military didn't have time to worry about them—so they were screening them out.

In 1968, the major defense systems were only worried about Soviet craft approaching the United States. According to Katchen, the North American tactical air defense system employed special filters in their radar network that cut out all unconventional objects or targets.

"Something that hovers in the air, then shoots off at five thousand miles per hour, doesn't interest us because it can't be the enemy," Katchen said. "UFOs are picked up by ground and air radar, and they have been photographed by gun cameras all along. There are so many UFOs in the sky that the Air Force has had to employ the special radar network to screen them out."

Alien Spacecraft Monitored *Apollo 11*'s Moon Landing

Three Russian scientists who were monitoring the historic Moon landing of the *Apollo 11* lunar module on

July 20, 1969, stated that they were not alone in their secret observation. Two alien spaceships were also present
to spy on the U.S. space mission firsthand.

According to Dr. Vladimir Azhazha, Professor Alexandr
Kazantsev, and Dr. Sergei Bozhich, Neil Armstrong told
Mission Control in Houston that two large UFOs were observing them as they landed the module on the Moon's
surface. Buzz Aldrin took pictures of the objects from inside the module as support of his fellow astronaut's report.

The UFOs set down near the Earthlings' module, but
flew away just minutes before Armstrong emerged from
the vehicle on July 21 to make his historic "one small step
for a man . . . one giant leap for mankind."

Maurice Chatelain, a former NASA consultant, has gone
on record confirming the Russian scientists' claims. According to Chatelain, the Apollo 11 encounter with UFOs
was common knowledge at NASA. Armstrong's verbal
report was censored, and Aldrin's motion picture film was
placed in a top-secret repository immediately after the astronauts returned to Earth on July 24.

Gigantic UFO Nearly Collides with
Space Shuttle *Endeavor*

Declaring the incident the most dramatic close encounter
in history, science writer William Kliner stated that he had
obtained a twenty-three-second tape from highly placed
NASA sources that shows the space shuttle *Endeavor* nar-
rowly avoiding a collision with a huge UFO.

According to Kliner, during the September 1997 near-
disaster, Commander David Walker is heard to say that
there is a "bogey" at three o'clock. Then: "God, what is it?
My God, it's coming right at us!"

NASA asks Walker what he has seen, and the astronaut shouts excitedly: "Oh, God! Get back. Move!" NASA asks for an explanation of what is transpiring aboard the *Endeavor*. Walker states: "Where? It's gone! UFO . . . spacecraft . . . huge . . . intelligent . . ." And the tape ends abruptly.

Kliner, who has published hundreds of articles on the U.S. space program over the past twenty-five years, said that he had never before believed in the existence of UFOs and the possibility that extraterrestrials might be visiting Earth. "But now I know better," he said. "Space aliens actually observed our shuttle astronauts as they orbited Earth."

NASA spokespersons have declined to comment, pending the outcome of an investigation "into the source of unauthorized information that might or might not have basis in fact."[7]

UFO ATTACKS ON EARTH'S INHABITANTS

Since the late 1940s, a disturbing amount of evidence has been steadily growing that implicates the UFOnauts in thousands of assaults, murders, abductions, and mysterious disappearances.

UFOs have been cited as the cause of radiation sickness, paralysis, and mental trauma. Some people who have approached alien craft have been seared, burned, even cremated.

UFOs have been sighted pursuing automobiles, attacking homes, and destroying aircraft. Hundreds of reputable eyewitnesses claim to have seen alien beings loading their space vehicles with specimens from Earth, including soil, water, animals, and struggling human beings.

A Beam of Light That Seared Away Human Flesh

Professor Felipe Machado Carrion told of the terrible experience of Joao Prestes Filho, a healthy, robust farmer in the state of São Paulo, Brazil, who was stunned and knocked to the ground when he was struck by a mysterious beam of light from the sky. According to Professor Carrion, the forty-year-old farmer made his way to the home of his sister, where he told his remarkable story to numerous friends and neighbors.

Eyewitnesses later told authorities that at first Filho displayed no trace whatever of any burns, either major or secondary, but within a matter of hours, the once vigorous man began literally to deteriorate before the eyes of his startled friends and family. Although at no time did he complain of any pain, his flesh took on the appearance of meat that had been cooked for many hours in boiling water, and it began to fall in lumps from his jaws, his chest, his arms, his hands. Soon his insides began to show and every part of his body had reached a state of ghastly deterioration.

Six hours after the farmer had been struck by the mysterious beam of light, he was dead. He had not even been able to reach a hospital before he was nothing more than an eye-bulging skeleton with strange, guttural sounds issuing from between clenched teeth.

Police investigation yielded no worthwhile clues. No marks were found at the site where Joao Prestes Filho was struck by the light. But, according to Professor Carrion, there were other sightings of mysterious lights in the sky, lights that performed "capricious and unexpected evolutions in the night skies."[8]

A Deadly Interplanetary Shootout
Leaves a Dying Human

On August 13, 1967, at 4 P.M., Inacio de Souza and his wife, Maria, were returning home to their farm at Santa Maria, between Crixas and Pilar de Golas, state of Goias, Brazil, where he was the manager. When they arrived, they saw a strange object shaped like a basin, only upside down. It seemed to be at least thirty-five meters in diameter, and it had landed not far from their house.

Between the UFO and their home stood three small, hairless men who wore tight-fitting, pale yellow close-meshed clothing. As these strangers watched the approach of Inacio and Maria, they pointed at them with their forefingers and started to run toward them.

Fearing an attack, Inacio shouted to his wife to run to the house. He withdrew his rifle from their vehicle and shot the alien intruder nearest to him in almost the same instant as one of the other beings directed a beam of green light at Inacio's chest. While the rifle bullet appeared to have little effect on his assailant, Inacio was knocked to the ground. Maria returned to defend him, grabbing his rifle and pointing it at their strange attackers.

The little men stood still for just a moment, as if considering their odds, then retreated to their craft, which took off vertically with what sounded to Maria like "the noise of a swarm of bees."

For the next two days, Inacio was nauseated, and he complained of numbness in his entire body. His hands trembled, and he felt as if he were on fire. Maria finally took him to Goiania, where the doctor attributed Inacio's burning sensation to accidental poisoning, most likely from ingesting a noxious plant.

Then Inacio related his incredible encounter to the doctor. Skeptical of such a tale, the physician nonetheless ordered various tests, including a hemogram. The grim results led the doctor to conclude that Inacio had leukemia and estimated that he had no more than two months to live.

The once rugged Inacio suffered a dramatic weight loss, becoming little more than skin and bones. He had pale yellow blots all over his body, and he was in great pain. Believing himself to be infected with some horrible contagion, he told his wife that she must burn his bed, mattress, and clothing upon his death—which occurred less than sixty days after the strange little intruder shot him with the beam of green light.

Searing Flames from the Sky

K.B., a respondent to our questionnaire, told of driving late at night on a desolate stretch of road in Oregon in July of 1963 when he sighted a strange, oval-shaped light high in the night sky. He wrote in his report:

I knew immediately that it could not be a star. It was much brighter than anything else in the sky—including the Moon—and it was moving in a peculiar zigzagging motion. I couldn't really tell how high it was when I first spotted it, but I soon became convinced that it was descending. And as it drew closer to the ground, it began to glow in different colors, first bright red, then blue, then yellow.

Then it seemed to be heading straight for me at just

above treetop level. I didn't know whether to try to run for it or to stop the car and get out.

Before K.B. could decide on either course of action, the UFO, which he estimated to be about sixty feet in diameter, moved over his automobile and seemingly sprayed it with some corrosive material.

"The smell was terrible, burning paint and scorched metal. I had been driving with my window down, and some of the stuff splashed on my elbow. It ate right through my windbreaker and burned my skin. I felt like acid had been dumped on me."

K.B. was only peripherally aware that the UFO had soared off into the night sky. He was now more concerned with staying alive, genuinely worried that the "acid" the glowing object had dumped on his car might dissolve the roof of his automobile and drip through on him.

He decided to make a run for the truck stop that he knew to be about fifteen miles ahead.

"When I pulled into the service area, everyone started yelling and asking me questions about what had happened to my car," K.B. said. "The roof was still kind of smoking, and most of the paint on the top of my car had been scorched off. I had no idea what to tell folks had happened to me. I didn't want anyone to think I was crazy or had been drinking, so I just told everyone that it was all a mystery to me."

K.B. treated his burned elbow with some ointment from the first aid kit that he kept in his car. "The next day when I went to my family doctor to have her check on it, she said that it looked like some kind of chemical burn."

The mechanics at the garage made a similar assessment

about the damage to his car's exterior. "The roof was really scorched, and there were burned-out splashes all over the side and hood. I had them sand the car down and repaint it."

Although neither K.B. nor his automobile was left greatly damaged after the strange ordeal, he still wonders why the UFO attacked him. "I sure wasn't doing anything that it could consider hostile. I was just driving along, minding my own business."

His Peaceful Approach Left Him Nearly Blind

On April 12, 1965, James Flynn, a forty-five-year-old rancher from East Fort Myers, Florida, was on a combination hunting and camping trip in the Everglades when he spotted a large, cone-shaped object that he later estimated to be between thirty and thirty-two feet tall and sixty-four feet wide. The object had three rows of square windows that reflected a dull, yellow light. The area under the vehicle gave off a reddish glow.

Unafraid of the unidentified vehicle, Flynn started his swamp buggy and began to drive the approximately quarter of a mile that separated them. When he was within a few yards of the craft, he switched off the buggy, doused the lights, and began walking toward the edge of the UFO's red circle of illumination. He raised an arm in what he considered a gesture of goodwill.

He was about six feet from the object when a beam of light shot out from under the bottom of a row of windows and struck him on the forehead. He instantly lost consciousness.

When the rancher awakened, he was alarmed to discover that he was blind in his right eye and had only partial vision in his left. In spite of his restricted vision, Flynn could see a circle of scorched ground where the cone-shaped object had been hovering. A number of cypress trees had been burned at their tops.

It was not until he walked into the doctor's office that Flynn faced the startling realization that he had been unconscious for twenty-four hours. However, the doctor was far more concerned with Flynn's loss of vision than he was with his patient's missing time.

Due to hemorrhaging in the anterior chamber, Flynn's right eye had the general appearance of a bright red marble. His forehead and the area around his eyes were inflamed and swollen. He was almost totally blind.

Upon his release from the hospital, Flynn accompanied researchers to the site of his attack. The physical evidence of the scorched cypress and the burned circle of grass was still there—and the Florida rancher was left with cloudy vision in his right eye and a depressed spot of about one centimeter in the skull area above the same eye.

Curiosity Brought Him Scorched Flesh

On May 20, 1967, Steve Michalak was out looking over some land just north of Falcon Lake, Manitoba, when the cackling of geese caused him to look up and see two objects coming from a south-southwesterly direction.

He remembered that the objects were glaring a bright red and one was moving only about ten feet off the ground. And then, to his astonishment, it landed.

Michalak estimated the object to be about thirty-five feet long, eight feet high, with a three-foot protrusion on top. It appeared to be constructed of stainless steel; he was awed by the apparent perfection of workmanship.

And then a door opened. All Michalak could see was a brilliant violet-colored interior. A peculiar whistling noise emanated from within, as if the craft were drawing in air. He watched the grounded UFO for half an hour before he decided to approach it.

As he drew nearer, he could hear voices coming from within the shiny shell. Multilingual, Michalak addressed the unseen occupants in English, Russian, German, Italian, and Polish. At the sound of his voice, the door in the craft's side closed, and the object began to move in a counter-clockwise direction.

Before the UFO took off, jets of heat came from a pattern of holes in the side of the object. These jets delivered painful burns to the Canadian and left him with a seared chest, the remnants of a shirt and an undershirt with a geometrically shaped burn on it, and a hat with a hole burned through it.

UFO Zings Teenaged Girl in Chile

In late February 1997, Maria Amparo Galvez of Puerto Arenas, Chile, was walking home from school when a glowing UFO suddenly appeared above her.

The startled teenage girl turned to run away and "was hit in the back by many small balls of light—flashes that peppered her back."[9]

Maria remembered nothing more of the frightening experience, but she reported that she awakened four hours later in a different location.

INCREDIBLE UFO ENCOUNTERS ON THE HIGHWAYS

His Pickup Truck Was Hoisted by a UFO

In December 1965, fifteen-year-old E.H. of Wisconsin claimed that a UFO actually raised the pickup truck he was driving and deposited it in a ditch. And there was evidence that seemed to bear out his story.

He was driving toward his farm at about 11:45 P.M. when he saw a large, bright light on the road about five miles west and two miles south of town. He said that the object seemed to cover the entire road and as he approached it, the engine and the lights on his pickup truck went out. The object, which had been hovering about six feet above the road, began to rise in the air.

The next few seconds were confused ones for the young man. He remembered that the red interior of the UFO began to glow and that what appeared to be sparks began to shoot out from the underside of the base of the object. He said that he saw "something" moving around inside the craft and that the "something" looked like a man. He is also certain that at this point his pickup began to rise right along with the flying saucer.

The next thing E.H. is certain of is that the truck, which had been headed north, was suddenly in the ditch on the opposite side of the road and pointing south. The teenager had had enough. He jumped out of the cab and started to run the rest of the mile and a half to his parents' home.

When his father returned with him to the spot where the pickup rested, he was unable to budge the vehicle, which was mired in deep snow. He decided to leave the task until morning.

And he also decided to reserve judgment on his son's wild story about a UFO. As well as he could determine from the illumination of his car's headlights, there were no tire tracks in the snow leading from the road into the ditch.

The next morning in the cold light of day, investigators

could find absolutely no trace of any wheel or tire marks leading from the road into the ditch. It all seemed to be just as the teenager had said: something picked up the truck, turned it around, and dumped it in a ditch.

A UFO Took Control of His Automobile

According to Leon W. of Michigan, a UFO took control of his automobile in September 1966 and drove him several miles out of his way. Leon first noticed the UFO when he was driving his girlfriend to her apartment. Both of them described the object as large and blue.

When the object lowered itself a few feet above the ground, Leon drove his car toward it to investigate. The object allowed him to come within a few yards, then it zoomed silently into the sky and disappeared.

Amazed to have witnessed a UFO at such close range, Leon and his girlfriend spent several minutes discussing just exactly what it was that they had seen and comparing their respective impressions of the object.

A short time later, as Leon was driving home from his girlfriend's apartment house, the round blue object suddenly reappeared. "It just seemed to take control," he said. "My car began to pick up speed. The brakes wouldn't work. The doors wouldn't open."

He tried desperately to steer his automobile, but the pressure of his hands on the wheel had nothing to do with where the vehicle actually went. The UFO stayed above his car for several miles, directing its course and speed by some devilish remote control.

When he was at last able to regain control of his automobile, he drove directly to the police station to report the incident. He said that he didn't feel that the police would issue a traffic ticket to the UFO, but it made him feel better to tell someone about the harrowing event.

Mystery Force Transports Couple from Argentina to Mexico

In late May 1968, Dr. and Mrs. Vidal attended a family reunion at the Rapallini home in Chascomús, Argentina, a town located near National Route 2. They had arrived in the late hours of the afternoon, enjoyed an elaborate dinner, then began the eighty-minute drive back to their residence at Maipú, a city in Buenos Aires province. Another couple—relatives and near neighbors in Maipú—decided to leave at the same time; and just a few minutes before midnight, both cars set out on Route 2.

The couple, who remained anonymous, arrived home without incident, but because of their agreement with the Vidals, they awaited the arrival of their relatives before retiring for the evening. After waiting for several minutes, they began to fear that the doctor and his wife might have met with an accident, so they got back into their automobile and began to retrace the route back to Chascomús. They drove the entire eighty miles back to the Rapallini residence without seeing a trace of the Vidals.

In spite of the lateness of the hour, they drove back to Maipú on Route 2, studying every foot of the highway. They had accepted the grim possibility that the Vidals might have overturned on the steep banks, and that, because of the night shadows, the wreckage had gone unnoticed on their first trip back.

Again, a long, late-night drive for nothing. And a visit to the Maipú hospital gained only the information that no accidents had been reported that evening.

Dr. and Mrs. Vidal had vanished without a trace—or so it seemed until nearly forty-eight hours later when Rapallini received a telephone call from Dr. Vidal, who said that he was calling from *the Argentine consulate in Mexico City*. There was an incredulous gasp and an exclamation from Rapallini, then Dr. Vidal continued with an apology that he could not provide any details at that time. Instead, he gave Rapallini the date and hour of their arrival so they might be met at the airport in Ezeiza.

An astonished group of friends and relatives gathered at the appointed hour to meet the flight from Mexico City. The Vidals still wore the same clothing that they had been wearing on the evening of the family reunion and their mysterious disappearance. Mrs. Vidal, the victim of a "violent nervous crisis," was taken directly from the airport to a private clinic.

Although Dr. Vidal said that he had been warned not to issue any public statements about their strange experience, he did relate enough details of their "interrupted journey" to friends and relatives for *La Razón* to piece together the bizarre story.

As everyone knew, the Vidals had left the city of Chascomús a few minutes before midnight and were traveling home on Route 2. They had been listening to the radio, and Dr. Vidal stated that he had been driving at a steady speed that would enable him to keep the tail lights of his relative's automobile always in view.

Then, shortly outside the suburbs of Chascomús, the Vidals found their car enveloped in a dense fog bank. He remembered slowing down, then there was only blackness.

In what seemed to be the very next moment, they were

blinking their eyes against bright daylight. When Dr. Vidal got out of the car, he saw at once that they were on a strange and unfamiliar road—and that every bit of paint had been scorched off the automobile's surface.

When he flagged down a passing motorist to ask where they were, Dr. Vidal was stunned to be informed that they were a short distance outside Mexico City. Somehow, in a manner far beyond their understanding, the Vidals' return trip to Maipú had been detoured to another nation, another continent, several thousand miles away from their destination.

Remarkably, their car's motor still worked, and they made their way to the Argentine consulate in Mexico City, where they gave a full report of their bizarre experience. It was there that a calendar informed them that what had seemed like a few moments of darkness before they awakened to a bright day had been a period of forty-eight hours.

Knowing that their relatives must be desperate with worry and concern, Dr. Vidal called the Rapallini family from the consulate. During their brief stay in Mexico City, the Vidals' automobile was removed to a laboratory in the United States for examination.

According to *La Razón*:

In spite of the halo of fantasy that the story of the Vidals seems to wear, there are certain details that do not cease to preoccupy even the most unbelieving:

The entrance of Vidal's wife into a Buenos Aires clinic; the proved arrival of the couple on an airplane that arrived nonstop from Mexico; the disappearance of the car; the intervention of the consulate; the serious attitude of the police in Maipú in regard to the event; and the telephone call from Mexico to the Rapallini family—which was confirmed by *La Razón*—make all this acquire the status of a matter worthy of being considered in these times of space adventures and fantastic appearances of flying saucers.[10]

A Frightening Near-Abduction in Western Australia

On January 21, 1988, Faye Knowles and her three sons, Sean, Wayne, and Patrick, were driving home to Perth on the Eyre Highway across the desolate Nullarbor Plain in southern Australia. Just before daylight, they sighted a bright white light ahead of them on the side of the highway. As they came closer, they saw that it was a large glowing object hovering just above the road. Sean, who was taking his turn at the wheel, swerved to avoid colliding with the UFO.

To their amazement, they soon passed another car that had a similar bright object directly overhead, apparently pursuing it. Curious, Sean made a U-turn, determined to follow the light and try to gain a clearer picture of just what peculiar phenomenon was taking place around them.

Then, as if the UFO resented being tailed by the Knowleses' automobile, it changed course and headed straight for them. Although Sean spun the Ford Telstar around and brought it to a speed in excess of one hundred miles per hour, the object had no difficulty overtaking them.

That was when the object seemed to settle on top of their car with a loud thud, and the Knowles family began to suffer strange mental torments, as if their "brains were being pulled from their heads."[11] Their two dogs also became agitated.

Wayne shouted at his brother to get off the road, but Sean had already made the horrible discovery that the Ford's steering wheel was under the control of the mysterious object above them. And even worse, the UFO was lifting them—car and all—above the highway.

Suddenly, what had seemed like the beginning of a dramatic, frightening UFO abduction changed scenarios: the object released the Knowleses' car. The Ford dropped an estimated ten feet, hitting the asphalt highway on its right rear quarter, exploding a tire on impact. As soon as Sean managed to bring the car to a screeching halt, the family got out of the car and hid in the brush at the side of the road until the UFO left the area.

INTERRUPTED JOURNEYS

The case of Betty and Barney Hill has become the prototypical "interrupted journey," the classic case of humans abducted, examined, poked, and probed by aliens from another world. Their story has been covered extensively in numerous books and magazine articles, and there has even been a made-for-television movie with James Earl Jones and Estelle Parsons playing Barney and Betty. Any individual with the slightest interest in UFOs will probably already be familiar with the case, but as a brief memory jogger, we will outline the details.

On September 19, 1961, Betty, a social worker, and Barney, a mail carrier, then in their forties, were returning to their home in New Hampshire from a short Canadian vacation when they noticed a bright object in the night sky. Barney stopped the car and used a pair of binoculars to get a better look at it. The light soon showed the well-defined shape of a disklike object that moved in an irregular pattern across the moonlit sky.

Fascinated, Barney walked into a nearby field to get a better look. He could now see it plainly, and he was able to perceive what appeared to be windows—and, from the windows, beings looking back at him. Knowing that he was being watched frightened Barney, and he ran back to the car, got in, and began to race down the road.

Then, for some reason, as if heeding some internal directive, he drove down a side road—where the Hills found five humanoid aliens standing in their path. Suddenly unable to control their movements, Betty and Barney were taken from their car and, in a trancelike condition, led to the UFO by the humanoids.

The sensational details of the Hills' story were recalled only while under hypnosis, for the couple had a complete loss of memory concerning the nearly two hours that they were the selected guests of the UFOnauts. Betty and Barney were returned unharmed to their car with the mental command that they would forget all about their abduction experience. The UFO then rose into the air and disappeared from sight, leaving the Hills to continue their journey home, oblivious to the whole event.

Perhaps the remarkable encounter would never have been brought to light except for two factors: they began to experience strange and disconcerting dreams that they could not understand, and they could not explain the unaccountable two missing hours in their journey home from Canada.

Betty decided to seek the help of a psychiatrist friend, who suggested that the memory of those lost hours would return in time, perhaps in only a few months. But the details of that unexplained "interruption" remained in a troubled limbo of fragmented memories until the Hills began weekly hypnosis sessions with Dr. Benjamin Simon, a Boston psychiatrist.

Under Dr. Simon's guidance, the couple revealed an astonishing pastiche of bizarre physical and mental examinations at the hands of an extraordinary group of medical technicians. The individual accounts of Betty and Barney agreed in most respects, although neither was made aware of what the other had disclosed until later. In essence, both told of being treated by aliens from space in much the same manner as human scientists might treat laboratory animals. Although they had been given hypnotic suggestions that they would forget their experience, their induced amnesia was apparently ruptured when they were rehypnotized.

Much has been made of the Hills' unsolicited alien medical examinations, and their eerie experience has provided the prototype for subsequent alien abductions with their requisite physical and sexual exams. However, in the larger view, the key to the whole event and the single aspect that may be most essential in giving their story credibility is the star map that Betty said she was shown while on board the UFO.

Under hypnosis in 1964, Betty, with little or no understanding of astronomy, drew her impressions of the map with a remarkable expertise that concurred with other, professionally drawn, star maps. As an important bonus, Betty's map showed the location of two stars called Zeta 1 and Zeta 2 Reticuli, allegedly the home base of the space travelers who abducted them. Interestingly, the existence of the two stars was not confirmed by astronomers until

1969—eight years after Betty remembered seeing the star map aboard an alien spaceship. As an added element to intrigue both those who believed in the Hills' interrupted journey and those who did not, the two fifth-magnitude stars, Zeta 1 and Zeta 2 Reticuli, are invisible to observers north of the latitude of Mexico City.

Will They Return for Lois and Her "Key"?

In 1988, Lois, a well-respected Arizona businesswoman, told us of an abduction experience that she had undergone in November 1978.

Lois and her friend Gina were driving from Denver to Phoenix when, while negotiating a lonely stretch of highway, they saw a hitchhiker standing at the side of the road. Although Lois said that she had never before picked up a hitchhiker under any circumstances, she found herself inexplicably slowing her automobile and stopping.

Even at a distance, there seemed to be something decidedly different about this hitchhiker. It was as if Lois knew him—as if she knew he would be standing at the side of the road waiting for her. He was dressed casually in a plaid flannel shirt and jeans. He was so clean-shaven that it was as if he had no facial hair at all. His hair was long and blond, and his eyes were a brilliant sky blue.

He leaned forward toward the window that Gina had opened. "I'm so glad you've come," he said in a soft, musical voice that sounded almost as if he were singing or chanting the words. "We've been waiting for you."

As strange as it seemed, Lois felt as if she had known the man all of her life. Her friend Gina, usually reserved around strangers—especially men—was smiling as though she were greeting an old friend. Neither woman offered any protest when the attractive hitchhiker opened a back door and got into the car.

Lois's memory became very sketchy after the pronouncement that "they" had been waiting for them. She doesn't remember driving her car off the highway. Instead, the car seemed to float toward a large craft that was hovering just above the desert. She does recall the stranger continually calming their apprehensions by speaking to them in soothing, loving tones.

Gina and Lois were separated. The attractive hitchhiker disappeared, and Lois was surrounded by smallish entities with large, staring eyes. Their mouths were straight lines that Lois never saw open, but she seemed to hear voices inside her head.

The entities removed Lois's clothing, and she was told that she must lie on a table so that she might be examined. She obeyed everything without question, as if she had no will of her own.

Throughout her life, Lois said that she had endured a number of physical illnesses. She found the beings' bedside manner no colder than that of the average Earthling physician. "Nothing they did hurt *that* much," she said. "They took some blood, some samples of hair and skin here and there. I was not married at that time and had no children. I had a sense that a lot of tests had to do with my fertility . . . or lack of it."

Lois was given a gown to wear. Her abductors continued to examine her clothing and the items in her purse. She was ushered into a room with a soft couch and a vast window that looked out toward a night sky. "It really seemed as though we were moving through space," Lois said. "It was as if we were traveling to another world."

She had no concept of how long she might have been in that room, staring spellbound at what seemed to be colors and lights swirling past the window. The next thing she remembered clearly was when an elderly bearded man in a robe entered the room. To Lois's perception, he looked like a "regular, normal Earthman." He was a bit above medium height and well proportioned. She was able to remember only snatches of their conversation.

She was informed that she had been taken on board the craft because she was one of them. In answer to her immediate queries of who he was and who the little beings with the big heads were, she was told that she would remember in the fullness of time.

She had been examined, the bearded entity explained, to see if she was well.

"Why do you care about me?" she wanted to know.

"Because you have the key."

"I have a key? What key do I have?"

"You will remember when the time is right."

In what seemed to be the next moment, Lois was waking in her car along a lonely desert road, far from the main highway. Gina was once again beside her. They were both hungry and thirsty. They looked at each other but said nothing.

After the two confused women drove to the nearest town, they discovered to their amazement that *five days* had passed. They hurriedly made telephone calls to friends and family who they knew would be worried about them.

In the years that have passed since their UFO abduction experience, Lois said that she and Gina have seldom exchanged memories of the remarkable alien encounter. "Gina refuses to discuss it at all," Lois remarked. "She re-

gards the whole thing as some kind of high spiritual encounter that should not be denigrated by analyzing it. She
believes that we were blessed and that we should let it go
at that."

Lois remains disturbed by what may actually have occurred during that missing time. And, as she continues to
discover, the psychic residue of the experience has not left
her. Shortly after her marriage, three years after the UFO
encounter, she began to experience poltergeist phenomena
in her home.

"Doors would open and close of their own volition.
Telephones would ring at weird times of the night, and
there would never be anyone there. Lights would blink on
and off. My poor husband went nuts with all these things
happening. He thought he had married a witch."

Lois had periodic dreams of the blond, blue-eyed hitchhiker, who would remind her that she had the "key."

One night when her first child was about five years
old, she awoke screaming, calling out in terror for her
mother. When Lois ran into the child's room, the little girl
sobbed: "Mommy, Mommy, they're in the house and they
want to see you. They say they've come for the key."

Lois swore to us that she had never told her young
daughter anything at all about her abduction experience.
"Yet here was my five-year-old daughter repeating the same
phrase that I had been told directly, that I had the 'key.'
Somehow the beings had contacted my daughter, perhaps
in her dreams, and managed to get her to pass on a message
to me."

After this bizarre contact, the nightmarish physical manifestations in their home became so violent that the family
was forced to move. As an additional tragic effect, Lois's
marriage ended.

Until she made the decision to contact us, Lois said that she had told no one of her abduction experience: "I have kept all this weirdness to myself. I have virtually suffered in silence for all these years. I have undergone a hell because of that experience. I still have no idea what they meant when they said that I had the 'key.' The whole thing has nearly driven me crazy."

A DOSSIER ON THE ALIEN INVADERS

Lois's interrupted journey contains a number of classic elements in UFO contact and abduction cases and includes an interesting, and not uncommon, mix of entities.

First, the two women are stopped by an attractive, almost angelic-appearing hitchhiker, who seems very familiar to them in ways they cannot articulate. Something in the innermost reaches of their psyches is stimulated by the appearance of this pleasant being with his reassuring manner.

Next, Lois and Gina are separated and introduced to smallish humanoids that resemble reptilian or insectlike creatures. It is these beings who perform some kind of physical examination on the abductees.

Finally, a monklike, robed figure is brought into the scenario to offer additional reassurance to Lois that she is unique, a truly significant person, who has just participated in an act that is part of a much grander scheme of future events.

If the invaders in our skies are truly extraterrestrial in origin, would they really look so very much like us? Or do they have the ability to appear in whatever guise best suits their larger purpose?

Just who our uninvited guests might be is perhaps the most intriguing aspect of the UFO enigma.

In May 1998, London's *Sunday Times* published a survey that stated that, of forty-two Anglican bishops, forty (95 percent) believed in the possibility of alien life-forms on other worlds. Thirty-one (74 percent) envisioned that some of those alien beings might be intelligent. Such opinions are at odds with traditional church dogma that dictates that humans are unique in the universe and created in the image of God.

Henry Richmond, Bishop of Repton, expressed a common wish when he said that he would like to think that extraterrestrial life-forms we might encounter would be humanlike, but he acknowledged that we Earthlings might have to adjust our concepts of intelligent life and recognize that even little green men could represent another order of nonthreatening sentient beings.

Michael Turnbull, Bishop of Durham, thought that the discovery of other intelligent beings in the universe could be a positive force that could open our species to the greater wonders of God's creation. While Bishop Turnbull's sentiments express an ideal response to a close encounter with an alien life-form, the truth is that over the past five decades human confrontations with otherworldly beings have created a far greater sense of fear than a sense of wonder.

Since the mid-1960s, when we began speaking with men and women who claimed alien encounters, we have assembled a dossier of the invaders that includes such entities as the following.

Little Gray Men in Green

From about 1950 on, the catch-all designation for alien invaders—is "little green men." Actually, the earliest description of these entities from UFO contactees in the 1950s was really that of beings with gray or grayish green complexions who stood about five feet tall and were dressed in one-piece, tight-fitting green jumpsuits.

The contactees at that time described the creatures as having extremely large heads with big, lidless, staring eyes, usually with slit pupils. Their noses were said to be flat or tiny stubs. Very often, witnesses cited only nostrils, nearly flush against a smooth face. They had no discernible lips.

On occasion, pointed ears were mentioned, but usually witnesses reported that the beings appeared to have no ears at all. The general appearance of the entities suggested some kind of reptilian or amphibian humanoid.

In the jargon of contemporary UFO investigators, these entities have evolved over the decades into the "Grays," the invading aliens most often named in abduction cases. Consistently, however, their smallish size, large eyes, and oversized skulls have invited comparisons with elves and the "wee people" of the past.

The Space Brothers and Sisters

These entities are described as tall (around six to eight feet), blond, light-complexioned, idealized Nordic types. In fact, rather than "Space Brothers," contemporary UFO investigators have renamed them the "Nordics." Back in the 1950s and into the 1960s, these beings claimed that their place of origin was Venus. Now they most often claim to be orbiting Earth in massive motherships.

The Space Brothers and Sisters appear as benevolent,

concerned beings who seek to direct the misguided human species along a more spiritual path. They are also extremely concerned with the environment of the planet and lecture against ecological abuses.

According to many contactees, the Space Brothers and Sisters have participated in miracles and dramatic healings. The obvious historical antecedents of these entities are the appearances of angels.

The Space Sister is often sighted independently of any UFO-like vehicle, and she is sometimes described as being transported to the contactee on a beam of light. Interestingly, the increase in sightings of the Space Sister is coincident with the raising of feminine consciousness throughout the world and the reported appearances of the Great Mother entity and Mother Mary in the last three decades.

The Sinister Brothers of the Shadow

UFO contactees around the world have reported frightening encounters with these very humanlike beings, who most often travel in groups of three. Most often referred to as the "Men in Black," these beings appear as normal-sized human males who frequently seem to have difficulty breathing. They are reported to have pointed chins, thick lips, dark complexions, and unusually long fingers.

Men and women who have been visited by these entities complain of their rude or rough behavior, but on occasion, the Men in Black lapse into silly or farcical conduct. They most often appear to have trouble with our time track and come dressed in outmoded styles of clothing, utilizing colloquial expressions no longer in vogue. The Men in Black, will, in fact, often ask the witnesses to state repeatedly the month and the year of their visitation, as if uncertain just when it is that they have manifested.

Sasquatch

In the mid-1960s, we made a case for the bizarre appearance of a large, smelly, apelike monster in association with many UFO sightings. The big hairy humanoids leave profuse tracks behind them, as well as a vile stench—but when a search party forms to capture the beasts, they appear to vanish into thin air.

In general, small, hairy bipeds are seen adjacent to grounded UFOs, and large creatures are sighted independently of any aircraft. Historically, these entities have been known to the native people for centuries. Whether one calls them Big Foot, Sasquatch, Skunk Apes, or Abominable Snowmen, they appear to be very much a part of the UFO mystery.

The Shape-Shifter

Very often associated with UFO sightings is a type of entity that seems capable of assuming any shape or size. Their one constant characteristic is partial or complete self-luminosity. Their eyes glow brilliantly. They most often have the ability to float or to fly.

The Shape-shifters may display any of the following characteristics (although seldom simultaneously): invisibility to the human eye while being recorded on radar; the ability to fade in and out of the spectrum of visibility; the capability of appearing to evaporate or disintegrate, accompanied by a foul stench; and the apparent lack of significant mass, weight, or density.

*   *   *

In the next chapter we take a closer look at some of these invaders and try to determine just how many of them really come from outer space and how many have been popping in and out of human history for thousands of years.

3

The Case for
Extraterrestrial Invaders

The possibility that the strangers in our skies might be extraterrestrial cosmonauts is the most exciting and appealing of all the theories concerning the true place of origin of the UFOnauts. Even if the ETs have come to invade us, we would have definite proof that we are not alone in the universe. This seems almost worth the possible hazards of hostile alien contact.

In the mid-1960s, very few UFO researchers spoke of paranormal explanations for the flying saucer mystery. The physical "nuts-and-bolts" theorists had a firm hold on the general public's imagination, and respectability in the UFO community demanded strict adherence to the extraterrestrial hypothesis. And even though Brad Steiger had come from the field of psychical research to investigate UFO reports, his treks into the hinterlands to interview UFO contactees from New York to New Mexico had begun to convince him that flying saucers from outer space had landed.

One summer night in 1967, Brad was enjoying a backyard cookout with a group of friends when someone spotted a peculiar, zigzagging light in the night sky. The principal topic of conversation that evening had been the UFO mystery, and now it appeared as though they were about to be the recipients of a command performance.

"That's no meteor or satellite," a sharp-eyed lady said with earnest conviction as she pointed out the object that was moving rapidly in its erratic course.

"And it is certainly no conventional aircraft," confirmed another member of the party. "Look at the way it moves—those right-angle turns."

Within another few moments, this UFO was joined by another lively light in the sky, then another and another. After three or four minutes, Brad and his friends were witnessing an astonishing aerial circus against the backdrop of a midwestern summer's night.

Brad remembers clearly that they all sat spellbound by the remarkable display of impossible aeronautics above them, and then after about fifteen minutes, one of the fellows said that he thought they might get an even better view if they were to drive down by the river.

Three of the group refused to go. They feared that they might be abducted by aliens if they left the safety of the neighborhood and drove to a secluded riverside spot. That left five of the group, and they all managed to squeeze into one car and head for the river.

It was as if a carefully planned aerial pageant celebrating the facile maneuvers of the UFO awaited them. As Brad and his friends stood there in the darkness and kept their eyes skyward, even the hungry mosquitoes could do little to distract them from the remarkable display above their heads.

After a routine of seemingly impossible flight patterns, six rather brightly glowing UFOs hovered opposite each other and appeared to shoot lightning-bolt-like beams of light at their partners.

"Are they exchanging energy or trying to shoot each other down?" someone asked.

No one answered. Who knew? The objects did not seem to wish to destroy one another, for the crackling lightning exchange continued for quite some time at a range so close that they could not have missed one another.

After several minutes of this strange procedure, three of the glowing UFOs descended in a falling-leaf motion downriver. The group watched them closely until the objects dropped below tree level.

Then, from another area even farther downriver, two UFOs began to *ascend* in that same peculiar falling-leaf movement. Once they had attained a certain altitude, however, the vehicles zoomed off at an astonishing speed.

That appeared to signal the conclusion of their performance. The four UFOs that remained within the field of vision suddenly moved quickly off to various positions in the night sky and froze, looking now like ordinary stars.

When the group finally returned to the backyard barbecue, they found their three friends huddled around the dying coals of the grill, greatly relieved that the hardy investigators had not been taken away to Alpha Centauri. Brad and the others had been gone for hours, and the more timid members of the party had never ceased praying for their safety.

No one thought of going home and falling asleep. Brad recalls how they sat in lawn chairs until dawn, discussing over and over again what they had witnessed on that extraordinary evening.

Then, in the full light of a glorious summer morning, one of their members said what all of them had perhaps been silently asking themselves: *"Did we really see what we thought we saw?"*

In the thirty-two years since that remarkable evening, Brad has often stated that he will *know* forever what he saw that night, and he will never forget that astonishing display of UFO maneuvers. But *what* was it exactly that they really saw? Was it truly an extraterrestrial flying circus? Or was it really an airborne squadron of playful elves . . . some unrecognized aerial life-forms . . . some awesome spirit beings or deceitful demons? *What?*

And whatever it is that millions of people have seen for the past fifty years, the most popular theory is still that our visitors originate from some extraterrestrial source.

FOUR ALIENS VISIT A FARM
NEAR THE ADRIATIC SEA

During the week of January 12, 1998, four aliens landed in a UFO on a farm just outside the Croatian city of Šibenik, a port on the Adriatic Sea. According to the newspaper *Vecernji List*, Jako Vrancic, an elderly farmer, well liked in his village and considered by all to be an honest man, encountered four aliens, who had the stature and build of human children.

Vrancic was herding his cattle when the UFO, appearing very much like a household flatiron, landed noiselessly in the pasture. The generous farmer offered to share his lunch with the four beings who emerged from the craft, but they indicated in broken Croatian that they weren't hungry.

After the aliens departed, Vrancic reported the incident and made it quite clear that he felt no fear of the UFO occupants, because he had seen such things on television.[1]

Although the skeptics might argue that the elderly

Croatian farmer had probably been watching too much television—especially science fiction programs featuring alien visitors—there are former military personnel who are ready to blow the whistle and declare that world governments have long been aware that our planet is under close scrutiny by extraterrestrial invaders. Bob Dean, a retired U.S. Army Command sergeant major, is a veteran of twenty-seven years of military service. He was an infantry unit commander in combat in Korea, Laos, Cambodia, and North Vietnam and served with Special Forces in South Vietnam. In the summer of 1963, Dean was assigned as an intelligence analyst at the Supreme Headquarters, Allied Powers, Europe (SHAPE) in Paris, and it was then that he learned things that would change forever his understanding of the true nature of the cosmos.

ASSESSING A UFO MILITARY THREAT
TO ALLIED FORCES IN EUROPE

Dean had been in Paris only a short time when he began hearing intriguing rumors about *The Assessment*, a study begun in February 1961 after fifty large, disk-shaped metallic objects flew in formation over Central Europe. Of course, similar objects had been sighted many times before, but on this occasion the UFOs almost caused the Soviets and the Allies to start shooting at each other—each suspecting the other of launching a full-scale air attack.

Bob Dean told us that he was at last able to see the top-secret document called *The Assessment* for himself. The study ended in 1964, and he was informed that each of the allied NATO countries had received a copy. According to Dean, the classified study reveals that our planet has been under surveillance by extraterrestrial visitors for hundreds or even thousands of years. SHAPE had concluded, however, because of the high level of technology demonstrated, whoever or whatever is behind the circular metallic disks must not be a real danger. By now, deduced the authors of *The Assessment*, if these beings were hostile or malevolent, they could easily have destroyed us, for our military had virtually no defense against their advanced technology. The committee that prepared the analysis could only conclude that the visitors must be watching or observing us— or, based on the growing numbers of sightings, landings, and abductions, planning to increase contact with us.

The huge number of reports detailed in *The Assessment* indicated that the UFOs possess the capability to cloak themselves so they may be seen when they want to be seen and remain invisible when they do not wish to be observed. Although the UFOs were often pursued by Allied fighter planes, the objects made fools out of our most technologically advanced aerial craft.

"They flew rings around us, constantly," Dean said. "It seems to me that it was almost as if the UFOs staged incidents to make the point that they were so advanced that it would be futile to combat them. Yet it seems apparent that they could have wiped us out long ago if that was their intention."

Dean told us of a huge metallic disk thirty meters wide that crashed near the Baltic Sea in a little town called Timmendorf, which was in the British zone. When the investigating British personnel figured out how to get inside the craft, they found twelve alien bodies, all smallish and gray in color.

An aspect of the autopsy report that most intrigued Dean was the determination that all twelve bodies were absolutely identical, as if they had all been cut from the same pattern. "Each of the extraterrestrial entities were 'living systems,' " Dean told us. "Each one possessed a lung system, a blood/circulatory system—yet they had no indication of being either male or female. There was no reproductive system."

According to Dean, the SHAPE report determined that there were four different and separate groups of aliens visiting our planet. Group One was referred to as the "Grays," biological androids or clones, smallish in height with oversized heads and huge, wraparound eyes. Group Two were the humanoids—that is, aliens who were very human in appearance. Group Three was composed of "taller Grays," beings with more humanlike heads, minus the large insect-type eyes. Group Four was considered basically reptilian, with lizardlike skin. Their eyes had vertical pupils, adding to their snakelike appearance. The investigating committee at SHAPE determined that if these four groups were not allied, they did most certainly seem to be aware of one another's existence.

From what Dean could ascertain, there seemed to be no accumulated knowledge in *The Assessment* of the place of origin of any of the four extraterrestrial groups. He did not recall seeing any references to any specific planets, galaxies, or areas of the universe in the documents, which were nearly a foot thick.

Dean did remember clearly that a number of the generals connected with SHAPE appeared quite unnerved by the fact that the Group Two aliens were so humanlike in appearance that they doubted anyone could detect any superficial differences. "If one of them sat next to any of us in a restaurant, dressed as we are, no one could possibly tell the difference," Dean said. "That fact so affected the generals that they wondered if these extraterrestrials could be walking the halls of SHAPE undetected—or anywhere else among us for that matter."

ROSWELL, NEW MEXICO: JULY 2–4, 1947

When we began active UFO research in the early 1960s, we would have been hard-pressed to have found six serious UFOlogists who placed a great deal of credence in the alleged crash in July 1947 of a flying saucer on a ranch located about sixty miles north of Roswell, New Mexico. The stories of a UFO that had experienced some kind of mechanical problems and nosedived into the desert, along with rumors of diminutive alien corpses found nearby, had been largely dismissed by all but the more stubborn true believers.

Every once in a while, though, stories would surface about the infamous Hangar 18 on Wright-Patterson Air Force Base that was said to hold the remains of the crashed Roswell flying saucer and the refrigerated corpses of the alien bodies discovered alongside the spaceship. We grimly recall one night in Los Angeles in the early 1970s when we were led from telephone booth to telephone booth, driven by the promise of being shown indisputable proof of the truth of the Roswell incident. Our mysterious informant, allegedly a secret government insider, insisted that he must know we were not being followed, so we were directed from one ringing telephone booth to another, like characters in a B spy movie, to pick up our new instructions. After a few hours of this, we abandoned the unproductive quest as another unfortunate aspect of UFO delirium and allowed the next telephone booth to ring on and on until our alleged informer got the message that he was now playing the game all by himself.

But today, in the 1990s, those once-controversial pieces of debris and the bodies of two to five extraterrestrial crew members retrieved by Major Jesse Marcel have been amalgamated and elevated into the very cornerstone of UFO mythology—and Roswell, New Mexico, has become the Mecca, the Graceland, for flying saucer buffs all over the world.

According to Major Marcel's memory, around 1980, he, as intelligence officer for the 509th Bomber Group, had been ordered to take a top-security unit to the ranch of Mac Brazel and collect the fragments of some aerial craft that had crashed on the land. Major Marcel and his crew discovered a strange, seemingly weightless material, broken into pieces that ranged in length from four or five inches to three or four feet. A number of the weird fragments were marked with some kind of hieroglyphics. The men brought back as many pieces of the material as they could gather to Roswell Army Air Field Base.

On July 8, 1947, Walter Haut, public affairs officer at Roswell, issued the press release stating that the Army had discovered the debris of a crashed flying saucer. The news that the Army had a downed saucer in its possession created a sensation. However, after the flying saucer fragments were shipped to Brigadier General Roger Ramey at the 8th Air Force at Fort Worth, Texas, the bits of an extraterrestrial craft were immediately transformed into the scraps of a collapsed high-altitude weather balloon. Although reports of retrieved alien bodies never made it into any military release in July of 1947, accounts of eyewitnesses having seen between two and five nonhuman corpses soon entered the UFO literature.

General Ramey is said to have silenced the story of the Air Force collecting flying saucer fragments, but retired General Thomas DuBose, who at the time of the Roswell incident was a colonel and a chief of staff to Ramey, recently told quite a different story. According to DuBose, the military investigators had no idea what Major Marcel had sent them, but then the word came down from Air Force headquarters that the story was to be "contained."

"We came up with the weather balloon story, which I thought was a hell of a good idea," he said. "Somebody got [a weather balloon], ran it up a couple of hundred feet and dropped it to make it look like it had crashed—and that's what we used."[2]

Lewis Rickett, who in 1947 was a master sergeant and counterintelligence agent stationed at Roswell air field, was among those military personnel who had actually been present at the crash site. "It was no weather balloon," he recalled in 1994. "The fragments were no more than six or seven inches long and up to eight to ten inches wide. They were not jagged, but curved and flexible. They couldn't be broken."[3]

Gathering Eyewitnesses Who Remember the Day the Aliens Died

Nuclear physicist and government cover-up enthusiast Stanton Friedman firmly believes that a UFO exploded in the area in early July 1947 and that the retrieved bits and pieces were shipped off to Wright Field [now Wright-Patterson Air Force Base] in Dayton, Ohio. He denies the official pronouncement that Major Marcel and his crew found only a downed weather balloon at the crash site. He also dismisses the theory that the debris was that of a crashed Japanese Fugo balloon bomb. It is Friedman's contention that Walter Haut, on direct orders from base commander Colonel William Blanchard, prepared the official press release that initiated the military conspiracy to conceal the truth of a crashed UFO from the public.

Some years ago, Friedman and author-researcher William Moore claimed that they had interviewed more than 130 men and women who had firsthand knowledge of the UFO crash at Roswell. By now, Friedman and other researchers who have made the Roswell crash the Holy Grail of their personal quests have located dozens more alleged eyewitnesses to the strange goings-on in July of 1947.

Friedman argues that Major Jesse Marcel was familiar with weather or military balloons and that he certainly would not have mistaken such ordinary and familiar debris for that of a downed alien spaceship. Nor would any of the military personnel or civilian witnesses have confused the alien bodies at the crash site for misshapen human remains.[4]

If It Was Only a Weather Balloon, Why Were Witnesses Being Silenced?

When Kevin Randle, a former captain in Air Force intelligence, began to investigate the Roswell legend, he wondered why the military had sought to silence civilian witnesses if all the fuss was only about the debris from a weather balloon. As he looked deeper into the Roswell story, he began to unearth substantial evidence that supported civilian claims that military representatives had visited the homes of witnesses and threatened them. Randle also maintains that the crash of the aerial object actually occurred on July 4, 1947, for it was on July 5 that Mac

Brazel visited Sheriff George Wilcox and reported the strange discovery that he had made on his ranch the day before.

Randle has determined that most accounts of eyewitnesses speak of five alien bodies found at the impact site north of Roswell. Additional evidence indicates that four corpses were transported to Wright Field and the fifth to Lowry Field to the USAF mortuary service. There are, however, numerous secondary accounts that maintain that one of the aliens survived the crash and was still alive when Major Marcel and his retrieval unit arrived on the scene. Some UFOlogists believe that as late as 1986 the alien entity was still alive and well treated as a guest of the Air Force at Wright-Patterson.

Randle and his associate, Don Schmitt, told of a March 1991 interview with a granddaughter of Sheriff George Wilcox who stated that not only did her grandfather see the fragments of the UFO crash, he also saw the little space beings. According to the woman, he had described the creatures as having gray-colored skin and large heads. They were dressed in coveralls of a silklike material. She also added that her granddaddy thought one of them was still alive. Later, she said, gruff and humorless military men visited her grandparents and warned them that they, their children, and their grandchildren would all be killed if they ever told anyone what the sheriff had seen at the crash site.

Randle and Schmitt located one Frankie Rowe, who had been a child of twelve at the time of the flying saucer crash. Her father, a lieutenant with the local fire department, told his family at dinner one night that he had seen the remains of "some kind of ship." He went on to state that he had also seen two peculiar bodies in bags and a third being walking around the crash site in a daze. He said that the creatures were only about the size of ten-year-old human children. If extraterrestrials were that size, he observed, people on Earth had nothing to fear.

Frankie Rowe also claimed to have been present one day at the fire station visiting her father when a New Mexico State Police officer was showing the firemen a strange piece of metal that he confessed he had confiscated from the flying saucer crash site when no one was looking. To the astonishment of all present, the trooper tossed the material onto a table, where it "unfolded itself in a fluid motion," looking very much like water flowing.

Everyone had a turn examining the alien metal, even Frankie, who remembered being able to crumple the material into a ball: "I couldn't describe what it felt like, because it didn't feel like I had anything in my hand. It didn't make a sound like aluminum foil or anything like that. It was thinner than the foil [from gum wrappers]."[5] After a while, some of the firemen got out knives and torches and tried to cut or burn the material. None of them could damage it in any way.

Then, according to Ms. Rowe, a group of military men arrived at their home and told her family that they knew all about the demonstration that she and her father had witnessed in the firehouse. The apparent leader of the men "didn't mince any words." He told them that if any of them ever talked about the incident again, the entire family would be taken out in the desert and no one would ever find them again.

Researchers Randle and Schmitt also located Glenn Dennis, who had been a Roswell mortician in 1947 and who had "blundered" into the army hospital on the night that the alien bodies had been recovered. According to Dennis, a "nasty red-haired officer" warned him that if he ever spoke to anyone about the crash or the alien corpses, "they will be picking your bones from the sand."[6]

A Convincing Account from a Roswell Mortician

In the November 1994 issue of *The American Funeral Director*, Glenn Dennis recalled the telephone conversation that he had with the mortuary officer at Roswell Army Air Base on Tuesday, July 8, 1947, when he was asked if he could provide three- or four-foot-long hermetically sealed caskets. An hour later, the officer called back to ask Dennis how to handle bodies that had been exposed out in the desert for four or five days. In each instance, Dennis was told the officer was asking about a "hypothetical" situation.

A short time after the peculiar telephone calls, Dennis had an opportunity to visit the base when he was called upon, in his capacity as an ambulance driver, to transport an injured airman to the base hospital. As he drove past two field ambulances, he looked into their open back ends and saw an enormous amount of a silvery, metallic material, two chunks of which were curved at the bottom in the manner of a canoe. He also noticed that the pieces were covered with odd markings, which he assumed were some kind of hieroglyphics.

Dennis stated in the article that he was a familiar figure at the air base, even accepted as an honorary member of its Officers Club. On this occasion, however, when he approached an officer unfamiliar to him and asked if, judging by the piles of silvery metallic material, help was needed with air crash victims, the man shouted at him to leave the base at once.

While he was leaving, two MPs grabbed him and brought him to the red-haired officer who warned him that somebody would be picking his bones out of the sand if he ever shot his mouth off about seeing the peculiar material.

As the MPs were escorting Dennis back to his hearse-ambulance, they met a female nurse in the hallway. The nurse, with whom he was well acquainted, held a towel over the lower part of her face, and Dennis at first thought that she had been crying. Alarmed by his presence, she told him to leave at once before he was shot.

Dennis indicated his two-man armed escort and said that he was leaving the base. As he was being ushered rudely down the hall, Dennis saw two men who also had towels over their noses and mouths.

The next day, the nurse called the funeral home and arranged to meet Dennis at the Officers Club. There she told him that a flying saucer had crashed in the desert and the Army had recovered the bodies of three dead aliens. When he had encountered the nurse and the two men, whom she identified as pathologists from Walter Reed Hospital in Washington, D.C., they had been performing an autopsy on the aliens. Until the bodies were frozen, she said, their smell had nauseated the medical staff.

Dennis said that the nurse became extremely emotional while describing the smallish beings with large heads and big eyes, and he thought it best to take her back to the nurses' quarters on base. He never saw her again. At first he was informed that she had been transferred to a base in England. Later, he was told that she had been killed in an airplane crash.

The Air Force Closes the Case with a Special Balloon and Falling Dummies

The United States Air Force chose June 24, 1997—the fiftieth anniversary of Kenneth Arnold's sighting in Washington State—to conduct a special Pentagon briefing to announce the release of its answer to the Roswell ruckus, *The Roswell Report: Case Closed.* In its explanation of the mystery, the Air Force claimed the alleged flying saucer fragments were pieces of a balloon that was used in Project Mogul, a highly classified intelligence-gathering operation that had been instituted immediately after the end of World War II to spy on the Soviets and to monitor their efforts to build nuclear weapons.

The alleged alien bodies seen near the Roswell crash site were actually artifacts from an Air Force project begun in 1953 during which the dummies were dropped from high altitudes in order to test parachute effectiveness. Civilian witnesses saw Air Force personnel collecting the dummies and mistakenly believed that they were seeing military units retrieving alien corpses. The six-year discrepancy between the Roswell event and the dummy dropping was officially explained as "time compression," that is, the witnesses became confused about the actual time reference and compressed their memory of the Roswell UFO crash in 1947 and their recollection of the smashed dummies in 1953 into the same scenario.

In Kevin Randle's opinion Project Mogul, though highly classified, does nothing to explain the events on the Brazel ranch. "There is too much testimony from too many firsthand witnesses. When all the data are examined, it is obvious to all that Project Mogul is inadquate as an explanation."

SOCORRO, NEW MEXICO: APRIL 24, 1964

On April 24, 1964, in Socorro, New Mexico, policeman Lonnie Zamora was pursuing a speeding car north on U.S. 85 when he heard a roar and saw flames in an isolated area where a dynamite shack was located. He decided to abandon the chase and drive to the spot where he believed an explosion had occurred.

After he had traveled a little-used road through an unpopulated area full of hills and gullies and arrived at the site, Zamora saw what he at first thought was an overturned automobile standing on its end. At this point he was about 800 feet away from the scene of the supposed accident. He saw two figures in coveralls, whom he assumed to be the occupants of the upended car.

Later, Zamora would state:

Thought some kids might have turned over. Saw two people in white coveralls very close to the object. One of these persons seemed to turn and look straight at my car and seemed startled—seemed to quickly jump somewhat. At this time I started moving my car towards them quickly, with an idea to help. The only time I saw these two persons was when I had stopped . . . to glance at the object. I don't recall any particular shape . . . or headgear. These persons appeared normal in shape—but possibly they were small adults or large kids.[7]

Zamora radioed headquarters to report the accident, then proceeded to drive closer to the automobile and its occupants. When he was about 150 feet from the gully, he stopped his patrol car to continue on foot.

By now he could clearly see that he had found something far more bizarre than an upended automobile. He saw a white egg-shaped object supported on girderlike legs that had smoke and flame issuing from its underside. He heard a loud roar and feared the object was about to explode. He turned and ran to shield himself behind the patrol car, bumping his leg and losing his glasses on the way.

> It was a very loud roar . . . Not like a jet . . . It started at a low frequency quickly, then the roar rose in frequency and in loudness—from loud to very loud . . . Object was starting to go straight up—slowly up. Flame was light blue and at bottom was sort of orange color.[8]

Crouching behind the patrol car and shielding his eyes with his arm, he watched the object rise to a point about fifteen to twenty feet above the ground. The flame and the smoke had ceased swirling around the object, and Zamora could see a design on its side. The markings were red and shaped like a crescent with a vertical arrow and horizontal line underneath. The UFO remained stationary for several seconds, then flew off in a southerly direction following the contour of the gulley.

Within minutes, Sergeant Chavez of the New Mexico State Police arrived in response to Zamora's earlier radio call. He saw no object, but he did take notice of some slight depressions in the ground and some burned brush in the area where Zamora had sighted the object.

The Air Force sent investigators from their project office at Wright-Patterson Air Force Base in Ohio. The investigation disclosed the following facts:

> There were no unidentified helicopters or aircraft in the area. Observers at radar installations had observed

no unusual or unidentified blips . . . There was no evidence of markings of any sort in the area other than the shallow depressions at the location . . . Laboratory analysis of soil samples disclosed no foreign material or radiation above normal . . . Laboratory analysis of the burned brush showed no chemicals which would indicate a type of propellent. . . .[9]

In a report of the Socorro case to arch UFO skeptic Dr. Donald H. Menzel, Dr. J. Allen Hynek, scientific consultant for Project Bluebook, the U.S. Air Force's official investigation of UFOs, wrote:

I wish I could substantiate the idea that it was a hoax or hallucination. Unfortunately, I cannot. I have talked at length with the principals in the sighting, and unless my knowledge of human nature is utterly out of phase, I would feel that [Lonnie Zamora] is incapable of perpetrating a hoax. He is simply a good cop . . . he resented the whole thing because it prevented him from getting his quota of speeders that day. He is not imaginative, sticks solidly to business, and is far from talkative. . . .

Major Quintanilla [Air Force officer in charge of Project Bluebook] is convinced that the Socorro sighting is neither a hoax nor a hallucination, but he feels that perhaps some sort of test object (war games, etc.) might have been going on. However, there is no record of such an event though he has tried to track this down through White Sands, Holloman Air Force Base, and a few others. I would like to go along with the hallucination idea if it weren't for the marks and burned patches . . . I have the word of nine witnesses who saw the marks within hours of the incident, who tell me that the center of the marks were moist as though the topsoil had been freshly pushed aside.[10]

BENTWATERS/WOODBRIDGE ROYAL AIR FORCE BASE, U.K.: DECEMBER 26–28, 1980

Christmas week of 1980 was quiet for the servicemen stationed at the Bentwaters base in England. Although the base was on British soil, Bentwaters was staffed primarily by U.S. military personnel, and it, together with nearby Woodbridge base, was designated a NATO base to be equipped with the most modern jet fighters.

On December 26, just after 9:45 P.M Greenwich Mean Time, several mysterious lights were sighted in the skies moving northward from Portugal toward Germany, then on to the southern English counties of Kent and Sussex. All along the objects' northern route, there were many witnesses, both human and technological, as radar operators monitored the UFOs. Then, when one of the objects crossed the English coast and appeared to "land" in Rendlesham Forest, near the strategic NATO military bases of Bentwaters and Woodbridge, tracking was lost.

Several members of the Bentwaters security force formed a patrol and entered Rendlesham Forest, where they found neither a crashed aircraft nor a fire, but a strange, glowing object that was hovering just above the forest floor. The members of the patrol described the object as metallic and triangular, several meters across, with a bank of blue and white lights.

And then, as bizarre as it might seem, the men seemed to become mesmerized by the mysterious object. One of the servicemen insisted upon attempting to enter the hovering craft, which was said to be about the size of a compact automobile. Although his fellows restrained him from actually making contact with the vehicle, he claimed to receive a telepathic message from occupants in the interior of the object, who told him that they would return on the following evening.

During the next two nights, more than fifty witnesses would become involved in what has come to be known as the Bentwaters Incident, a UFO case that many investigators consider more substantial than Roswell because of the close encounter that occurred between U.S. military officers and alien beings.

Airman First Class Larry Warren, who was just nineteen at the time of the incident, was stationed with the 81st Security Police at Bentwaters-Woodbridge. He had been on leave in Germany during the onset of the mysterious invasion of the base, and hadn't been informed about the strange lights that had landed just outside the base on the two previous evenings.

In his lecture presentations and in personal conversations, Warren tells how he had just returned for duty to his command post when he was told to jump into the back of a pickup truck. In the front seat sat a lieutenant and a sergeant and in the back with Warren were other personnel of his rank or lower.

Warren recalled that when they entered Rendlesham Forest it was as if they were entering a vacuum. "Things were unusually silent. Nothing felt right."

When they reached a clearing, the men were asked to maintain radio silence, though Warren could hear considerable chatter coming in over the airwaves from other military personnel stationed in various positions throughout the forest. The group of airmen walked about a mile into a farmer's field within Rendlesham Forest until they were told to set up a number of battery-operated lights.

Warren next noticed that just over a slight rise was a strange mist that seemed to have some kind of definition to it. The peculiar fog bank was about fifty feet in diameter.

There were flashbulbs going off and movie and video cameras taking pictures. Warren saw British police officers, U.S. and U.K. armed forces personnel, and a few civilians.

Then a red light came in from the direction of the North Sea and exploded over the cluster of fog on the ground. As if by magic, the fog bank was replaced by a machine of some sort. Warren found it difficult to give a detailed description of the object as it changed its shape depending upon the angle from which one looked at it. It seemed to shimmer with light that created a kind of rainbow effect, and there were tubes and pipes protruding from its surface.

Later, Warren remembered that some of the personnel there said that there were symbols on the UFO. "I don't recall," he said. "It was very hard to look at it directly. You could best see this device with your peripheral vision, then you could see its shape, but otherwise it would just distort."[11]

At this point, a staff car arrived and several officers got out. None were in uniform, but Warren recognized Lieutenant Colonel Gordon Williams, wing commander of the 81st Tactical Group. A glowing, bluish gold ball of light came from the UFO, hovered about one foot off the ground, then moved slowly and deliberately toward the group of officers. The glowing ball stopped about ten feet away from the craft, and Warren could distinguish three smallish beings within the light.

"They were living nonhuman beings, and they didn't

come out of a hatch," Warren recalled. "They were just there, separate from this *thing* on the ground. I'm really reticent to say 'craft,' because I don't quite know what it was—but it wasn't built in Detroit, I assure you."[12]

Very slowly—and to Warren's eye, somewhat nervously—Lieutenant Colonel Williams left the other military men and walked toward the entities until he stood about five feet from them. For a period of time, the wing commander looked down at the beings while they stood looking up at him. Although he could not hear any conversation, Warren firmly believes that Lieutenant Colonel Williams and the aliens communicated with one another.

Warren remembered later that some of the witnesses to the incredible event ran away. Others reacted "very intensely to the presence of the craft and the beings." Warren thinks that he stayed in the woods for about forty-five minutes, but he contends that everything became rather hazy after the appearance of the aliens.

The next day, all military personnel who were present at the site were warned to remain silent about what they had seen. They were made to sign papers and were debriefed in an underground facility. Bluntly, the men were told to keep their mouths shut, and they were reminded that "bullets were cheap" if anyone decided to talk.

In 1996, Larry Warren and Peter Robbins coauthored *Left at East Gate: A Firsthand Account of the Bentwaters-Woodbridge UFO Incident, Its Coverup and Investigation*. It is Warren's hope that the book will encourage other airmen who were present that night to come forward to tell what happened on that incredible evening in Rendlesham Forest.

ABDUCTED BY EXTRATERRESTRIALS

While such incidents as those at Roswell, Socorro, and Bentwaters-Woodbridge are offered as evidence that the alien invaders have arrived, the accounts of missing time and abductions by extraterrestrial medical teams bring home a particular kind of fear to the common folk of Earth.

Terror and Missing Time for Three Kentucky Women

During the night of January 6, 1976, three Kentucky women, known to their friends and neighbors as being of the highest moral character, were abducted by a UFO crew and put through a torturous ordeal that lasted for more than an hour. Forty-eight-year-old Elaine Thomas; Louise Smith, forty-four; and thirty-five-year-old Mona Stafford, who all lived in or near Liberty, Kentucky, were returning home from a late supper around 11:30 P.M. when they saw a disklike object as big as a football field. The object appeared to be a metallic gray, with a glowing white dome, and a row of red lights around the middle. The women could also see three or four yellow lights underneath the craft.

Suddenly Louise Smith, who was driving, screamed that she no longer had control of her automobile, which accelerated to eighty-five miles per hour. At that point the three women lost consciousness for the next eighty minutes.

Later, under hypnosis, Elaine Thomas remembered that she had been placed on her back in a long, narrow incubatorlike chamber. There were small, dark figures standing near her that she estimated to be about four feet tall. One of them placed a blunt instrument against her chest that caused her a great deal of pain. Something that she could not see encircled her throat. Each time she tried to speak, she felt as though she were being choked. Frightened, she believed that the small humanoids were going to suffocate her.

During the hypnosis session, Louise Smith recalled being in a hot, dark place. Something had been fitted over her face, and she begged whoever had covered her eyes to let her see where she was. When her captors complied, however, she immediately closed her eyes in terror at the frightening appearance of the humanoids and the bizarre environment in which she found herself.

Mona Stafford remembered lying on a table in what seemed to be some kind of operating room. Her right arm was pinned down while three or four figures in white gowns sat around her. Mrs. Stafford said that at one point it felt as if her eyes were being pulled out of her skull. At another time, her stomach had been blown up like a balloon. She also reported that a number of aliens pulled at her feet, then bent them backward and twisted. She remembered that she finally screamed out that she couldn't take any more of their torture.

Such painful details as these were revealed later under hypnosis. The only thing that the three friends knew for certain the night of their abduction was that they arrived at Louise Smith's home at 1:30 A.M. They should have been there around midnight. They had lost one hour and thirty minutes.

Mrs. Smith complained that her neck hurt. When Mona Stafford examined it, she saw a strange red mark like a burn that had not blistered, about three inches long and an inch wide. Elaine Thomas's neck had the same type of mark on it. Frightening memories of having seen a huge UFO began to flood back into their minds.

The three frightened women called a neighbor, who had them go into separate rooms and draw what they thought the strange UFO had looked like. The three drawings were very much alike.

Although the peculiar burn marks disappeared in about two days, the three women still could not account for the missing time—nor could they recall more about that night than having seen a UFO overhead and Louise Smith screaming that she could not control her rapidly accelerating automobile.

Only after a number of sessions with Dr. Leo Sprinkle, a professor of psychology, an accomplished hypnotist, and an experienced UFO investigator, did the women recall the details of their abduction. In his opinion, it would have been impossible for the women to have faked their reactions of extreme horror and pain. He also said that their ordeals during the time of their abduction were similar to reports given by other UFO abductees.

"The Most Amazing Case of All":
Sex on Board a Flying Saucer

There are currently numerous accounts in circulation of human-alien sexual interaction during abduction experiences; one of the earliest of such reports came from Brazil and was originally published in the magazine *O Cruzeiro*. Dr. Olvao Fontes, one of the original investigators of the incident, stated that the abductee, Antonio Villas Boas, was a twenty-three-year-old farmer near the town of Francisco de Sales in the state of Minas Gerais.

Antonio and his brother Joao first saw the UFO one

night through Antonio's bedroom window. Light from the object penetrated through the slats of the shutters and shone down between the tiles. Antonio described it later as resembling the light of an automobile headlight shining downward.

About nine days later, the strange lighted object seemed to focus on Antonio for a second time as he was plowing a field. Again his brother witnessed an aerial light shining so brightly that it hurt his eyes.

On the next night, October 15, 1957, Antonio was plowing alone when an egg-shaped object came at him and hovered over his tractor. A few minutes later, when the object landed, Antonio observed three metal legs being lowered to support the weight of the craft on the plowed soil.

Antonio admitted that he was frightened and had begun to run when four or five occupants emerged from the craft. One of them grabbed his arms, but he managed to wrench himself free. He had not gone far, however, when three other beings got hold of his arms and legs and lifted him off the ground.

The young farmer was a well-muscled man who said later that his abductors were about his height (five-foot-four) and strength. In his deposition, he protested that under ordinary circumstances he could have come out on top in a one-to-one encounter.

Antonio screamed for help as the weird kidnappers carried him toward the egg-shaped craft. His shouts seemed to arouse the beings' curiosity, for they stopped and studied his facial expression each time he made a sound.

Once inside the vehicle, Antonio was brought to a brightly lighted room. Two of the UFOnauts retained their hold on his arms while others gathered around him, apparently discussing their catch. Antonio later told Dr. Fontes that the aliens' speech sounded to him like a series of doglike barking noises.

After the beings had finished their verbal analysis of Antonio, the young farmer was stripped naked despite his protests and his struggles. Deciding that it would go easier on him if he complied with their wishes, he permitted himself to be thoroughly examined.

He remembered clearly that a chalice-shaped flask with a nozzled tube was applied to his chin, and some minor surgery was performed that left a scar still visible to Dr. Fontes four months after his abduction. Antonio also recalled that another tube was applied to his side, and he saw his blood slowly entering the chalice until it was half full. After that withdrawal was completed, the aliens bled him again from the opposite side of his chin, leaving Antonio with two facial scars.

Antonio later recalled that the beings were dressed in tight-fitting coveralls made of a thick but soft gray cloth. There was no clear separation between the snug coveralls and the shoes, which were strangely turned up at the toes. The coveralls continued right up to the neck, where they joined a helmet of the same color. Three round, silvery tubes emerged from the helmet and ran backward and downward, curving in toward the ribs.

His abductors wore five-fingered gloves at all times, and on each crew member's chest Antonio remembered a round shield, which from time to time gave off a luminous reflection.

When the beings at last finished their ostensible medical examination of Antonio, he was left alone to rest on a couch. He had not lain there long before he became aware that a gray smoke had entered the room from some tubes protruding from the walls. The smoke had a disagreeable, suffocating odor, and Antonio was forced to relieve his nausea by vomiting in a corner of the room.

After a few more minutes, he began to breathe easier and the nauseating odor seemed less offensive. The door to the room opened, and a well-proportioned and totally naked woman walked in to join the young farmer on the couch. In spite of the stressful bloodletting and skin sampling that he had just endured, Antonio was embarrassed to find himself responding to the alien woman's frank sexual advances.

Later, Antonio told Dr. Fontes and other investigators that the beings must have somehow doused him with an aphrodisiac to have made him enter into a rapid sexual union with the alien woman. He described her as having large blue eyes that seemed to slant outward, a straight nose, high cheekbones, a nearly lipless mouth, and a sharply pointed chin.

After the sexual act had been consummated, an alien male entered the room and barked to the woman. Before she left, she turned to Antonio and pointed to her stomach and to the sky.

Antonio's clothing was returned, and the alien male indicated that he should get dressed. It was clear to Antonio that his abductors were finished with him.

The next day, Antonio became ill. His eyes began to burn and a series of sores broke out on his arms and legs. In the center of each of the sores was a little lump that itched. Two weeks later, his face became speckled with yellowish spots.

Gordon Creighton, a former British consulate officer in Brazil, subsequently offered a few observations regarding the Antonio Villas Boas incident, labeling it "the most amazing case of all." He noted that the male aliens who left the craft to abduct Antonio wore helmets with pipes coming from a device located on their backs. The female, who did not leave the UFO, wore no such device, presumably because she never left the aliens' controlled environment. Antonio did survive inside the craft, but . . .

> Let us not forget that he did have an attack of violent vomiting. . . . Does this perhaps mean that their atmosphere, although disagreeable to us, can nevertheless be tolerated by us, and is not fatal? That, by contrast with this, our atmosphere is impossible for them?
>
> In such a case, would not the obvious solution be to breed a mixed race, a new race which would have inherited some of our characteristics, including our ability to live in a mixture of 80% nitrogen and 20% oxygen? A new race, in brief, which is destined to live here, and to populate the vast uninhabited areas of Brazil?[13]

An interesting, albeit unsettling theory. Yet if the seduction was part of an alien program of interbreeding, then that implies that they brought one of their women whose egg is ready to be fertilized to an Earthman for insemination. And if that is what they did, then we really cannot be talking about an *alien species* at all, for if pregnancy is to start during a sexual act, the male and female must be of the same species.

Either we have met the aliens and they are us—or they are somehow our counterparts in another dimension of time and space.

Or maybe the whole alien abduction phenomenon is

something else altogether. A something else very ancient and very familiar.

In 1994, researchers at a major U.S. university asked 697 people chosen at random five questions designed to ascertain whether they might have had experiences associated with UFO abduction. Intrigued that 3.4 percent of the sampling gave responses to questions regarding sleep paralysis, missing time, and sensations of flying through the air that seemed representative of the abduction phenomenon, two experts interpreted the results as indicating the possibility that 8.7 million Americans have been abducted by extraterrestrials.

On the other hand, James Pontillo's study of alien abductions involved an examination of the long history of encounters with demons, witches, fairies, and other entities and led him to conclude that there was no evidence to indicate that alleged alien abductions had any objective reality.

"It is apparent that alien abductions are the continuation of an ancient ongoing cycle of religio-mythic beliefs," he stated. "The 'seed events' consist of routine medical and gynecological procedures, hypnagogic and hypnopompic (sleep-related) imagery, and causative traumas such as sexual assault. These events are then reconstructed in accordance with historical and cultural precedents as well as modified by modern-day medial influences. The driving force behind this creation of abduction accounts lies in the extensive use of hypnotic recall in unsupervised investigations conducted by Extraterrestrial Hypothesis proponents."[14]

UFOs, ESP, and the Power Within Us

We do believe that there is an objective reality to some abduction cases. We maintain, however, that this reality is quite different from the experiences that many abductees and UFO researchers insist occurred.

The abduction phenomenon seems to be a modern adaptation of the mystical voyages to the fairies' Middle Earth magical kingdom or the classic incubus-succubus exploitation of human sexuality. Even the much vaunted "scars" and "markings" displayed by the abductee as physical proof of the experience have their antecedents in the so-called "witches' mark" left by Satan after he had claimed his own during a Black Sabbath.

Flying saucers and shields, glowing orbs and chariots, the appearance of grotesque entities, the unexplained mutilation of livestock, and a wide variety of alien life-forms stalking humans or walking among them can be found in the supernatural traditions of all cultures throughout all of human history.

Claims of teleportation, clairvoyance, telepathy, and miracle healings after a visitation by a heavenly being or after contact with an extraordinary entity who arrived in a glowing orb are familiar phenomena dating back to the earliest of our planet's civilizations, and were standard fare in global folklore long before the modern era of flying saucers began in 1947.

On June 30, 1998, the Society of Scientific Exploration of Stanford, California, announced that it had sponsored a nine-month study of UFOs staffed by a nine-member panel of physicists and astronomers from such institutions as the German Aerospace Center, the University of New Mexico, and France's University of Bordeaux. Such an independent review of the UFO mystery by an interdisciplinary group of scholars is the first of its kind since 1968. Although the panel of scientists did not find hard evidence that convinced its members that extraterrestrial intelligence was visiting Earth, it did concur that the UFO enigma in general contained enough unexplained and unusual phenomena to merit careful exploration.

The late author-publisher Ray Palmer devoted his entire life to an exploration of the strange, the unusual, the unknown. He was cofounder of *Fate* magazine and the editor-publisher of *Flying Saucers* and *Search* magazines. Once, in a private conversation with us, he expressed his opinion that the ultimate answer to the UFO mystery was to be found on our own planet, rather than some extraterrestrial source.

"I think the truth behind such things as UFOs and ESP could force the scientists, the clergy, the AMA, and the educators to revise most of their cherished concepts of what makes the universe tick," he said. "I believe that there is a basic reality behind the UFOs and paranormal phenomena. I believe these things have a common place of origin— an area not commonly concerned with the five senses— something within each of us. Perhaps those who harnessed this power in the past became the 'masters' who could control time, space, and physical matter.

"When it comes right down to it, we really don't know much about ourselves. But people sense that such things as UFOs really do exist."

We certainly do not rule out the extraterrestrial hypothesis altogether, and we most emphatically believe that there is an intelligence at work behind the UFO mystery. In the next chapter, we explore the increasingly popular theory that an ancient terrestrial occult society developed an advanced society thousands of years ago and has been utilizing the UFO as a means of steadily working toward global domination—a New World Order—with or without the alliance of extraterrestrial entities.

4

The Sorcerers' Triumph

Some years ago, a former naval intelligence officer told us that he had seen certain government documents that proved to him that UFOs are real and that an official cover-up had been set into motion. His subsequent research into the UFO enigma convinced him that certain terrestrial secret societies had been interacting with UFO intelligences for thousands of years.

Our informant is not alone in his conviction. An increasing number of UFO investigators firmly believe that certain secret societies and government agencies behind our terrestrial power structures have been communicating with alien intelligence and receiving guidance from them. Some theorists go so far as to declare that every major improvement in our culture, our science, our technology, literally every major turn that humankind has taken through history has been because of this behind-the-scenes alien manipulation.

Principal among these secret societies and perhaps the group most often named as the conduit for alien control of world governments is the Illuminati, a secret society supposedly founded in 1776 by a German law professor named Adam Weishaupt. However, persistent researchers claim to have traced the history of the Illuminati back to the ancient Temple of Wisdom in Cairo.

As we can see in this 1876 quote from Benjamin Disraeli, British prime minister, the concern over interference by secret societies in the affairs of government was considered very real long before our present-day paranoia: "The governments of the present day have to deal not merely with other governments, with emperors, kings, and ministers, but also with the secret societies which have everywhere their unscrupulous agents, and can at the last moment upset all the governments' plans."

If, as the argument goes, an ancient secret society of alchemists and/or superscientists developed a technology that they managed to keep hidden from outsiders, the matter in perpetual debate is whether the Secret Ones are benevolently guiding us to a time when they may share their accomplishments more openly or whether they await the appropriate moment to conquer the entire world.

MYSTERIOUS ADVISERS WHO MOVE IN AND OUT OF HUMAN HISTORY

Helvetius, the grandfather of the celebrated philosopher of the same name, was an alchemist who labored ceaselessly to fathom the mystery of the "philosopher's stone," the legendary catalyst that would transmute base metals into gold. One day in 1666 when he was working in his study at the Hague, a stranger attired all in black, as befitted a respectable burgher of North Holland, appeared and informed him that he would remove all the alchemist's doubts about the existence of the philosopher's stone, for he possessed such magic.

Helvetius decided to humor the man, who appeared very simple and modest in his demeanor. The stranger immediately drew from his pocket "a small ivory box, containing three pieces of metal, of the colour of brimstone, and extremely heavy." With those three bits of metal, he told Helvetius, he could make as much as twenty tons of gold.

The alchemist examined the pieces of metal "very attentively," and seeing that they were very brittle, "he took the opportunity to scrape off a small portion with his thumbnail."

Helvetius then returned the three pieces of metal to his mysterious visitor and entreated him to perform the process of transmutation before him. The stranger answered firmly that he was not allowed to do so. It was enough that he had verified the existence of the metal to Helvetius. It was his purpose only to offer him encouragement in his experiments.

After the man's departure, Helvetius procured a crucible and a portion of lead, "into which, when in a state of fusion, he threw the stolen grain he had secretly scraped from the philosopher's stone. He was disappointed to find that the grain evaporated altogether, leaving the lead in its original state."

Thinking that he had been made the fool by the mad burgher's whimsy, Helvetius returned to his own experiments in attaining the philosopher's stone.

Some weeks later, when he had almost forgotten the incident, Helvetius received another visit from the stranger. "Please do explain further the process by which you *pretend* to transmute lead," the alchemist goaded the man. "If you cannot do as you claim, then please leave me at once."

"Very well, I shall show you that that which you most

desire does truly exist," the stranger said, consenting to perform a demonstration of the philosopher's stone for the skeptical Helvetius. "One grain is sufficient," he told the alchemist, "but it is necessary to envelope it in a ball of wax before throwing it on the molten metal; otherwise its extreme volatility will cause it to vaporize."

To Helvetius's astonishment and his boundless delight, the stranger transmuted several ounces of lead into gold. Then he permitted the alchemist to repeat the experiment by himself, and Helvetius converted six ounces of lead into very pure gold.

Helvetius found it impossible to keep a secret of such immense value and importance. Soon the word of the alchemist's remarkably successful experiments spread all over the Hague, and Helvetius demonstrated the power of the philosopher's stone in the presence of the prince of Orange, and many times afterward, until he had exhausted the supply of catalytic pieces that he received from the mysterious burgher.

And search as he might, Helvetius could not find the man in all of North Holland nor learn his name. And pray as he might, the stranger never again visited Helvetius in his study.[1]

HIDDEN BENEFACTORS OF HUMANKIND— OR POTENTIAL SLAVEMASTERS?

Down through the centuries, very mysterious beings have appeared at certain moments in human history and provided convincing demonstrations that "impossible" inventions *are* possible. The "respectable burgher of North Holland" appeared "modest and simple" to the alchemist

Helvetius. The black-garbed stranger did not appear to be alien or the least bit unusual in his appearance. It was his incredible knowledge that startled and inspired the alchemists of Helvetius's day, and though these learned and determined men never did acquire the philosopher's stone that would transmute lead into gold, they did fashion the seeds of the science of chemistry that has accomplished so many transmutations of the human environment and the human condition in the last three hundred years.

Out of the smoky laboratories of the alchemists, Albert le Grand produced potassium lye, Raymond Lully prepared bicarbonate of potassium, Paracelsus described zinc and introduced chemical compounds in medicine, Blaise Vigenere discovered benzoic acid, Basil Valentine perfected sulfuric acid, and Johann Friedrich Boetticher became the first European to produce porcelain. We can but wonder if they, too, received visitations from mysterious black-garbed burghers.

While each of the above is an important discovery, there are rumors that lying amidst the musty pages of certain ancient alchemical laboratories there are recorded experiments with photography, radio transmission, phonography, and aerial flight. Throughout the Middle Ages and the Renaissance, there were many scholars who claimed that they had received late-night visits from mysterious members of a secret society that had accomplished the transmutation of metals, the means of prolonging life, the knowledge to see and to hear what was occurring in distant places, and the ability to travel across the heavens in heavier-than-air vehicles.

Numerous European occult societies have been at least partially molded around the belief that a secret society centuries ago achieved a high level of scientific knowledge that they carefully guarded from the rest of humanity. According to these occult groups, certain men of genius in ancient Egypt and Persia were given access to the records of the advanced technologies of the antediluvian world. Many hundreds of years ago, these ancient masters learned to duplicate many of the feats of the Titans of Atlantis.

The decision to form a society within a society may have been based on the members' highly developed moral sense and their recognition of the awesome position of responsibility that the discovery of such applications of ancient knowledge had placed upon them. They may have decided to keep their own counsel until the rest of the world had become enlightened enough to deal wisely with such a high degree of technical accomplishments.

From time to time, the secret society may decide the time is propitious to make one of its discoveries known to the "outside world." Such intervention in the affairs of humankind is usually accomplished by carefully feeding certain fragments of research to "outside" scientists whose work and attitude have been judged particularly deserving. When these scientists accomplish the breakthroughs in their research, they credit the success of the experiments to their own diligence, and the secrecy the society prizes so highly is maintained.

On the other hand, the secret society may feel little or no responsibility of any kind to those humans outside of their group. They may be merely biding their time until they turn the great mass of humanity into their slaves. For hundreds of years, certain scholars have worried about global conspiracies being conducted in secret by such groups as the Knights Templar, the Rosicrucians, the Vril, the Thule, and the Illuminati—who may all be waiting until the propitious moment to achieve complete world domination.

Some students of the history of alchemy have stated that crumbling, yellowed records of the alchemists remain in dusty libraries—more than 100,000 ancient volumes written in a code that has never been sufficiently deciphered. If certain master magicians, disciples of the Titans, individuals of exceptional intellect, power, and wealth, actually did achieve a high degree of technical accomplishment several centuries ago, then they could very well be responsible for a good many of the strange and mysterious vehicles seen in our skies. And if alien life-forms apprehended their advanced technology at the end of the previous century, then they might have established an alliance with the society of humans that easily appeared to be the more advanced and worthy to receive the benefits of their extraterrestrial superscience.

THE MARVELOUS AIRSHIP OF 1897

The year was 1897. Many of the world's most learned men and women were filled with pride over a host of new technological accomplishments. Science had gone about as far as it could go, and it was poised confidently on the brink of the twentieth century.

To list only a few of the most notable inventions and discoveries:

In 1893, Karl Benz and Henry Ford built their first four-wheeled automobiles.

Thomas Edison's Kinetoscope (1889) was among the first practical systems of cinematography, and in 1895, Louis and Auguste Lumière presented the first commercial projection. In that same year, Wilhelm Roentgen discovered X rays, Marconi invented radio telegraphy, and Konstantin Tsiolkovsky formulated the principle of rocket reaction propulsion.

In 1896, William Ramsay isolated helium, Ernest Rutherford accomplished the magnetic detection of electrical waves, and Henri Becquerel discovered radioactivity.

The Royal Automobile Club was founded in London in 1897, and cars were going faster every year.

There were as yet no heavier-than-air aerial vehicles to occupy the efforts and the interests of potential aviators, and a good number of brilliant scientists of great reputation doubted that it was aerodynamically possible to build such a flying machine. The future of balloon transport seemed promising, and gondolas could be attached to carry passengers. With all the other marvels of science, how could anyone bemoan the lack of heavier-than-air flying machines?

And yet, in March of 1897, a bizarre aircraft, often described as resembling a cone-shaped steamboat, was seen flying across the United States and later throughout the world. (Note that the German Count Ferdinand von Zeppelin did not build his famous airship until 1898.)

Could some anonymous American inventors have beaten Count von Zeppelin to the drawing board with a much more impressive vehicle, a forerunner of the modern passenger plane? Or did extraterrestrials disguise their spacecraft as composite, awkward, bulky terrestrial vehicles and their UFOnauts as conventional humans in order to survey the planet undetected as aliens? Or was a secret terrestrial society of master magicians once again displaying their superiority over the outsiders?

A Secret Weapon to Help Free Cuba

On April 7, 1897, "good reliable citizens" of Wesley, Iowa, sighted a cone-shaped airship "with windows in the side through which shone bright lights." The witnesses were unable to discern "in what manner the ship was propelled or what sustained it in the air,"[2] but the craft was low enough to the ground that some thought they had heard voices coming from its interior.

On April 15, the airship landed two miles north of Springfield, Illinois, and a woman and two men who appeared to be normal humans emerged from the craft. The ship's occupants explained that they had landed to repair their electrical apparatus and searchlight equipment.

A member of the airship crew also made the first of many references to their perplexed audiences about traveling to fight the Spanish and assist in freeing Cuba. Since the Spanish-American War had not been declared (April 25, 1898) and the rallying cry of "Remember the *Maine*," shouted in outrage over the sinking of the U.S ship in Havana Harbor, had not yet been heard, the airship occupants, whoever they really were, were exactly one year out of time sync with those who saw their aerial maneuvers.

In Waterloo, the Curious Were Kept Back with a Rifle

By April 17, the airship returned to Iowa and set down outside Waterloo. The "stranger in charge" of the airship seemed all too human as he brandished a rifle to keep the curious several hundred yards from his machine.

Journalists described the airship as being about forty feet long and constructed like a giant cigar, "with winglike attachments on the sides and a steering apparatus in the rear."[3] The machine had a cupola on its roof, and the bizarre craft appeared to have been fashioned of heavily varnished canvas.

Although his rifle kept the crowds from approaching too near, the captain of the air vessel was not totally hostile. He explained that he was on a 'round-the-world flight, but had been forced to land for repairs. One day, he promised, he would return and give the folks of Waterloo a free exhibition.

Just Call Me Smith

During April 21–22, the airship barnstormed Arkansas and Texas. On April 21, John M. Barclay of Rockland, Texas, took his Winchester rifle in hand when the airship landed in a pasture adjacent to his house shortly before midnight. Barclay later described the craft as "oblong-shaped with wings and side attachments of various sizes and shapes."

"Never mind about who I am," an emerging occupant told Barclay. "Just call me Smith."[4] Then he gave the astonished Texan a ten-dollar bill and asked him to get the crew lubricating oil and some tools.

When Barclay requested a quick peek inside the craft, Smith told him that they could not allow it. But if Barclay did as they requested and brought them the oil and the tools, they would appreciate his kindness and call on him sometime in the future to take him on a special trip.

A Brilliant Inventor from St. Louis
Suspended the Laws of Gravity

On that same evening, in Harrisburg, Arkansas, ex–state senator Harris was awakened about one o'clock in the morning by the airship and surprised its crew at his well. The leader of the aeronauts, an elderly gentleman with a dark, silken beard that hung down near his waist, said because Senator Harris seemed like an intelligent man, he would divulge the secret of his airship.

The bearded captain's uncle had been a brilliant inventor from St. Louis who had discovered the secret of suspending the laws of gravity. After his uncle's death, the aeronaut had spent nineteen years creating the airship that the senator now saw before him. However, because the craft was not quite perfected, they preferred to travel at night to avoid detection. Once they had accomplished a successful voyage to the planet Mars, they would put the airship on public exhibition.

Remarkably, the captain, for all his genius at creating gravity-suspending airships, was out of time sync in regard to the war between the Americans and the Spanish, which in conventional linear time would not be declared until 1898, a full year *after* he spoke with Harris. Furthermore, he told the confused senator that he had on board a four-ton Hotchkiss gun and ten tons of ammunition that he had planned to use to "kill out" the Spanish army if they *had not surrendered when they did.*[5] Since the Spanish-American War ended when the U.S. Senate ratified the Treaty of Paris in 1899 and the captain referred to the surrender of the Spanish, he was speaking from a time perspective two years in advance of his interaction with Senator Harris. Then to further baffle the senator, the airship captain made a reference to their going to aid the Armenians in Constantinople to resolve a bloody conflict that had actually taken place in 1896, the year *before* the visitation.

In the 1990s, UFO dogmatists say that the 1897 airship occupants could not have been extraterrestrials because they did not look like the "Grays." Amazingly, those big-headed, huge-eyed, gray-skinned reptilelike entities have so captured the imagination of the public and the researchers alike that it is currently de rigueur that any being wishing to qualify as an ET must manifest as a Gray.

We agree that the airship occupants of 1897 were quite likely not extraterrestrials—unless, of course, they were the Shape-shifters and could appear in any guise acceptable to their human percipients. We do believe that the various inventors and their crews could well have been representatives of a hidden terrestrial society who set out on a mission whose motives and goals remain somewhat fuzzy from our human perspective.

We Come Not from Heaven, but from Iowa

On April 24, a prominent Texas farmer named Frank Nichols was awakened at midnight by a strange whirring sound and looked out of his bedroom window to behold "brilliant lights from a ponderous vessel" that had landed in his cornfield. Leaving his house to investigate, he encountered two men who asked permission to draw water from his well.

Nichols, a very religious man, believed that he might be entertaining heavenly visitors who had come from the skies in a most peculiar chariot, so he readily granted the "angels" permission to draw all the water they required.

The airship visitors informed the farmer that they came not from heaven, but from a small town in Iowa, where five such airships had been constructed. The craft themselves, they explained, were built of a newly discovered material that had "the property of self-sustenance in the air."[6] The motive power was a highly condensed electricity. Even as they spoke, Nichols was told, an immense

stock company was being formed and within another year
such air machines would be in wide usage.

A Busy Flight Schedule for the Airship

Throughout the following weeks, landing and contact
reports came from areas all across the United States. Always, the talk was of "secret inventions," a concept that
was ably abetted by the airship occupants themselves, who
appeared as ordinary humans to each of the many witnesses. During the summer months of 1897, airship sightings were reported from other parts of the world as well. In
July and August, mysterious aerial objects were seen over
Sweden and Norway. On August 13, what appeared to be
the same aerial craft was sighted off the coast of Norway
and over Vancouver, British Columbia, on the same day.

After a Twelve-Year Absence,
the Airship Returns in 1909

The mysterious airship disappeared from the skies for
twelve years. No stock company was formed to make mil-
lionaires of people who wished to invest in the bearded inventor's marvelous flying machine. For a time, concerned
individuals speculated whether the affable crew might
have crashed into the Atlantic during one of their overseas
flights to Europe. Then the wonderful airship of 1897 was
forgotten.

The craft returned to stimulate interest in heavier-than-
air flying craft on March 24, 1909, when a police constable
in the town of Peterborough, England, reported having
heard a sound "similar to a motor car" overhead. Looking
upward, he spotted an airship with a powerful light that
was "traveling as fast as an express train." The constable
emphasized that it was not a balloon.

On May 18, C. Lethbridge, a resident of Cardiff, Wales, was walking home from the town of Senghenydd when he came upon a landed airship, a strange craft with wheels on the bottom of its carriage and a "whirling fan" at its tail. Mr. Lethbridge also encountered two occupants, who wore heavy fur coats and fur caps fitted tightly over their heads. He admitted to being somewhat frightened, because when they became aware of his presence, they jumped up and "jabbered furiously in a strange lingo"[7] that was unfamiliar to the Welshman.

Whoever Built the Airship, It Was Not the Wright Brothers

As you may be well aware, Orville and Wilbur Wright accomplished the historic first flight with a heavier-than-air vehicle in 1903 when their craft managed to stay aloft for twelve seconds and travel 120 feet. Although the progress in aeronautics would be remarkably rapid, in 1909 the flight across the English Channel by Louis Blériot was considered a major accomplishment. After eleven years of steady improvements, Count von Zeppelin had a number of airworthy dirigibles, but they had such a restricted flying range that great difficulties were encountered in making successful flights from Germany to England.

The identity of the aeronauts—whether members of a secret society of alchemists or extraterrestrials in disguise—who traversed the skies of Great Britain and as far away as New Zealand in 1909 remains as much a mystery today as it was at the turn of the century, for there simply were no known aircraft that could come anywhere near to replicating their flight schedule.

A Triumphal Return to the United States

The airship remained over New Zealand for six weeks, but by September, it was ready to return to the United States after a twelve-year absence. There was one reported overflight in the New England area in August, then the airship disappeared until the night of December 12, when residents of Long Island heard a buzzing sound, resembling the rattle and hum of a high-speed motor coming from the starlit skies above them.

On the very next evening, the airship returned to one of its favorite haunts, the area around Little Rock, Arkansas. Inhabitants from Mabelvale to Little Rock reported strange illuminated objects moving through the air and "cylindrical shafts of light"[8] being directed at them from above.

"Airshipitis" Afflicts the Citizens of Massachusetts and Rhode Island

By December 16, the airship had revisited New England, hovering over Potowomut and Providence, Rhode Island. On that same evening, ex-councilman B. W. Johnson said that he spotted the airship hovering over the southwestern part of Marlboro, Massachusetts, and claimed that the craft came down so low that he could hear a man speaking from within its interior.

Thousands of residents in various cities of Massachusetts and Rhode Island watched spellbound as the airship cavorted in their skies on the night of December 22. In Worcester, crowds watched it maneuver over the city for more than fifteen minutes and estimated its speed at between thirty and forty miles per hour while it swept the heavens with a searchlight of "tremendous power."

In Willimantic, Connecticut, the *Daily Chronicle* said that last-minute Christmas shoppers "forgot what they had come for and stood on the sidewalk and even in the middle of the street," looking upward at the brilliant light in the sky and hoping to see the return of the airship.

On Christmas Eve, the *Providence Journal* declared that an attack of "airshipitis" afflicted thousands of people: "Every star was an airship; every light in the sky was an aeroplane; and some were disappointed because they couldn't ring in the moon as a dirigible."

The Airship Heads South, Then Flies Away Forever

As 1910 drew near, the airship moved to the southern and northern portions of the nation. The town of Huntington, West Virginia, received an early morning visit on December 31, 1909.

For three successive days, thousands of Chattanooga, Tennessee, residents sighted a mysterious white airship traveling over their city and heard the sound of its engines. On January 12, 1910, the first day of its appearance, the aerial vehicle also visited Huntsville, Alabama, but the next morning it was back again in Chattanooga. The craft crossed over the city for the third time about noon on January 14, then disappeared over Missionary Ridge.

What appears to have been the last reported airship sighting came from Memphis, Tennessee, on January 20. A number of witnesses saw a craft flying very high in the air and traveling at a high rate of speed. It crossed the Mississippi River into Arkansas, veered slightly to the south, and rapidly disappeared.

Perhaps the members of a secret society no longer felt that it was necessary to inspire the "outsiders" to pursue the science of aeronautics, for by 1910 there had already been an International Aviation Competition held in Rheims, France, a flight from the deck of a seagoing cruiser, and a takeoff from water by a floatplane, and the first woman pilot had obtained her license. In just four more years, in August 1914, German and Allied pilots would begin to utilize the wonder of heavier-than-air flight by shooting at each other from their biplanes.

Some UFO researchers maintain that the mysterious airship was merely a charade conducted by a secret society, such as the Illuminati, who had combined forces with certain alien intelligences to test the psychological responses of typical humans to the prospect of flying machines well in advance of their known technology. The airship would eventually be revealed in the 1940s as the circular spacecraft that it actually was. By then, the world would be softened by two terrible world wars and be vulnerable to global invasion.

IN THE 1990S, PARANOIA RULES THE UFO SCENE

A recent poll revealed that 74 percent of Americans believe that the government is deeply involved in conspiracies and cover-ups that the majority of its citizens will never even find out about. Large numbers of UFO buffs, right-wing conservatives, and evangelical Christians are in agreement that there are all kinds of shameful secret agendas and systematic atrocities against unsuspecting citizens going around—and a good many of them involve secret societies and alien intelligences.

The most prevalent conspiracy theory contends that the government learned the truth about UFOs at the site of the Roswell crash in 1947 when the military recovered alien corpses. A secret group known as Majestic 12 keeps the president and other world leaders briefed on the progress of alien activity on Earth. While the governments of the planet officially deny the existence of UFOs to prevent panic among the masses, the chief executives are well aware of the existence of extraterrestrial involvement in world affairs.

A secret arm of our government, in association with the Illuminati, made a deal with the alien invaders to trade advanced extraterrestrial technology for such Earth treasures as water, minerals, cattle—and certain of its citizenry. UFO abductions are conducted by aliens as a species-monitoring program. Physical examinations of humans and crossbreeding attempts involving preselected men and women are allowed by our government as a treaty concession.

Just as certain rumors and bits of gossip may be based upon some germ of truth, so might a number of the current crop of conspiracy theories contain varying degrees of reality and veracity. After all, many men and women of intelligence and trustworthiness believe in one or more of the following UFO conspiracies and, when pressured, they can present strong and passionate arguments for their beliefs. As researchers in the field, we will withhold final judgment until we have accumulated more facts regarding the following UFO and alien conspiracy theories.

- At the United Nations' recent World Food Summit, world powers declared their goal of restricting the sale of fertilizer for agriculture in Third World countries. This is part of a secret society's plan to depopulate the Earth, starve the masses, and kill off huge numbers of people in order to make the takeover of the planet by their alien allies that much easier.
- The National Security Office in Washington, D.C., is a

Gestapo-like organization that has already begun building crematories and concentration camps. They will soon employ a high-tech human tracking system and begin to arrest and incarcerate all those who oppose their policies or offer resistance to the conquering extraterrestrials.

- Foreign troops are now stationed and operating on American soil and an entire German *Luftwaffe* occupies an air force base in New Mexico. U.S. government officials have betrayed their citizens and have handed over control of the military to foreign interests. The German airmen are commanded by former Nazi officers who worked with the aliens in constructing the Foo Fighters of World War II.

- The devilish Order of Skull and Bones virtually owns the CIA and the State Department. These monstrous men helped bring both the Marxist Communists and the Nazis to power, and they work today to build a Fascist New World Order in league with alien intelligences that have been working quietly behind the scenes.

Satan's Legions Are Arriving in UFOs

As we approach the year 2000, many fundamentalist religious sects have become obsessed with fears concerning the Millennium and Armageddon, the great final battle between Good and Evil. Such an obsession has created a mind-set of suspicion that has many members of these groups identifying Satan's minions as aliens arriving on UFOs.

The UFO buffs themselves have begun seeing treacherous agents of the secret government behind every tree. Men in Black have been joined by Black Helicopters, and once-benign Space Brothers have been largely replaced by nasty alien doctors who want to perform painful physical examinations aboard motherships and steal human ova and sperm for their genetic experiments in creating a new hybrid species.

Mysterious Black Helicopters Hover over America

Hundreds of men and women have recently reported being harassed and spied upon by mysterious unmarked black helicopters. If you are involved in serious UFO research, many believe, you are certain to be under surveillance by a hovering black helicopter.

According to "informed" individuals, the black choppers are the property of a clandestine national police force that will soon begin to wage bloody warfare against all Americans who oppose the secret government, whose agents have signed a document that has turned over control of our nation's military forces to greedy and power-hungry international bankers, the Secret Brotherhood of the Illuminati, and their alien allies.

NASA Has Covered Up Evidence of Alien Life Found on the Moon and Mars

Recently, NASA gadfly Richard Hoagland has charged the space agency with a conspiracy to cover up information that should rightfully be revealed to the public. Rather than accusing NASA with never having been to the Moon or to Mars as some conspiracy theorists do, Hoagland insists that not only have the astronauts been there, but they have been covering up the discovery of ruins and various artifacts that would change the history of Earth as we know it. Especially intrigued by the so-called Mars Face, a fascinating sphinxlike object that appeared on numerous NASA photographs of an area named Cydonia during the *Viking 1* orbit in 1976, Hoagland has demanded that the agency come clean about its conspiracy to keep important discoveries from the public.

In April 1998, NASA's Mars Global Surveyor spacecraft made three sweeps near Mars and sent back photos to debunk theories that ancient civilizations constructed the face—and especially, perhaps, to defuse Hoagland's steady clamoring for NASA to confess the details of their cover-up. The new pictures showed only an innocuous pile of rocks, completely devoid of the shadowed eye sockets and profile of the previous portraits of the Mars Face.

Hoagland was undaunted. Within hours of the release of the new NASA photographs of the face, Hoagland's website declared, "Honey, I Shrunk the Face!" Presenting a detailed criticism of the techniques employed in obtaining the featureless photographs, he argued that "without appropriate and meticulous documentation of the entire process—from taking the photographs at Mars, to receiving, enhancing, and displaying them back here on Earth—no one can make a scientific assessment of what's waiting at Cydonia ... We are still 'light years' from gaining access to such crucial, verifiable documentation."

Hoagland insists that NASA has been covering up the discovery of mind-boggling artifacts for decades. Not long ago, Hoagland unearthed a 1960 NASA-commissioned report by the Brookings Institute that recommended that any future discoveries of alien life be kept from the public in order not to disturb the evolutionary flow of twentieth-century civilization. Such a document fueled Hoagland's charges that there had been a "deliberate thirty-year-old superpower cover-up" to deny the world's people true information about the astonishing discoveries on Mars and the Moon.

UFO Abductees Are Really Victims of Secret CIA Projects

The CIA's highly classified MK-Ultra project involves the training and indoctrination of selected, multiple-personality assassins. These people are not only programmed to kill, but after repeated torture and hypnotic brainwashing sessions are given selective "memories" that include intense recall of UFO sightings and abduction experiences.

CIA medics employed by the U.S. government are implanting high-technology devices in the brains and ears of selected subjects. Such devices, directly or indirectly, stimulate brain centers, fostering mental imagery of UFOs.

UFOs and the New World Order

A few years ago, when President George Bush began speaking about a New World Order to beef up his campaign for reelection, evangelist Pat Robertson, who was briefly a presidential candidate, passionately spoke out that "new world order" was actually a code for a secret group that sought to replace Christian society with a worldwide atheistic socialist dictatorship.

Bush, the conspiracy buffs charged, was a member of one of the world's most devilish and powerful secret societies: the Order of Skull and Bones. What was more, according to these same buffs, Bush was linked to the Bilderbergers and the Trilateral Commission, dangerous elitist organizations.

At about the same time that President Bush's alleged secret affiliations were being exposed, a number of fundamentalist evangelists began to take their first real notice of the UFO phenomenon and saw the mysterious aerial objects as the "signs in the skies" referred to in apocalyptic literature and in the book of Revelation. It was a short leap for many evangelists to begin to blend accounts of UFOs with the secret societies of top U.S. government officials, politicians, corporate chairmen, international bankers, and many others who sought to bring into being the dreaded "New World Order."

According to the proponents of this cosmic conspiracy, when President Reagan gave his famous "alien invasion" speech to the entire United Nations General Assembly in September of 1987, he had already secretly advised representatives of the 176 member nations that the leaders of their respective governments must meet the demands of the technologically superior extraterrestrials or be destroyed.

As Reagan said in his speech: "I occasionally think how quickly our differences worldwide would vanish if we were facing an alien threat from outside this world. And yet I ask you, is not an alien threat already among us?"

A plan agreed to by the aliens and the world leaders decreed that shortly before the year 2000 a carefully staged "alien invasion" will convince the masses of the world that a real-life *Independence Day*–type attack is about to begin. People of all nations will believe their leaders who say that it has been learned that the aliens are a benevolent species and that unconditional surrender to them is for everyone's own good.

Immediately following the "surrender" to the aliens, the united leaders will form a One World Government, a New World Order, thus fulfilling biblical prophecies about a return to the days of Babylon. The aliens will reveal themselves as demonic entities that delight in doing Satan's work. The planet will be in torment and turmoil until Jesus returns to deal the final blow to the minions of evil.

* * *

A vast number of cultures—from that of the Vikings to Hitler's Germany—have believed in an underground empire inside the Earth. Couple this belief with the theory that the UFOnauts are the descendants of a prehistoric Earth civilization that developed space flight, emigrated to another planet, and return periodically to monitor the motherworld, and we have a hypothesis regarding the UFO enigma that is even more ancient and integral to our species' evolution than a terrestrial secret society.

5

UFO Mysteries Undersea and Underground

There are persistent legends in nearly every culture that tell of an Elder Race that populated the Earth millions of years ago. The Old Ones, who may originally have been of extraterrestrial origin, were an immensely intelligent and scientifically advanced species who eventually chose to structure their own environment under the surface of the planet's soil and seas. Those human witnesses who claim to have encountered and communicated with representatives of the Elder Race describe them as humanoid, but extremely long-lived and giving evidence of predating our species by more than a million years.

The Old Ones usually remain aloof from the surface dwellers, but from time to time they leave their underground caverns or their undersea bases in their aerial machines in order to perceive what kind of mess *Homo sapiens* is making of things. Throughout history, they have also been known to visit certain of Earth's movers and shakers in order to offer constructive criticism and, in some cases, to give valuable advice in the material sciences. They have also developed a somewhat nasty reputation for kidnapping human children to rear as their own.

The Buddhists have incorporated *Agharta*, a subterranean empire, into their theology and fervently believe in its existence and in the reality of underworld supermen who periodically surface to oversee the progress of the human race. According to one source, the underground kingdom of Agharta was created when the ancestors of the present-day secretive cave dwellers drove the Serpent People from the caverns during an ancient war between the reptilian humanoids and the ancient human society. To the contemporary UFO researcher, the Serpent People were probably extraterrestrial aliens seeking to colonize Earth.

In his book *Shambala*, author and adventurer Nicholas Roerich wrote of his curiosity about the universality of the legends of the underpeople: "You recognize the same relationship in the folklores of Tibet, Mongolia, China, Turkestan, Kashmir, Persia, Altai, Siberia, the Urals, Caucasia, the Russian steppes, Lithuania, Poland, Hungary, Germany, France; from the highest mountains to the deepest oceans . . . They tell you how the people . . . closed themselves in subterranean mountains. They even ask you if you want to see the entrance to the cave through which the saintly persecuted folk fled."

Throughout the world, Roerich emphasizes, one hears the same "wondrous tale of the vanished holy people. . . . Great is the belief in the Kingdom of the subterranean people."

THE NAZI QUEST TO FIND THE ENTRANCE TO THE INNER EARTH

Lest the reader dismiss such theories of an underground elder race as quaint notions from an unsophisticated and romantic past, it must be noted that in April 1942, Nazi

Germany sent out to the island of Rugen an expedition composed of a number of its most visionary scientists to seek a military vantage point in the hollow earth. Although this expedition, led by Dr. Heinz Fischer, an infrared expert, left at a time when the Third Reich was putting maximum effort in its drive against the Allies, Goering, Himmler, and Hitler are said to have enthusiastically endorsed the project. Steeped in the more esoteric teachings of metaphysics, the fuehrer had long been convinced that Earth was hollow and that a master race lived on the *inside* of the planet.

The Nazi scientists who left for Rugen had complete confidence in the validity of their quest. They believed they would be able to photograph the British Fleet with infrared equipment by shooting upward at a forty-five-degree angle. At the same time, such a coup as discovering an opening to the inner world would not only provide them with a military advantage, but it would go a long way in convincing the masters who lived there that the German people truly deserved to mix their blood with them in the creation of a hybrid master race to occupy the surface world.

UFOS FROM THE HOLLOW EARTH

Dr. Raymond Bernard's *The Hollow Earth* has become the classic in the rather tenuous field of proving the existence of an inner Earth. In his introduction to the book, Dr. Bernard promises to prove that "the earth is hollow and not a solid sphere . . . and that its hollow interior communicates with the surface by two polar openings. . . ."

Dr. Bernard's *magnum opus* discloses that Rear Ad-

miral Richard E. Byrd flew *beyond* rather than *over* the
North Pole and that his later expedition to the South Pole
passed 2,300 miles *beyond* it. According to Dr. Bernard,
the North and South Poles have never been reached because they do not exist. In his view, the nation whose explorers first locate the entrance to the hollow interior of the
Earth will become the greatest nation in the world.

And, in Dr. Bernard's opinion, there is no doubt that the
mysterious flying saucers "come from an advanced civilization in the hollow interior of the earth." In the event of a
nuclear world war, Bernard states, "The hollow interior of
the Earth will provide an ideal refuge for the evacuation of
survivors of the catastrophe."

THEORIES OF THE HOLLOW EARTH
AND LEGENDS OF ATLANTIS

Almost from the initial sighting of UFOs in the modern
era, certain researchers, spawning numerous theories, have
identified the mysterious aerial vehicles as originating from
the Hollow Earth and have suggested that its inhabitants
might well be the descendants of the survivors of Atlantis.
Among the theories most often cited are the following.

- The UFOs are piloted by an ancient humanoid race that
  antedates *Homo sapiens* by at least a million years. Their
  withdrawal from the surface world survives in the collective human unconscious as the legend of Atlantis.
- Atlantis was an actual prehistoric world that created a
  superscience and destroyed itself in civil war. The sur-
  viving Atlanteans sought refuge from radioactivity by

retreating under the Earth's crust. They have continued to monitor the new race of surface dwellers and accelerated their observation after the detonation of the first atomic bombs.

- Extraterrestrial beings established a colony on Earth about 50,000 years ago when *Homo sapiens* was establishing itself as the dominant aboriginal species. They gave primitive humankind a boost up the evolutionary ladder, then grew aghast at humanity's perpetual barbarism and left the surface world to establish underground and undersea bases from which to observe how their cosmic cousins would develop without direct interference and assistance.

THE ANSWER TO THE UFO MYSTERY LIES WITHIN OUR OWN PLANET

The late Ray Palmer, editor of *Flying Saucers* and *Search* magazines, once told us that after decades of research he was personally convinced that the answer to the UFO mystery was to be found on our own planet, rather than outer space.

The more one thinks of the extraterrestrial thesis, the more impossible it is to prove. UFOs have been seen in the skies since man's prehistory, and today there seems to be a virtual traffic jam of objects coming in from somewhere. It seems, to me, difficult to conceive that ours should be the only planet of any interest to extraterrestrial life-forms.

The supposition that the saucers have an Earth base and may be manned by an older terrestrial race brings the cosmic concept down to reality. Geographically speaking, our own atmosphere is a heck of a lot closer than Alpha Centauri![1]

THE "CELEBRATED RUMPUS" OF
THE SHAVER MYSTERY

Shortly after Kenneth Arnold's June 24, 1947, sighting of nine disk-shaped objects captured the world's imagination and set millions to thinking about extraterrestrial visitors, Ray Palmer began running installments of the famous Shaver Mystery in *Amazing Stories*, the popular Ziff-Davis science fiction magazine that he then edited. Publication of the series touched off what *Life* magazine (May 21, 1951) characterized as "the most celebrated rumpus that ever rocked the science fiction world."

The Shaver Mystery told of a race of misshapen subhumans named Deros who dwelt within a vast cave system of underground cities. The Dero, original inhabitants of the lost prehistoric world of Lemuria, remain in control of the fantastic technology of this vanished civilization and are responsible for much of the evil on the surface world above them. The Dero take sadistic pleasure in tormenting the human race, and the malformed creatures are kept under control only by the intervention of the Tero, a more benign group of subsurface dwellers.

Richard Shaver, the author of the stories that appeared in *Amazing Stories* over the course of four years, claimed that he had actually been in the caves and that he continued to maintain communication with the Tero. In many of his articles he warned that the Dero were becoming more numerous and had scattered the benevolent Tero with their ceaseless attacks. The perverted Dero did not have the requisite intelligence or moral sense to use the machines of Lemurian superscience responsibly, and they had taken possession of "vision ray machines" that could penetrate solid rock, together with technological units that could accomplish instant teleportations. In addition, they were controlling mental machinery that could produce "solid" illusions, and, of course, the aircraft that the simple surface dwellers referred to as flying saucers.

What was Ray Palmer's opinion about the Shaver Mystery some twenty years after he had stirred up such a "rumpus" in *Amazing Stories*?

I don't discount the reality of underground cultures. One can find reference to them in the most primitive oral traditions right up to contemporary accounts. As for Richard Shaver, I believe that . . . he is correct— there may be underground civilizations which may still be in existence today.

When the Shaver Mystery was running in *Amazing Stories*, some FBI agents came to visit Shaver and spent two days with him. They told Richard that his stories were 25% correct!

Isn't that fantastic? The FBI comes to tell Shaver that the stories I am running as science fiction are 25% correct! Boy, I would like to know which 25% they were referring to![2]

UNIDENTIFIED SUBMARINE OBJECTS

Although there are some witnesses who claim to have seen UFOs ascending from caves or other openings in the earth, such accounts are extremely sparse compared to the vast number of reports received from those who have witnessed strange aerial craft entering and leaving large bodies of water. What is more, the mystique and the possibility of undersea USO (Unidentified Submarine Object) bases seem to grow more convincing with each passing year.

Massive USO Rises Next to Oil Rig in December 1997

In December 1997, a massive craft was seen emerging from the sea next to an oil platform in the Gulf of Mexico. According to engineer Jeremy Packer, the sighting was witnessed by 250 oil-rig workers.

At about 7:58 A.M., Packer said that everyone got frightened when they heard a rumbling noise that they knew couldn't be the engines that ran the platform bore. Looking toward the west, they sighted twenty-five to thirty helicopters on maneuvers. This was not unusual, Packer said, except that the rig commander said that he had not received the usual alert regarding Coast Guard operations in the area.

Then, according to Packer, they all saw something that totally changed their lives. All of the helicopters stopped in midair and a huge metal cigar-shaped object about the size of the oil platform surfaced beneath them. The massive craft, about as long as two football fields, soared straight out of the water and into the air, where it hovered above the helicopters for about two minutes.

Packer described the object as concave on its underside with four large domes on its bottom. The topside of the cigar-shaped craft was encircled by beautiful lights of every imaginable color.

And then, as if someone had turned off a light switch, the giant craft disappeared. One second everyone was studying the object through binoculars or telescopes; then, in the literal blink of an eye, it was gone.

As an interesting sidenote, Packer said that the crew noticed that their watches were thirty minutes later than the actual time when they got back to the mainland.[3]

RAAF Pilot Clashes with USO Five Years Before Roswell

In mid-February 1942, Lieutenant William Brennan of the Royal Australian Air Force (RAAF) was on patrol over the Bass Strait south of Melbourne, Australia, on the lookout for Japanese submarines or long-range German U-boats. Fishermen in the area had reported mysterious lights bobbing on the sea at night, and after the Japanese attack on Darwin on February 19, the Allied High Command was urging the strictest vigilance.

About 5:50 P.M. on a sunny afternoon the air patrol was flying a few miles east of the Tasman Peninsula when a strange aircraft of a glistening bronze color suddenly emerged from a cloud bank near them. The object was about 150 feet long and approximately 50 feet in diameter. Lieutenant Brennan saw that the peculiar craft had a dome or cupola on its upper surface, and he thought he saw someone inside wearing a helmet.

There were occasional greenish blue flashes emanating from its keel, and Lieutenant Brennan was astonished to see, "framed in a white circle on the front of the dome, an image of a large, grinning Cheshire cat."[4]

The unidentified aerial craft flew parallel to the RAAF patrol for several minutes, then it abruptly turned away and dived straight down into the Pacific. Lieutenant Brennan emphasized that the USO made a dive, not a crash, into the ocean, and he added that before the craft left them, he noticed what appeared to be four finlike appendages on its underside.

The Force Invited Him to Become One with Them

In the summer of 1969, Englishman John Fairfax rowed his way across the Atlantic, docking in Fort Lauderdale after six harrowing months alone on the sea. When asked by journalists to name the most impressive thing that had happened to him during the ocean adventure, Fairfax replied rather reluctantly that the answer to that question would have to be the appearance of objects that could not have been anything other than flying saucers.

Emphasizing that he had never believed in such things, he went on to explain that there was much more involved in his experience than simply observing UFOs. There was a *force* he told reporters; it was as if the objects kept asking him if he wanted to come with them.

"And I was fighting [the force] and saying back, 'No, no, no,' " Fairfax said.

> It was like telepathy, like being hypnotized. I was hypnotized once, voluntarily. It was like that.
>
> I had lit a cigarette. Then these luminous saucers swooped down over the ocean, rose and swooped down again. There was this magnetic feeling. When they had gone, I realized the cigarette had burned my fingers.
>
> I don't believe in flying saucers, but there is nothing else they could be.[5]

Fairfax sternly rejected proffered explanations that he might have seen Venus or some other bright stars. He stressed that the objects were ten times brighter than Venus and said that the UFOs were too bright and too large to be stars or planets and their flight pattern too irregular to have been those of satellites.

An Undersea Mechanic Made an
Unauthorized Adjustment

In 1948, Professor Auguste Piccard brought his unmanned bathyscaphe up from a record descent of 4,600 feet under the surface of the ocean.

Professor Piccard and his crew were so excited by their successful mission that it took them a moment to become cognizant of a very peculiar thing. Although the bathyscaphe had suffered no actual damage from the intense pressure of the record descent, its aluminum radar mast had been neatly removed, as if a skilled underwater mechanic had accomplished a clean theft.

An Undersea Camera Captures the
Image of an Impossible Artifact

The U.S. ship *Eltanin*, owned by the Military Sea Transportation Service, was specially designed for use in the National Science Foundation Antarctic research program. On August 29, 1964, the *Eltanin* was a thousand miles west of Cape Horn, and its crew of highly trained specialists were busily engaged in photographing the ocean floor, which reaches a depth of 13,500 feet in that area. A uniquely designed camera, housed in a metal cylinder, was being pulled along by a cable.

Later that day, when darkroom technicians developed the exposed film, they found that the camera had captured the image of a bizarre device jutting out of the muck of the ocean floor. A central mast supported four series of cross rods, which made the object look like a cross between a television antenna and a telemetry antenna. The cross rods were spaced at ninety-degree angles and showed white knobs on their extremities.

Although all scientific logic argued against such an assessment, the mysterious object appeared to be manmade and definitely seemed out of place in the anticipated natural environment of the ocean floor. The *Eltanin*'s specially designed camera had been built to bounce along the seabed and to take photographs at regular intervals. It was only a fortunate, albeit puzzling, accident that the peculiar artifact had been photographed.

When the *Eltanin* docked at Auckland, New Zealand, on December 4, 1964, a reporter questioned Dr. Thomas Hopkins, senior marine biologist on board, about the eight-by-ten prints of the underwater anomaly. Dr. Hopkins estimated the object to be about two feet high and specified its point of discovery as being on the 45,000-mile fault-line rift that encircles the planet. He went on to comment that the device could hardly be a plant, for at that depth there is no light. Without light, of course, there can be no photosynthesis and plants cannot live. For obvious reasons, Dr. Hopkins was reluctant to declare the object to be of human manufacture.

When asked if the thing might be some strange coral formation, Dr. Hopkins replied that if it were, it was of a kind unknown to any of the experts on board the *Eltanin*. Again, he expressed his reluctance to pronounce the object to be manmade, for that would bring up the problem of how it got there.

Masters from an Undersea Kingdom

In 1969, Dr. Roger W. Wescott, chairman of the anthropology department at Drew University in Madison, New

Jersey, published *The Divine Animal*, in which he presented a well-reasoned theory that extraterrestrials landed on Earth ten thousand years ago, fully intending to teach humankind a better way of life. But when Earth's dominant species continued to demonstrate their avaricious and destructive nature, the extraterrestrials gave up in disgust and withdrew to establish undersea bases.

Although these cosmic tutors were temporarily thwarted in their attempts to build a better world here on Earth, they did not give up hope for all time, and they emerge from time to time to conduct certain spot checks to see if humans are advancing intellectually and becoming less barbaric. Such monitoring forays explain the sightings of UFOs that have been reported for thousands of years.

Dr. Wescott also suggested that when the UFOnauts withdrew from the Earth's surface, they took some humans along with them to train and to tutor according to their advanced extraterrestrial principles. Dr. Wescott conjectures that some of these specially tutored humans might have been returned to the surface at certain intervals to become leaders. Some of these apprentices worked to change humankind for good, while others, corrupted by a combination of their secret knowledge and the malleability of the less advanced surface humans, brought additional chaos and confusion to the world. Dr. Wescott speculates that such individuals as Buddha, Jesus, Muhammad, Genghis Khan, and Attila the Hun might have been sent up to the surface by the UFOnauts with varying degrees of success.

The anthropologist believes that the space travelers were viewed as gods by our human ancestors. He believes that the UFO beings sincerely wished to teach developing humankind, but as the human species began to master the environment, they also began to desire more material goods and became willing to wage wars to obtain the goods they didn't possess. In his theory, human greed and aggressiveness disgusted the masters from space and caused them to withdraw from humankind and to establish undersea bases where they could still observe the species but live comfortably apart from it.

In Dr. Wescott's view, such a theory helps to explain two of the most widespread and persistent legends found among nearly all peoples and all cultures: (1) there was a time when gods walked the earth and tutored humankind, and (2) there was a land called Atlantis, whose thriving civilization met with catastrophe and sank beneath the sea.

Of course both legends could be distortions of an actual event, which was not truly a catastrophic destruction of a continent, but an orderly withdrawal of the "gods," the cosmic teachers, as they transferred their bases from the land to the sea floor.

Dr. Wescott concedes that he has no firm evidence to support his hypothesis, but he suggests that the many reputable sea captains who have seen UFOs going in and out of the ocean might well be seeing aerial vehicles from undersea bases constructed by advanced beings.

An Incan Shaman Guides Us to a Mountain Lake Home for UFOs

We asked similar questions about ancient gods, cosmic teachers, and the true nature of UFO reality on a night spent somewhere not far from the sacred Incan city of Ollantaytambo in Peru. After talk over dinner turned to accounts of UFOs, our shaman guide said that he would take us to a sacred lake where every night one could see such objects entering and leaving the water. The only condition to his taking us was that we maintain the continued secrecy of the location.

So on an extremely dark night, the Incan shaman took us to this secret location, where we did, indeed, see numerous illuminated UFOs emerge from the lake's surface, descend beneath the waters, and bob around the night sky in their peculiar zigzag flight pattern.

In spite of the chill in the night air, there were barefooted villagers walking about in the darkness, carrying grain and water to their families in jars atop their heads. What did they think the glowing objects were that they regularly saw entering and leaving the lake? *Spirits of the grandfathers,* answered some. *Angels,* replied others. *The Old Ones,* declared a few.

Among our group of adventurers, the answers were equally varied: *The Space Brothers. Aliens who have a base in the lake. Some really weird natural phenomenon. Survivors of an ancient culture who exist in secret underwater and subterranean bases.*

Perhaps each of the Peruvian villagers and each of the seekers of mystery from the United States had a piece of a most complex puzzle.

Two Mystery Submarines Escape the Argentine Navy

Early in February 1960, the Argentine navy, with the assistance of United States advisers, alternately depth-bombed and demanded the surrender of submarines thought to be lurking at the bottom of Golio Nuevo, a forty-by-twenty-mile bay separated from the South Atlantic by a narrow entrance. On a number of occasions, the Argentines declared that they had the mystery submarines trapped. Once, they even announced that they had crippled one of the unidentified subs.

There were at least two mystery submarines, and they both had peculiar characteristics. They were able to function and maneuver in the narrow gulfs for many days without surfacing. They easily outran and hid from surface vessels. And in spite of the combined forces of the Argentine fleet and the most modern U.S. sub-hunting technology, they were able to escape capture and destruction.

Skeptics of the bizarre undersea chase accused the Argentine navy of timing a dramatic search for mystery submarines with the evaluation of the new navy budget by the Argentine Congress. However, UFO researchers enumerated the many reports of strange vehicles seen entering and leaving the sea off the coast of Argentina. In their opinion, the unknown objects were underwater alien craft rather than terrestrial submarines.

A USO Visits New York City's East River

At 3 A.M. on July 15, 1960, the 24,000-ton Panamanian-flag tanker *Alkaid*, with a full cargo of crude oil, was struck by a USO as it passed under the Williamsburg Bridge in New York City's East River. The collision tore a massive gash in the starboard side of the big ship, forcing the captain to beach her near the United Nations building. Later, the *Alkaid*, on the verge of capsizing, was towed off to a dock.

After two days of Coast Guard hearings and an investigation by the Army Corps of Engineers, whose job it is to keep the harbor waters clean, no explanation could be found for the *Alkaid*'s mysterious collision with a USO. Nor could any object be found in the harbor that would have been capable of piercing the tanker's steel hull.

Something Unseen Sank the *Ruby E.*

For many years now we have received regular reports from shrimpers of UFO harassment. The account of Ira Pete, owner of the *Ruby E.*, a 67-foot shrimp boat, who had his vessel sink under mysterious circumstances in the first week of July 1961, is considerably more serious than the accounts of UFOs surfacing beside the shrimp boats or buzzing around the crews.

According to Pete, he was fishing in the Gulf of Mexico off Port Arkansas with his two-man crew when something hooked into the boat and ripped off its stern. Fortunately for the three shrimpers, there was another fishing vessel close by.

A USO Eludes Australian and New Zealand Warships

On November 14, 1961, Australian and New Zealand warships were conducting naval exercises off Sydney Heads when a large unidentified submarine object interrupted their maneuvers. There was no visual sighting of the craft, and the interloper eluded the fleet with speed and ease until contact was lost.

The official response to those who had questions about the mysterious intruder was that it was an "unidentified object."

Something Big Rammed the *Hattie D.*

On February 5, 1964, the 105-foot yacht *Hattie D.* was rammed by an underwater object near Eureka, California. Ten men and one woman were lifted from the fast-sinking yacht in a dramatic Coast Guard helicopter rescue.

The survivors all agreed that the *Hattie D.* had been run into by something big made of steel. When crewman Carl

Johnson was informed that no submarines were reported in the area and that the yacht had sunk in 7,500 feet of water, he adamantly replied that he didn't care how deep it was in that area—and he knew that whatever "holed" the yacht had been a very long piece of steel.

A Submarine Where a Submarine Could Never Be

On January 12, 1965, Captain K., an airline pilot on a flight between Whenuapai and Kaitaia, New Zealand, spotted a USO when he was about one-third of the way across Kaipara Harbour. As he veered his DC-3 for a closer look at what he had at first guessed to be a stranded gray-white whale in an estuary, it became evident to him that it was a metallic structure of some sort.

Captain K. saw that the object was perfectly streamlined and symmetrical in shape. He could detect no external control surfaces or protrusions, but there did appear to be a hatch on top. Harbored in no more than thirty feet of water, the USO was not shaped like an ordinary submarine. Captain K. estimated its length to be approximately 100 feet with a diameter of 15 feet at its widest part.

Later, the New Zealand Navy stated that it was impossible for any known model of submarine to have been in that particular area due to the configuration of the harbor and coastline. The surrounding mudflats and mangrove swamps would make the spot in which Captain K. saw his USO inaccessible to conventional undersea craft.

It Wasn't a Large Mechanical Shark

On July 5, 1965, Dr. Dmitri Rebikoff, a marine scientist making preparations to explore the Gulf Stream's depths, found himself faced with a most unusual challenge when he detected and attempted to photograph a fast-moving undersea USO on the bottom of the warm-water stream that flows from the Florida Keys to Newfoundland and onward to northern Europe. Dr. Rebikoff told Captain L. Jacques Nicholas, project coordinator, that the object was pear shaped and moving at approximately three and one-half knots.

The peculiar object was moving beneath various schools of fish, and at first, judging from its size, Dr. Rebikoff thought it to be a large shark. As he monitored it, however, he noted that the USO's direction and speed were too constant for a shark.

The marine scientist theorized that the object was mechanical and running on robot pilot, but since they were unable to receive any signal from the USO, he really had no idea what it might have been.

A USO Plunges into Shag Harbor

On October 3, 1967, the main topic of conversation among the residents of Shag Harbor, Nova Scotia, was the 60-foot-long object with a series of bright portholes that had been observed gliding into the harbor and submerging into the ocean. Within twenty minutes several constables of the Royal Canadian Mounted Police were on the scene, attempting to reach by boat the spot where about a half-mile offshore the sizzling USO was seen to float, then submerge beneath the surface of Shag Harbor.

A Coast Guard boat and eight fishing vessels joined the constables in time to observe a large path of yellowish foam and bubbling water. Divers from the Royal Canadian Navy searched the area for two days, but found no physical evidence of any kind.

The Halifax *Chronicle-Herald* quoted Squadron Leader

Bain of the Royal Canadian Air Force as commenting: "We get hundreds of [UFO] reports every week, but the Shag Harbor incident is one of the few where we may get something concrete on it."

A Mysterious Submarine with a Blue and White Glow

Captain Julian Lucas Ardanza of the Argentine steamer *Naviero* was some 120 miles off the coast of Brazil on the night of July 30, 1967. The time was about 6:15 P.M., and the *Naviero* was running at seventeen knots. Captain Ardanza was enjoying his evening meal when one of his officers, Jorge Montoya, called him on the intercom to report something strange near the ship.

According to reports in the Argentine newspapers, Captain Ardanza emerged on deck to view a cigar-shaped shining object in the sea, not more than fifty feet off the *Naviero*'s starboard side. The submarine craft was an estimated 105 to 110 feet long and emitted a powerful blue and white glow. Captain Ardanza and the other officers could see no sign of periscope, railing, tower, or superstructure on the noiseless craft. In his twenty years at sea, Captain Ardanza said that he had never seen anything like it.

Chief Officer Carlos Lasca ventured that the object was a submersible UFO with a brilliant source of illumination. The seamen estimated the craft's speed at twenty-five knots, as opposed to the *Naviero*'s seventeen.

After pacing the Argentine steamer for fifteen minutes, the unidentified submarine object suddenly submerged, passed directly under the *Naviero*, and disappeared into the depths of the ocean, glowing all the while it dove deeper and deeper.

* * *

The sea has always held its share of mysteries, but the continued reports of unidentified submarine objects add a dimension of otherworldly intrigue to the even greater mystery of the UFO phenomenon.

6

Merry Pranksters from the Magic Theater

Although the hypothesis may seem bizarre to some and fanciful to others, a good number of UFO researchers have drawn extensive parallels between the magical machinations of elves, fairies, and other paraphysical entities and the actions of alleged extraterrestrial beings. Whoever the fairy folk may truly be, throughout history they seem to have coexisted with humankind as a companion species and to have participated somehow with *Homo sapiens* in some as yet undetermined evolutionary design.

A BIZARRE BARTER WITH TWO MERRY ELVES

Forty-year-old Rosa Lotti lived on a farm in a wooded area near Cennina, a village near Bucine in the Italian province of Arezzo. On November 1, 1954, the mother of four had an encounter in the forest with two small beings who emerged from a small craft.

It was 6:30 A.M., and in one hand Rosa carried a bouquet of carnations to present at the altar of Madonna Pellegrina and in the other she clutched a pair of stockings. As she entered a clearing, she saw a barrel-shaped object that immediately attracted her curiosity. It looked like two bells joined together, and it was covered with some kind of metallic material that appeared more like leather.

Two beings the size of children suddenly emerged from behind the craft. Rosa saw that they had friendly expressions on their faces and were dressed in one-piece gray coveralls that covered their entire bodies, including their feet. Their outfits also included short cloaks and doublets, which were fastened to their collars with little star-shaped buttons. Helmets crowned their small but normal faces.

The two little strangers were vigorous and animated, and they spoke rapidly in a tongue that sounded to Rosa very much like Chinese. There were words like *liu*, *lai*, *loi*, and *lau*.

She vividly remembered their magnificent eyes, full of intelligence. Their facial features were not terribly un-usual, but their upper lips were curled in such a manner that they always appeared to be smiling. Their teeth were slightly protuberant, and to a countrywoman such as Rosa, their mouths appeared rabbitlike.

The older-looking of the two tiny men continually made a sound that she interpreted as laughter, and he startled her when he snatched away her carnations and one of the black stockings that she had been carrying. When Rosa re-covered from her shock, she remonstrated with him, and he returned two flowers after he had wrapped the others in the stocking and thrown the bundle into the barrel-shaped object.

As if in exchange for the stocking and the carnations, the little men stepped away from Rosa and appeared to be fetching two packages from inside the object. But before they could return with their gifts, she took advantage of the moment to escape.

The frightened woman ran through the woods for several seconds before she dared to glance back over her shoulder. When last she looked, the little men and their vehicle were still there.

Rosa told her story to the village *carabinieri*, her priest, and others who knew the woman to be absolutely truthful and free of foolish fantasies. The experience of Rosa Lotti has entered the annals of UFO research as a classic close encounter of the third kind. However, three or four centuries earlier, Rosa might have told all who would listen about her strange experience with the magical little people who, from time to time, emerged from their underground kingdom—and she might have been perfectly correct.

UFO OCCUPANTS SAMPLE THE SOIL IN NEW JERSEY

It was a rather warm night for January that evening in 1975 when George O'Barski drove home from the small liquor store that he owned and managed. It was about 2 A.M. as he moved through North Hudson Park on the New Jersey side of the Hudson River. Then, strangely, his car radio suddenly developed a lot of static.

When seventy-two-year-old O'Barski tried to adjust the station, the radio went dead. At about the same time, he began to notice a droning sound, a bit like the noise a refrigerator makes. The car window was down partway, because of the unseasonably warm weather, so he could clearly hear the peculiar sound.

Then he saw a round object, about thirty feet in diameter and six to eight feet high, coming down from the sky. The object itself was dark with a dome on top and had several lighted vertical windows around the main section of the body of the craft. Each window was about a foot wide and four feet long, spaced about one foot apart.

O'Barski said that he saw nothing at any of the windows other than the illumination, which was about the intensity of household lighting. He also noticed a lighted strip around the object at the base of the dome.

According to O'Barski, the object moved into the nearby park, parallel to his car, and came to rest about one hundred feet from him. At first the object appeared to hover approximately ten feet above the ground, then it settled to about four feet over the grassy area. He could not determine whether the object rested on legs or any kind of platform.

A lighted square opening suddenly appeared, and nine to eleven humanoids scrambled down the steps, "like kids coming down a fire escape." The occupants were all about three to four feet tall and seemed to be wearing dark coveralls, "like little kids with snowsuits on."

Each being also wore a helmet that was round and dark. They also seemed to be wearing gloves.

As the smallish beings descended the steps, each carried a small, dark bag and a small shovel. Each bag appeared to have a string or handle attached to it.

The little humanoids apparently knew their mission well, for they had no sooner reached the ground than they began digging rapidly in various locations near the UFO. The whole procedure lasted less than two minutes. The beings put the soil samples in their bags, climbed the steps once again, and within moments the craft took off, totally disappearing within twenty seconds.

O'Barski said that the UFOnauts did not act like robots, but moved about very much like humans. Although they did not seem to notice him as he observed them, he gradually became frightened that they might see him and capture him as another specimen to accompany the soil samples.

In concluding his report, O'Barski said that he had been held up in his liquor store many times by hoodlums with pistols and knives. He had been plenty scared during those robberies, but "nothing like this, ever. I was petrified!"

THE LITTLE PEOPLE ALWAYS HAVE THE POWER

When she was eleven years old, Lisa S. of New Jersey said that she was taken by fairies, the little people, to a special place where she received instructions that had a bearing on her future life experiences.

"I remember that it was a warm July night in 1983," Lisa said. "I was eleven years old, just approaching my twelfth birthday, when I was awakened one night by one of the little people asking me to go with him in the woods. I thought to myself, 'How will I get out the window and join him?' Before I knew it, I was floating off my bed and going *through* the window.

"Outside, waiting for me, was a being that I somehow knew as a very old and dear friend of mine. I felt so happy and elated to see him. I remember becoming very excited when he told me that we were going to go somewhere special and magical."

As an adult undergoing hypnotic regression, Lisa stated that she began crying hysterically at this point in her memory of the event. The "little people" had managed to erase all recollection of her magical journey.

"They have the power!" she sobbed to the hypnotist. "They always have the power!"

In subsequent visits, Lisa recalled, the little people that she had once assumed were fairies or elves told her that they were beings from an extraterrestrial world. What is more, the entities informed her that she and her sister also came from another galaxy and that they volunteered to come to Earth in a long-ago time before humans had yet evolved on the planet.

WELCOME TO A MUCH MORE COMPLEX UNIVERSE

Lisa S. is certainly not alone in her confusion over whether she was dealing with fairies, the traditional little people, or with extraterrestrial UFOnauts from some other galaxy. There are many UFO researchers who believe that the two entities are one and the same. There are other students of the phenomenon who maintain that there never really have been any visitors from the stars. It has been the wee people from the magical middle kingdom who have been tricking us foolish mortals with such elaborate deceptions for the last fifty or sixty years—just as they have been hoodwinking us with other fancies for four or five thousand years before the modern era.

What such seemingly disparate phenomena as the UFO, the appearance of wee people, the visitations of angels, and the manifestations of such archetypal images as Mother Mary throughout the world mean to us is that we are part of a larger community of intelligences, a much more complex hierarchy of powers and principalities, a potentially richer kingdom of interrelated species—both physical and non-physical—than most people are bold enough to believe.

Shakespeare made fairies famous in a number of his masterworks. He is largely responsible for the concept of the wee folk as mostly benign—mischievous, perhaps, but never evil. Alexander Pope wrote lovely passages ideal-izing fairies, but once satirically remarked that he be-lieved many of the woodland sprites were possessed by the souls of deceased socialites who even after death re-fused to give up earthly amusements. Sir Walter Scott em-phasized the beauty of the fairy realm and the struggle of the fairies to achieve humanlike souls. The famed poet William Butler Yeats had a nearly obsessive interest in the paranormal and strongly believed in fairies.

And it was, of course, the creator of Sherlock Holmes, Sir Arthur Conan Doyle himself, who came to the defense of Elsie Wright and Frances Griffiths in the famous and controversial Case of the Cottingly Fairies in 1917. He be-came convinced that fairies are genuine psychic phe-nomena and that just as some people can act as mediums and others have unusual powers of ESP, so do others—especially certain children—have the ability to see fairies.

Concerning fairies, Doyle theorized that they are con-structed of material that emits vibrations either shorter or longer than the normal spectrum visible to the human eye. Clairvoyance, he believed, consists, at least in part, of the ability to see these vibrations.

FAIRIES—OUR MULTIDIMENSIONAL COUSINS

Traditionally, the fairies are a race of beings, the counterparts of humankind in physical appearance but, at the same time, nonphysical or multidimensional. They are mortal, but lead longer lives than their human cousins.

In most traditions, especially in the British Isles and Scandinavia, the fairy folk were supernormal entities who inhabited a magical kingdom beneath the surface of the earth. In *all* traditions, the fairy folk are depicted as possessing many more powers and abilities than *Homo sapiens*, but, for some unexplained reason, they are strongly dependent on human beings—and from time to time they seek to reinforce their own kind by kidnapping both children and adults. Tales of folk being abducted by smallish beings did not begin in the last few decades.

Fairies have always been considered very much akin to humans, but also as something other than mortal. They have never been popularly conceived of as spirits, although some biblically influenced authorities have sought to cast the fairies in the role of the rebellious angels who were driven out of heaven during the celestial uprising led by Lucifer.

Most of the ancient texts declare that the fairies are of a middle nature, "between humans and angels." Although they are of a nature between spirits and humans, they can intermarry with humans and bear half-human children.

One factor has been consistent in fairy lore: the "middle folk" continually meddle in affairs of humans, sometimes to do them good, sometimes to do them ill.

C. S. Lewis, author of many classic books on spiritual matters, once suggested that the wee folk are a third rational species. The angels are the highest, having perfect goodness and whatever knowledge is necessary for them to do God's will; humans, somewhat less perfect, are the second; fairies, having certain powers of the angels but no souls, are the third.

Medieval theologians seemed to favor three possible theories to explain the origin of fairies: (1) they are a special class of demoted angels, (2) they are the dead or a special class of the dead, or (3) they are fallen angels.

Since the beginning of time, the human race and the ultradimensional race of fairies have shared this planet, experiencing a strange, symbiotic relationship. There have been misunderstandings, false legends, and many hurtful acts done in the name of ignorance and prejudice. There are some humans who do not believe in their supernatural companions—and there apparently are some of the woodland gentry who do not believe in the value of all human beings.

COMMUNICATING THROUGH THE SUBCONSCIOUS

We perceive the Other, whether of terrestrial or extraterrestrial origin, as communicating with us essentially through the subconscious mind. That is why experiences with these entities seem to happen more often, and most effectively, when the percipient is in an altered state of consciousness—and that is why UFO experiences, fairyland adventures, angelic visitations, and so forth, sound so much like dreams. They are really occurring when the percipient is in a dreamlike state. The conscious mind of the percipient remembers certain highlights of the experience—or interprets the symbols and lessons in a consciously acceptable manner—but the actual teaching mechanism and the important information have been indelibly etched upon the subconscious.

MAKING CROPS GROW FROM
ROUGH AND BARREN SCOTTISH SOIL

The story of the Findhorn trust community has been told many times. The entire world has come to marvel at the accounts of human interaction with nature beings that resulted in extraordinarily large vegetables and fruits being produced from the rocky, barren soil of northern Scotland.

In the summer of 1970 several members of the community began to receive a series of messages that dealt with the nature of new energies unfolding and penetrating Earth. This communication came from a presence that identified itself as "limitless love and truth."

While in meditation, one of the community, Dorothy Maclean, received the insight that "all of nature was infused with the divine intelligence which was embodied by beings living on higher vibratory dimensions from the physical." Ms. Maclean recognized these beings as the *Devas* (Sanskrit for "shining ones"), elementals or nature spirits, and they told her that they were of an order of evolution existing parallel to humanity and that they wield vast archetypal formative forces that energize and externalize the processes and forms of nature.

She was further told that far too many citizens of the western world had lost their sense of oneness with nature, thereby greatly increasing the very real danger that they would destroy the world. However, the Devas promised that, in the new cycle that is dawning, humanity will once again learn to live in harmony with all life-forms on the planet.

Ms. Maclean was instructed that an initial step in this process was the recognition by the community that the Devas did indeed exist. Next must be a demonstration that the people of Findhorn were willing to cooperate with them. She was told to contact these beings and to seek their help in the garden, for they possessed the energies required to make barren soil fertile and productive. The community did as the entities directed, and within a very short time, the world was marveling at their preternaturally large produce.

In 1975, we met with David Spangler, a director of the Findhorn Foundation, and asked him if he felt that the Devas, the nature spirits, were benignly concerned with the welfare of human beings. He replied:

> The majority of them are benignly concerned about our welfare, but I would say that what they are primarily concerned about is the maintenance of harmony and wholeness, a synergistic state with Earth. They recognize that humanity as a species is a necessary and vital part of the synergistic state. Therefore, the health of humanity is their concern, because it reflects the health of the planet. Also, humanity wields forces at the moment which bear directly on the health of the planet.
>
> In some sense, there's concern for us along the line of self-enlightenment, coupled with an awareness that if their kingdoms are going to prosper, humanity has to

prosper in relationship to those kingdoms. At the same time, there's a definite impression that humanity is important, but not indispensable.

Sometimes we get the feeling they're saying, if humanity doesn't get it together, a whole different evolutionary cycle may take over—which will move us out of the picture, at least in our present state.

The entities weren't really that concerned about Findhorn raising vegetables as much as they were concerned with getting across the point of their existence. They felt it was a real necessity that humanity alter its conception of reality so as to include their existence.

When we asked about our relationship to these entities, he answered:

We're first cousins to each other, sort of like humanity and the ape. We seem somehow to have a common ancestor . . . But even that isn't exactly true. Humanity itself has other antecedents which are not of this planet.

It is my understanding that the elements of what now constitute human nature and human potential—ingredients that went into the mix out of which we are now emerging—are not derived from this planet, either spiritually or otherwise, but come from other sources. In a way, humanity is an evolutionary cycle unto itself, which has overlapped to some extent with Devic evolution or nature spirit evolution—and to some extent evolution of a transplanetary nature.

HOW DO YOU TELL A FAIRY FROM AN ALIEN?

For the past five decades, various UFO researchers and eyewitnesses to alleged alien activity have been convinced that they had conclusive proof that extraterrestrial beings truly exist. For perhaps the past four thousand years, various scholars and eyewitnesses to alleged fairy activity have felt that they have garnered persuasive evidence that the Little People exist.

The fairies are said to be able to enchant humans and to take advantage of them in numerous ways, to marry humans or cast a spell on likely young men or women and have their way with them sexually. They often seem intent upon kidnapping children and adults and whisking them off to their underground kingdom. Those who return from the magical kingdom have experienced missing hours, days, weeks—even years.

On the other side of the coin, it must be said that fairies have also been reported to help farmers harvest their crops or assist housemaids in cleaning a kitchen. There are accounts of fairy folk guiding humans to achieve material successes with their apparent ability to divine the future. Stories are told of fairy midwives who stand by to assist at the births of favored human children and remain to guide and tutor the individuals for the rest of their lives.

Certainly, the same things may be said of the alleged alien beings who have involved themselves with *Homo sapiens*. The UFOnauts have been reported to hypnotize— to employ some kind of mind control—in order to make Earthlings more malleable. There have recently been dozens of reported cases in which humans were whisked away inside space ships and experienced missing time upon their return. It has been suggested that hundreds of thousands of men and women have been abducted and probed sexually in what has been argued is an attempt to create a hybrid species.

On the positive side, certain contactees have claimed beneficial interactions with aliens that have permitted them to make major scientific discoveries, accomplish medical breakthroughs, and to achieve great material success. Many individuals claim to have been healed after their contact with extraterrestrials, and they have expressed their belief that the aliens are generally benevolent in their intentions toward humans.

So you tell us: "How *do* you tell a Fairy from an Alien?" The answer may simply lie in the cultural and technological biases of the beholder.

ISRAELI ABDUCTEE GETS
SPRINKLED WITH FAIRY DUST

In our modern era, there is no question that the Wee Folk, whoever they may be, continue their bizarre patterns of incongruous behavior, including the abduction and harassment of humans.

During a period of heavily reported UFO activity in Israel in September 1996, sixty-two-year-old Uri Sakhov claimed that he was seized by two short, green-skinned beings while he was on his way to the local post office.

According to Sakhov, his attackers grabbed him by his collar and hair and hauled him into an egg-shaped craft. The Israeli said that his assailants spoke in a language completely unfamiliar to him and that before they released him, they sprinkled him with yellow dust.

Associated Press accounts of Sakhov's abduction and dusting stated that the yellow substance did not appear to be soil from the area. If these entities were extraterrestrials, then apparently they had adopted the centuries-old fairy folk tradition of sprinkling dust on their unwilling guests.

THE OLD BURYING-A-POT-OF-GOLD TRICK

Perhaps the most widely familiar bit of fairy lore is depicted in the scene in which a farmer comes upon a fairy circle that has been pressed into the grass of the meadow the night before by the merry dancing feet of the Little People. Filled with wonder, and perhaps a bit of fear, he follows the sound of a shovel slicing sod and comes upon one or more of the Wee Folk digging in the earth.

The farmer has heard all the stories about fairy gold, so he naturally surmises that the Wee Ones are burying their booty. He manages to snatch one of the woodland gentry and forces him to confess that they were, indeed, hiding their gold.

The farmer rejoices in his good fortune. But then he considers the grim fact that unsavory folk might see him hauling the treasure and rob him. And since he would be quite conspicuous walking about with a fairy in his clutches, he frees the elf and marks the spot so that he will be able to return after dark and find it again with little effort.

The tale has been told with endless variations, but most often the denouement finds the farmer eagerly returning with a sack and shovel to find that the fairies have altered or confused the spot in some manner to make the excavation of their gold impossible. However the story ends, it remains essentially the account of a fairy outwitting an avaricious human.

Less widely known to the general reader are the many stories of humans who come upon fairies at work or play and are whisked away by them to the underground fairy kingdom, from which they may return much later as elderly folks who think that only a day or so has gone by. Or perhaps they never return at all.

From our contemporary UFOlogical viewpoint, it is likely that the fairylike beings are not digging for gold at all. Rather, they may be UFOnauts obtaining soil, mineral, and legume samples who do not wish their activities known. Consider how the following account might have been related as a fairy tale if it had occurred four hundred years ago.

A Tragic Variation on an Ancient Theme

On August 17, 1962, Rivalino da Silva, a miner from Diamantina, Brazil, came upon two strange beings approximately three feet tall engaged in digging a hole.

Startled by da Silva's sudden approach, the tiny manlike creatures ran into the bushes. While the miner stared into the brush, attempting to identify the bizarre strangers, he was further amazed to see a fiery, hat-shaped object ascend into the sky.

Completely baffled, da Silva continued on his way home, trying his best to integrate the whole weird business into something that made sense according to his prior life experiences.

The next day, after he had slept on it and was still convinced that he had truly seen what his senses told him had taken place before his very eyes, he told his friends and fellow miners what he had witnessed on his way home from work the day before. Most of them laughed at him and believed that he was joking.

But shortly after dawn of August 20, da Silva's twelve-year-old son Raimunda was awakened by strange voices. The boy swore later that he heard them say, "Rivalino da Silva is in here. He must be destroyed."

Then Raimunda saw his father moving as if entranced. He opened the front door and walked toward two large globes that hovered about six feet off the ground. The peculiar objects hummed and blinked with an eerie illumination.

Raimunda screamed at his father to come back, to stay away from the floating globes, but the man continued to walk toward them. Before the boy could make a move to grab his father and shake him out of his strange trance, the globes emitted a heavy, yellowish smoke that completely enveloped his father's form.

When the smoke cleared, the mysterious floating globes had disappeared—and so had Rivalino da Silva.

Raimunda and his two younger brothers, Fatimo and Dirceu, ran to the police station, sobbing out the unbelievable tale of their father's disappearance. The police began an immediate investigation.

At the da Silva home, investigators found a strange, cleanly swept area in the dust that was about sixteen feet in diameter. They could find no sign of footprints or tracks in the vicinity. The officers did find a few drops of blood about 160 feet from the house, but even though laboratory analysis established that the blood was human, it did not appear to be da Silva's.

Police began to operate on the premise that the twelve-year-old boy had murdered his father and had somehow hit on an ingenious method of disposing of the body. They tried to break Raimunda's account of his father's disappearance, but they soon became convinced that the boy was terrified by what he had witnessed and that he sincerely mourned his lost father. Later testing by psychologists demonstrated that Raimunda seemed incapable of murder.

Continued investigation of the bizarre disappearance turned up a fisherman who reported that he had seen peculiar illuminated globes hovering above the da Silva home on the evening of August 19. Da Silva's miner friends told police about his claimed encounter with the two little men. Baffled by accounts of the strange events that had preceded Rivalino da Silva's disappearance, the police officially closed the case as unsolved.

Place this story in a different time and cultural context, and you might easily have a fairy tale of a workman who came upon two Little Folk burying their gold. After failing to trick them into giving up their treasure, he is whisked off to the fairy kingdom in a mysterious golden coach, never to be seen again.

SOMEONE KEEPS MAKING "FAIRY CIRCLES" IN FARMERS' FIELDS

Farmers in various sections of the United States and Canada have repeatedly told us that flying saucers passed over their farms with such regularity that they could set their watches by them. We have traveled to a number of these homesteads and "set our watches" by the brightly illuminated objects that suddenly appeared over our heads.

On many of these occasions, we also spotted a number

of scorched circular areas on the farmers' property. There is no question that some agency is still making those "fairy circles" in fields and pastures throughout the world, and they show no signs of stopping. In the early 1970s, a UFO researcher told us that his group had amassed a file of more than sixty thousand such sites. Undoubtedly, in 1999 the number of UFO touchdown areas is much higher.

A Peculiar Series of Burnt Circles Near a Power Line

Some years ago, a lineman employed by an Iowa power and light company told us that he had noticed a series of "burnt circles" near one of their power lines. When he made inquiries of the farm family who lived nearby, they openly stated that they had seen "flying saucers" hovering over the power line and landing in their nearby pasture.

Many UFOlogists theorize that the reason UFOs are often reported hovering near power lines is because the vehicles are somehow drawing electrical energy from them. Our call to the manager of the power company produced a courteous reply that there had been no undue outages or any sign of unnatural power loss or depletion along any of the area serviced by their lines.

During other UFO flaps, similar inquiries to managers of power companies have produced identical responses. Perhaps rather than drawing power from the lines, the normally "cloaked" objects are made visible by electro-magnetic emanations from them.

Because we were committed to an upcoming book-promotion tour, we called our friend and research associate Glenn McWane, who readily agreed to conduct a preliminary investigation of the case.

A Farm Where "Odd Things" Happened on a Regular Basis

McWane found the farm, located in Clayton County, Iowa, to be literally covered with scorched circles. The greatest concentration of the circles were found along the power line.

In addition to the scorched areas, McWane noticed indentures that could certainly have been caused by some kind of landing device.

Mr. and Mrs. S.H. were very friendly individuals who had apparently come to accept the regular visitations of the UFOs to their farm with little emotion. McWane assessed Mr. S.H. as a successful farmer, "level-headed, calm, not likely to jump to excitable conclusions." During his military service, Mr. S.H. had served at various missile sites around the United States.

Mrs. S.H. freely admitted to McWane that "odd things" had been occurring on their farm for about two years. And all the neighbors had seen the "odd things" as well: strange lights in the sky at night and sometimes weird noises coming from the fields and pastures.

Then, early that spring, their sons, aged eleven and eight, had seen a round, red object hovering over the power line. The older boy climbed a tree for a better view while the other watched the object cautiously from around a corner of the barn. Seemingly aware of their presence, the object directed a red beam of light at each of the boys.

The more courageous eleven-year-old remained in the tree to watch the object while his little brother sought sanctuary in the farmhouse. According to the older boy, the object rose higher above the power line, then descended again to land behind a clump of nearby trees.

Understandably, neither parent chose to investigate the

boy's story that evening, assuming that he had made it up to frighten his kid brother.

But the next morning when they looked behind the patch of trees, they found a circular burned spot and the impressions of what they came to believe must be landing gear.

When McWane visited the farm, each member of the family told him that the objects had reappeared on numerous occasions.

"They usually land in late afternoon, around five P.M.," Mrs. S.H. explained. "In the winter months, it can be pretty dark by then. There's been only one exception to their five o'clock arrival. One Sunday an object landed about two o'clock."

In his report to us, McWane said that according to the family and the neighbors who have witnessed the landings, "the UFOs are not seen until they are relatively close to the ground. Then—bang!—they suddenly appear and lower themselves to earth." He added:

It would seem that the objects are somehow able to remain invisible until they descend to a certain altitude. Or, to conjecture a bit, they may be entering our dimension through a doorway that just happens to be open on the S.H. farm.

It may be, as some UFOlogists suggest, that the UFOs come from another world existing outside our space-time continuum and that they are most often seen in areas wherein these "doorways" exist. Such a theory might explain how UFOs have suddenly disappeared with our Air Force jets in close pursuit.

At any rate, my opinion is that if a mysterious "someone" did not want to be observed by a lot of people, the area in which the S.H. farm is located would be a perfect spot to conduct secretive activities. It has heavily wooded areas, and a river runs through the farm. There is also a large cave in the area.

HEALED BY A WEE UFONAUT'S HAND

During our forty years of researching the UFO mystery, we have gathered numerous accounts of miraculous cures that were accomplished after a visitation by ostensibly the same sort of small humanoid beings that have been named as the villains in other accounts. Perhaps these entities have the good and the bad, the cruel and the compassionate, the concerned and the indifferent, in their world, just as we humans most certainly do in our society.

- One evening in 1986, Richard T., bound by injuries to a wheelchair, was enjoying the solitude of a beach near La Jolla, California, when a hundred-foot-long, cigar-shaped UFO appeared and hovered above him. Richard has only a dim recollection of both him and his wheelchair being lifted into the spacecraft. He has some memory of smallish humanoids with large heads and enormously large, slanted eyes working over him. At no time did he experience fear, only a kind of euphoria and peace.

  Richard lost all sense of time, but when he regained full consciousness, he was seated inside his van, his wheelchair neatly tucked away in the back.

  Amazingly, over the next few weeks, the condition for which the doctors had extended no hope began to reverse itself—until he was finally able to walk again with the help of a cane.

- A native of Finland had been troubled by a congenitally enlarged liver, and he had been told repeatedly that it could never become normal. A few years ago, however, as he was skiing in a remote area, he was caught in a white beam of light from an egg-shaped UFO.

    Although he had no memory of any kind of interaction with alien beings, he was disturbed by the fact that he seemed to have experienced missing time after he sighted the UFO. During a complete physical examination by his doctor, it was discovered that his liver had been reduced to a normal size.

- In 1973, a formerly toothless, eighty-year-old farmer in Brazil was pleasantly surprised to discover that he had new teeth growing in his jaws within two months after his abduction by four small entities in a silver, circular-shaped craft.

Our friend Dr. Edith Fiore has said that about half of the cases of abduction that she has investigated have involved healings due to operations and/or treatments conducted by the alien beings.

In the September 1997 issue of *Fate*, Preston E. Dennett claims to have unearthed more than one hundred cases of UFO healings. Dennett quotes Dan Wright, manager of the Mutual UFO Network Abduction Transcription Project, as saying, "Almost one-third of the subjects reported some type of physical effect as a direct result of one abduction episode or another . . . Curiously, in four cases, the subject was either told by an entity or separately concluded that the beings' 'reconstructive surgery' had repaired some medical problem."

Dennett observes that the wide range of cancer cures attributed to UFO entities is truly remarkable. In addition to uterine cancer and childhood leukemia, other cases have involved throat, stomach, skin, and breast cancer. In fact, Dennett writes:

> Approximately 10 percent of all healing cases on record involve cancer cures. UFO investigator Richard Boylan, Ph.D., who uncovered one cancer cure, says . . . "I can tell you in a general way that one woman . . . was cured of a cancerous growth on her uterus. A surgeon who examined her later could find no trace of the previously diagnosed cancer."

AS WITH ANY POWERFUL ENERGY, PROCEED WITH EXTREME CAUTION

Well-intentioned and earnest men and women often write to us asking how they might establish contact with alien intelligences from other worlds, beings from the Fairy Realm, entities from other dimensions, or angels from the higher planes. We always advise extreme caution to these folks, who truly may not be aware of what they are asking.

To seek to make contact with any form of multidimensional intelligence—whether elf, guardian angel, spirit guide, or space entity—without first undergoing an extensive program of study, self-examination, and disciplined training can be very risky. To open your psyche to these energies before you have achieved a high degree of spiritual balance is to run the risk of setting destructive forces loose on you and your household or inviting a parasitic, disruptive intelligence into your soul.

To demonstrate our point, we present herewith the experience of a group of very able, highly intelligent young men who thought that they could successfully interact with the UFO mystery and become masters of the universe.

Five Bright College Students Seek to Master UFO Energy

Bill Fogarty saw a UFO in the early 1970s when he was a twenty-year-old college junior at the University of Indiana at South Bend. One night a short time later, he mentioned his sighting to the members of an informal group that got together one evening a week to discuss politics, philosophy, and art. The discussion became freewheeling as members argued the pros and cons of the reality of flying saucers and the possibility of extraterrestrial life-forms.

That night on his way home, Fogarty sighted another UFO. He was reluctant to mention this second sighting, thinking that his friends would hardly find it credible, given the topic of the evening's lively discussion. The next day, however, he was astonished to learn that four other members of the group claimed to have witnessed a low UFO overflight that night as they drove back to their respective apartments.

In his written report to us, Fogarty emphasized that he and his friends were all physically fit, nondrinkers, and nondopers. Two of them were Vietnam War combat veterans. Each of the five prided himself on maintaining a cool, analytical approach to all aspects of life, and all were especially skeptical of anything that smacked of the occult or the bizarre.

And yet each of them swore that he had seen what was unmistakably an object in the night sky that he could not identify as a conventional aircraft, an ordinary celestial manifestation, a weather balloon, a bird, or anything else that could have been flying above them.

Four nights later, two of the five saw another UFO. Then, on the next evening, Fogarty and the other two saw a brightly glowing object overhead as they returned around one o'clock from a movie.

"We decided to form a splinter group in order to focus on the UFO phenomenon," Fogarty said. "We were well aware that the main group of culture vultures would mock us for our flying saucer experiences, so we headed for an all-night pancake house to compare notes and thoughts on our subjective responses while undergoing the experience of encountering what certainly appeared to us to be unknown phenomena."

It was not long before the five of them had a group sighting of a UFO. From that evening on, they instituted nightly sky watches.

"We all witnessed UFOs cavorting in the midnight sky," Fogarty said. "On one occasion I stood within ten feet of two nocturnal lights hovering silently in midair. Later, we heard rappings in the dark, hollow voices, heavy breathing, and the crushing footsteps of unseen entities. Strangely enough we were all able to maintain our cool toward the phenomena occurring around us. Maybe we had been chosen for some kind of special interaction with higher beings. Perhaps, secretly, we were beginning to view ourselves as masters of two worlds."

After all, Fogarty pointed out, they were all dean's list students, all athletic young men, normally balanced emotionally, mentally, sexually. "I guess we felt that modern Renaissance men such as ourselves should be able to deal rationally with such phenomena and stay completely in control of the situation."

But then, suddenly, the manifestations became more aggressive and hostile. Just when they thought they were capable of exercising control over the invisible forces emanating from the UFO, the apprentice wizards found that not only were they far from being the equals of the unseen visitors, they were also in danger of losing control over themselves.

One night invisible energies swept through the home of one group member, pounding on the walls, yanking furiously at the bedposts, striking the startled young man in the face, terrorizing his entire family. Some of the group were followed by automobiles that seemed a bizarre mixture of styles and models.

Within the next few months, the number of harrowing incidents directed against the students increased and expanded to include strange, dark-clad, nocturnal visitors in the apartments of several of them.

Radio and television sets switched on by themselves. Doors opened and closed—although when they were tested, they were found locked.

One member of the group made the extraordinary claim that he had been teleported one night from his bedroom to the middle of a forest on the outskirts of the city. "As preposterous as all this might sound," Fogarty stated, "I'm sure that most of us accepted all of these experiences as true, since we had all undergone some incredible encounters. We had all lost our sense of perspective."

Fogarty admitted that he had begun sleeping with a light on and a .38 special under his pillow. Another of the five invested heavily in weapons and began running with a group that offered sacrifices to Odin. A third was "born again" into fundamentalist Christianity. The remaining two dropped out of college a month before they would have graduated with honors.

By the time that he made his report to us, Bill Fogarty had had several years to consider the big question of what it all had meant, the bold quest of five bright young men to tackle the UFO mystery and to seek to become one with its energy.

"I think the five of us believed that we had entered a kind of game, a contest, a challenge, a testing experience," he said. "The trouble was, we just didn't know all the rules.

"Modern society doesn't prepare its youth to play those kinds of games. Modern society doesn't tell its kids that there is another reality around them. Our educators have ignored the individual mystical experience and the other dimensions that can open up to those who enter altered states of consciousness—whether it be through drugs or through accidentally stumbling into the twilight zones."

Bill Fogarty recalled that at first he had the feeling that they were dealing with some kind of energy emanating from outer space, from some alien world, but he now believes that they somehow activated some energy that is a part of this planet. "I think we might have triggered some kind of archetypal pattern with our minds. Maybe that's what magicians have tried to do since Cro-Magnon days— interact with and control the energy with their minds."

But how had such intelligent, resourceful young men lost control of their experiment? Why had they ended up paranoid, frightened, or converted to widely disparate philosophies?

Bill Fogarty's answer was honest and direct: "Because we weren't magicians obviously. We had no idea just how deadly serious the game could become. It really is a game for wizards, not for some smart-ass college students who believe that their brilliant intellects and the theories in their physics books can provide an answer for everything."

He Became the Entity's "Reference Point" on Earth

A much worse scenario than that experienced by Bill Fogarty and his friends was that of a young man named Mark, who believed that he had made contact with an extraterrestrial being. After a period of increasingly dramatic interaction, this entity agreed to grant Mark certain concessions in return for allowing it to use his body.

The being did not give itself a name, saying only that it was a multidimensional being whose substance was totally energy. While its essence permeated the entire universe, it could, by effort of will, concentrate its force and be at any point in the cosmos for the purpose of making contact with beings still bound to the physical plane. Its reason for making the contact with Mark was to enable it to have a point of reference on Earth.

The entity had originally represented itself to Mark as neutral in the affairs of humans. But, tragically, by the time Mark realized the entity's true nature, he was forced to remain committed to the contract that he had made.

According to Mark's friend Bob: "The being at last identified itself to Mark as 'Asmitor,' and his description of it was very similar to those H. P. Lovecraft uses in his stories of the Elder Gods and the Old Ones. The entity was infinite in its expanse, a tenuous network of energy that stretched throughout the universe, but which had consciousness and the ability to concentrate itself at any one point on this level of reality, but only when expressly invited—or, in Mark's case, unknowingly invited. Mark had opened the door to the entity by his use of psychedelics without proper protective preparation."

Mark learned that there were two types of entities, essentially equal in power and scope, perpetually at war over the ownership of the physical universe. Mark was led to believe that Asmitor and his forces would win the next great battle and that he would be rewarded by receiving some of the spoils of war.

Such beings as Asmitor needed human points of reference on the earth plane of reality because the more points they had, the better they would be able to fight against the opposing force, which was also working to gain its own points of reference on the planet. "Apparently, these entities were not able to perceive our level of existence directly," Bob concluded, "but only indirectly through the minds of their servitors."

Mark became disenchanted when most of the powers that Asmitor promised him failed to materialize. He was unable to levitate objects; he had no demonstratable powers of telepathy; the curses he levied upon his enemies seemed to have no effect. But the deceitful Asmitor was now so completely in control of his body that Mark felt the only way to achieve freedom from the entity was to destroy himself by committing suicide.

Although the name "Asmitor" had meant nothing to Bob when Mark had first identified it, after his friend's death Bob chanced across it in a medieval text on magic: "It was—I believe—in the works of Agrippa [1486–1535], a German soldier, physician, and an adept in alchemy, astrology, and magic. I am convinced that Mark had never read this book; and I am also convinced that he did not simply make up this name. In my opinion, my discovery of the name was a piece of corroborating evidence to indicate that rather than a case of insanity, Mark's case was one of true demonic possession."

Bob has become a very serious student of magic and mysticism, and he stated firmly that he has come to believe in entities from other planes of existence. Although he personally refers to these beings as the "Secret Chiefs," he concedes that they might just as easily be called angels, masters, guides, UFO beings, or even gods, who operate from another plane of being to influence humankind's development and to direct it in ways that are not always comprehensible to the people being subtly manipulated: "The overall goal of these beings may be incomprehensible to us—or from a human and very limited point of view, may seem to be evil. Human value judgments really don't apply on these levels . . . We must accept that [the Secret Chiefs] are a natural development of the universe and that they exist with as much validity as we do."

Bob reminded us of the line in C. S. Lewis's *Screwtape Letters* in which a demon declares that once humankind has produced the true materialist magician—an individual who will worship what he calls "Forces" without acknowledging the existence of *consciousness* behind those Forces— the demons may then consider that they have won the eternal battle between good and evil.

"Too many modern materialistic scientists fit this description," Bob observed.

In the next chapter we face a challenge as daunting as determining which intelligences are from outer space and which are an indigenous Fairy Folk. In the matter of distinguishing between angels and aliens, the problem is complicated by the fact that they are both extraterrestrials.

7

From Heaven Above
to Earth Below

On a segment of the July 8, 1997, broadcast of the *700 Club*, Pat Robertson, television evangelist and head of the Christian Coalition, suggested that if such entities as space aliens truly existed, they were quite likely demons trying to lead people away from Christ. Furthermore, he referred to Deuteronomy 17:2–5, which commands the Old Testament Children of Israel to stone those who worship other gods that might come from the heavens.

Robertson went on to state that the UFO beings receiving so much attention in the media were really demonic intelligences, and he reminded his audience that there were fallen angels as well as angels of the Lord.

Referring to the common descriptions given by UFO contactees and abductees, the evangelist said that demons could easily appear as "slanty-eyed, funny-looking creatures." To pay undue attention to such beings or to elevate them to positions of importance in one's life, Robertson warned, was a "clear violation of God's word."[1]

While the head of the Christian Coalition worries about fallen angels masquerading as UFOnauts, reports from Russia tell of religious fanatics who believe that the UFO entities are angelic messengers sent directly from God.

Angered by the research of Russian UFOlogists that generally portrays the beings as space intelligences from other physical worlds rather than heavenly guides, the members of several sects have taken to threatening UFO investigators—telling them to repent and cease their research at once. Many UFOlogists have been savagely beaten, and in October 1995, A. Zolotov, scientist and UFO researcher, was murdered because he persisted in his investigations.

Are the UFOnauts angels or aliens? Are they heavenly forerunners of Christ's return or benevolent extraterrestrials intent upon correcting our errant Earth? Are they demonic servants of the Antichrist come to assist in the harvesting of condemned souls or malevolent entities from another galaxy come to reap the spoils of a conquered planet?

Throughout the course of human history there have always been accounts of other intelligences—humanlike in appearance, yet somehow different, seemingly superhuman—interacting with the struggling and evolving species of *Homo sapiens*. These "Others" have been called Angels, Devas, Star People, Light Beings, and, on occasion, demons and devils, as well as gods and overlords. Whatever the name applied, the various activities ascribed to these entities have remained constant through the ages and consistent from culture to culture.

The mysterious supernatural visitors are seen riding in fiery chariots, moving within mysterious globes of light, driving strange aerial vehicles, or appearing suddenly in blinding flashes of light. Sometimes they appear benevolent, like friendly travelers one might encounter on a lonely road. On other occasions, they have been accused of abduction, kidnapping, rape, even murder.

Their place of origin has been declared to be heaven, hell, other worlds, other galaxies, other dimensions. But as the philosopher Voltaire once observed, "It is not known precisely where angels dwell—whether in the air, the void, or the planets. It has not been God's pleasure that we should be informed of their abode."

These beings are proclaimed to be so much more than human—and yet, there is always something very familiar about them that expresses itself to the deeper levels of the human psyche.

And the fact that their presence among us seems to be increasing as we near the millennium and what some religionists foresee as Armageddon, the final great battle between Good and Evil, these eerily familiar angels or aliens are increasingly declared to be the supernatural warriors of the Apocalypse.

QUESTIONING THE MOTIVES OF THE ANGELS IS AN AGE-OLD DILEMMA

Historians have observed that angels and spiritual beings are always very popular characters in apocalyptic writings. Theologians say that this is so because angels have been placed in charge of the cosmic order of the universe and that times of crisis summon them into the fray. Skeptics dismiss explanations of the current reports of angels and aliens as merely the externalized projections of fearful men and women who fantasize the images of benevolent beings in order to assuage the terror of existence in our contemporary world of chaos and conflict.

In nearly all accounts of angels, the beings seem to be paraphysical in nature—that is, they are both material and nonmaterial. Although they apparently originate in some invisible and nonphysical realm or dimension or vibrational level, they are seen to manifest as solidly in our reality as the humans whose lives they seek to affect.

MICHAEL FOUND IT ALWAYS PAYS
TO LISTEN TO HIS GUARDIAN

Michael of Seattle was five years old, alone in the wooded area near the family home, when he heard someone call him by his first name.

He turned around to see a tall, slender, silver-haired, pale-skinned man with light blue eyes. At his waist was a belt buckle shaped like a "glittery pyramid."

The strange man opened his arms to the boy, and inside his head Michael heard the being say, "I am pleased with you, my son."

Michael recalled that such a salutation puzzled him. "You are not my father," he told the stranger. "Who are you?"

The silver-haired entity laughed and told him: "In time you will come to know me. I am all you are, have been, and will become."

At that moment, Michael remembered, he was distracted by the voice of his father calling to him.

When he looked back to the stranger, he was astonished to see him fading from sight. "Don't forget me," the entity said. "Always remember me."

Michael stated firmly that he never has forgotten the

being: "From that day forward, he has come to me in my dreams or by voice only. He tells me things that are about to happen to myself, family, or friends. He sometimes warns me of things before they occur. It always pays to listen to him."[2]

THE SPACE BROTHERS: ANGELS IN STARSHIPS

Noel, a musician from California, said that he has endeavored as a child, teenager, and adult to live as Christ would have him live. He testified that he loves God first, Christ second, the Holy Spirit third, his parents fourth, with humankind following after them. In spite of what seems to be a most orthodox and conventional Christian faith, Noel also stated that he believes in the reality of UFOs, other intelligences in the cosmos, and the strong possibility that Christ will return in a space vehicle.

Noel was eight years old and riding in the company of his parents near a Nike missile base when they sighted six UFOs. From that point forward, his family agreed that Earth was being visited by beings from another planet.

Visits to Giant Rock, a mecca for UFO enthusiasts, in Landers, California, during the mid-1950s and '60s introduced him to George Van Tassel and that colorful figure's belief in the benevolent Space Brothers. According to Van Tassel, he had traveled with the Brothers in their beamships, and he commented that although the benign visitors from outer space looked just like us, they would seem like angels to humans. There were, in fact, a number of the Brothers who had been living among humankind for quite some time.

Over the years, Noel, now in his early fifties, has had numerous dreams in which he envisions himself aboard the beamships with the space beings. Always, he says, the Brothers and Sisters are warm and friendly, truly "angels in starships."[3]

TWO GLOWING OBJECTS AND A SHINING, SILVER HUMANOID

Pat, a schoolteacher from Ohio, recalled the summer day when she was eleven and saw two strange, glowing objects hovering above the lake near their home.

"That night something awakened me," she said, "and I saw a shining, silver humanoid being standing at the foot of my bed. I remember at first feeling the sensation of undistilled terror, but that soon changed to awe and wonder as I watched the being disappear."

Pat did not see the entity again until that Thanksgiving when she accompanied her father to take her grandmother home after her holiday visit with the family.

"Dad and I wound up on a dark, winding road," she recalled. "It was icy and slick because of a sleet storm. Dad asked me to roll down the window and to watch to make certain that we didn't slide off the road and down the steep banks."

Pat remembers feeling very frightened, and it was obvious that her father was nervous and concerned for their safety. There was a very real possibility that they could slip over the edge of the highway and crash and freeze to death.

"It was cold, and my face was numb and stinging as I

looked into the darkness from the open car window," Pat said.

"Suddenly I saw directly behind us and just above us a brilliant white light with a bluish center. I did not hear a voice, but I was unmistakably getting a message from the light . . . or from something. And I knew somehow that the message was something connected with myself—in the future or in the past.

"I survived that frightening, freezing night with the deep certainty that the white light had told me, 'I am.' "

Pat said that it was not until many years later that she learned the significance of the *I am* concept in theology, as exemplified in the experience of Moses when the voice from the burning bush identified itself as *I am that I am*. But from that childhood Thanksgiving evening onward, Pat was keenly aware that there was within and without the very essence of her being an aspect that exists in the now, in the past, and "will do so for all time."[4]

CAN ALIENS ALSO SERVE AS GUARDIAN ANGELS?

Is it possible that entities from UFOs are serving as guardian angels or spiritual guides for certain men and women of Earth?

Or are we only confusing heavenly angelic guardians as alien beings because our advanced technology and our contemporary culture find extraterrestrial entities easier to accept than messengers sent from God?

In both the Old and the New Testaments we are told that angels are divided into two vast hosts: one, obedient to God and active in good ministries for humankind; the other, intent on annoying and harming humans and bringing about their enslavement.

Such a division may remind the metaphysically minded of Edgar Cayce's concept of the primal warfare on Atlantis between the beneficent Children of the Law of One and the evil Sons of Belial. Belial, by the way, happens to be Hebrew for "person of baseness," and is often used to designate the prince of the dark angels, Satan.

BIBLICAL ANGELS ARE CORPOREAL BEINGS DWELLING ON A HIGHER PLANE

As used in scripture, the term "angel" indicates an office, rather than a person. An angel (*angelos* in Greek; *malach* in Hebrew) is simply a messenger, one who is sent to accomplish whatever mission has been assigned to him or her.

Even a casual student of the Bible can readily testify that angels are referred to as actual beings and not simply as impersonal influences. Angels ate with Abraham, were lusted after by the Sodomites, grasped Lot by the hand.

While angels steadfastly refuse to be worshipped by humans, they never turn down hospitality. By the same token, they fed prophets in the wilderness and undertook the great task of distributing manna, "angel's food . . . the bread of the mighty," to the wandering Children of Israel.

In relation to God, the Supreme Being, angels stand as courtiers to a king. They themselves are not gods, but are created beings, as subject to God's will as are humans.

And this would seem a good place to clear up an age-old misconception that humans become angels when they die. We're not denying folks an afterlife of playing harps and singing with the angels, but the true angelic ranks were formed long before humankind was scooped from the dust of Earth.

Although angels are frequently called spirits, it is often implied in the Bible that they do possess corporeal bodies, but dwell on a higher plane of existence than humans. When seen on Earth, angels have always appeared youthful, physically attractive, commanding. They are, in fact, described the same way UFO contactees of today describe their "Space Brothers and Sisters."

Even though angels have throughout history been often mistaken for ordinary humans when judged by their appearance alone, those who have confronted them have often felt the physical effects of their majesty. One touch of an angel's hand crippled Jacob. The single stroke of an angel's staff consumed Gideon's offering. Zacharias was deafened by an angel's spoken word. Daniel's men fell quaking at the sound of an angel's voice.

Their appearance is often sudden and accompanied by a bright light. Saul of Tarsus and the guards about Jesus's tomb were blinded by their heavenly light.

Whenever angels appear, they are described as strong, swift, splendid, subtle as the wind, elastic as the light. No distance wearies them, and no barriers hinder them. An angel entered the fiery furnace to keep Shadrach, Meshach, and Abednego cool, and another entered the lion's den with Daniel and closed fast the jaws of the beasts.

In the teachings of Islam, there are three distinct species of intelligent beings in the universe. There are first the angels (*malak* in Arabic), a high order of beings created of Light; second *al-jinn*, ethereal, perhaps even multidimensional, entities; and then human beings, fashioned of the stuff of Earth and born into physical bodies.

The Qur'an suggests that while a certain number of jinn act benevolently toward humans and may even serve as guardians and guides, the great majority of the ethereal entities are dedicated to performing devilish acts against humankind. Normally invisible to the human eye, they are capable of materializing in our three-dimensional world; and while in the physical plane, they are notorious for kidnapping human children and seducing adults into acts of sexual intercourse.

ANCIENT SUPERBEINGS OR SPACE TRAVELERS?

In an analysis of the works of fifty writers of antiquity, W. Raymond Drake, author and scholar, shows how these early authors provide evidence of superbeings from other worlds. He found references to such celestial phenomena as airborne lights, shields, fiery globes, strange ships, and warriorlike "men" with the ability to fly. In addition, there were mentions of two or more "moons," two or more "suns," new "stars," falling lights, unknown voices, "gods" descending to Earth, and "men" ascending to the sky.

Drake strongly believed that the old gods of Egypt, Greece, Rome, Scandinavia, and Mexico were not simply manifestations of lightning and thunderbolts. Nor did he think that these oft-cited beings were disembodied spirits and anthropomorphic symbols. In his opinion, the gods of old were actual spacemen from other worlds.

Drake pointed out that the Roman hero Romulus was said to have been borne to heaven by a whirlwind, that his successor, Numa Pompilius, employed magic weapons, and that the classical writers Livy, Pliny the Elder, and Julius Obsequens refer often to mysterious voices, celestial trumpets, and men in white garments hovering in airships or descending to Earth.

"By some strange twist of the human mind," Drake once mused, "we worship prodigies in old Palestine as manifestations of the Lord, yet scoff at identical phenomena occurring at the same time only a few hundred miles away."[5]

HIS RESCUING ANGEL CAME FROM A UFO

When Bobby of Asheville, North Carolina, was five years old, he ignored his mother's warnings and ran out into a street after his toy race car.

"Too late I saw the semi truck bearing down on me," he said. "I froze, not knowing what to do. When I was able to move, I stumbled over my own feet and fell directly into the path of the truck."

Bobby, now thirty-two, remembers that it was as if time suddenly slowed "way down." A husky man with straw-colored hair materialized from nowhere and pulled him away from the huge tires just in time.

"He rolled me to the side of the street, right up against the curb, then reached down and rubbed my head affectionately. 'It's not your time yet, Bobby,' he said. Then everything went back to normal time, and my mother was screaming, picking me up, and crying about a miracle."

In 1982, Bobby had a sighting of a UFO while he was vacationing in Wisconsin. "I thought right away of the angel who had saved my life when I was a little kid. I got the same kind of feeling when I saw that UFO."[6]

THE BIBLE CONTAINS A WEALTH
OF UFO CONTACT STORIES

Certain UFOlogists have suggested that the Judeo-Christian Bible is the greatest record of UFO-contactee stories ever assembled. Without wishing to offend the religious beliefs of any of our readers, we acknowledge that scripture is filled with accounts of glowing aerial vehicles, angels walking among humankind, and certain humans receiving prophetic messages. And it does appear that a similar kind of contact and communication exists today between the UFO entities and an ever-growing number of humans.

If we can accept the possibility that the Bible is a remarkable collection of UFO-contact stories, then perhaps Armageddon, the predicted final battle between the Forces of Light and Darkness, may also address itself directly to our times. For while many UFO contactees believe their interaction with "Space Brothers and Sisters" to be totally benevolent, it cannot be denied that some of the space beings have deceived and embarrassed their human channels.

And then there is the uncomfortable matter of UFO abductions and what would at worst appear to be hostile activities—or at best, disrespect for humankind. Once again we are reminded of St. Paul's warning in his letter to the Ephesians (6:12) that we are warring against "sovereignties and the Powers who originate the darkness in this world, the spiritual army of evil in the heavens."

Traditionally, the wilderness has always been the habitat of evil spirits. The spiritually strong and disciplined may willingly enter the desert or the forest on their vision quest to test their mettle against the dark side of the Force, to wrestle with Satan. Today, thousands of UFO abductees claim that they have encountered negative, reptilian, demonic entities in the wilderness.

THE HUMAN SOUL—PRIZE OF A COMING WAR OF THE WORLDS

According to Persian and Chaldean tradition, the *Ahrimanes* are the fallen angels, who out of revenge for being expelled from heaven continually torment the apex of God's creation, the human inhabitants of Earth. The old legends have it that the Ahrimanes finally decided to inhabit the space between the Earth and the fixed stars, which is called *Ahrimane-Abad*.

Military and aviation historian Trevor James Constable has come to the conclusion that it is the Ahrimanic powers that are trying to seize control of our planet. He believes that Inner Space, not Outer Space, is the invasion route chosen by the Ahrimanic powers.

According to Constable, a fifth column inside the human mind makes external force unnecessary. In his view, Washington and the major political capitals of the world have already been conquered by "inner space invaders," and he warns, "Continuing ignorance of these malefic, invisible, but all-too-real forces will bring disaster not only to America, but to human evolution and to the destiny of man as a free being."

Constable reminds us that according to the ancient traditions the Ahrimanic powers have for centuries held as their goal the total enslavement of humankind. If they are unopposed, the Ahrimanic entities will overwhelm humanity and take evolution wholly under their control.

What the human species must realize is that in the struggle for mastery of Earth, we human beings are at once the goal of the battle and the battleground.

The choices we make, Constable says, and the extent to which we utilize balancing forces to neutralize the Ahrimanic attacks, will bring us victory or defeat. "The stakes in this battle are not the territory, commercial advantages, or political leverage of ordinary wars," he stresses, "but the very mind and destiny of humankind."

Free will dictates that humankind has the right to decide whether or not life on Earth will be surrendered to the Ahrimanes, and Constable underscores that the challenge presented by these dark forces will be a very grim one:

> UFO technology portends the kind of confrontation that lies ahead. Man faces a bewildering armory of advanced technical devices, transcendental abilities, and mind-bending powers. Armed only with mechanistic thought and an unbalanced technology ... the human posture for meeting this stupendous and unavoidable event is both unstable and inadequate.[7]

Constable agrees with the many other serious scholars of apocalyptic thought who have taken the time to assess the importance of these so-called latter days: all depends upon the expansion of human awareness.

> If man can be shown where the battlefield is, the nature of the terrain, and the ways in which he is already being assaulted in this inner war, then the right tactics and strategy can be brought to bear against the inimical forces.

The objective of the Ahrimanic powers is to pull

down all humanity. To this end, whatever political systems and philosophies exist among men are simply
manipulated.[8]

Humans are constantly being seduced into doing the
work of the nether forces because they simply do not acknowledge that such forces exist, let alone recognize how
they work *into* and *upon* Earth life.

"Incomprehension of spiritual forces and the institu-
tionalized denigration of the spirit in formal education
make humanity pitifully vulnerable to dehumanizing, life-
negative, and destructive trends," Constable says, and he
adds, "Entities riding etherically propelled vehicles and
obviously in mastery of psychic control in all its forms de-
vise contact encounters with ingenuous human beings
who can be used in various ways to serve certain ends . . .
[producing] chatter and bewilderment.[9]

The overall consequence of such depraved encounters,
wherein humans are set upon by the Ahrimanic humanoids,
Constable decrees, is that

The world is led to believe that material craft are involved, if convinced at all. And if not convinced, then
the contactee is another "flying saucer nut." Either way,
the world gets a lie overlaid with confusion and ridicule
while the humanoids depart from view.[10]

The Ahrimanic deceivers are everywhere, Constable
warns, "unrecognized and often aided by humans who
don't know that the Devil is indeed alive and well—and
coming to Earth within the lifetime of millions now living."

If Constable is correct, then one would certainly wish to
be cautious about taking an alleged UFOnaut's or angel's

word for anything pertaining to Earthly matters. One would certainly be wise to "test the spirits," so to speak, and attempt to determine if the counseling entity serves the Dark Side or the Light Side of the Force.

And such caution should be doubled in reports of UFO encounters, for in Constable's opinion, the Ahrimanic messengers inject themselves into such events in order to sow confusion, disorientation, and distrust among UFO investigators.

Trevor James Constable is not alone in suggesting that the UFO beings may be etheric, rather than physical entities, who have as their goal the ultimate enslavement of the very soul, mind, and destiny of humankind.

Other investigators of the UFO mystery insist that a mass invasion of Earth would already have taken place if it had not been for the intervention of other, more benevolent interplanetary beings. A kind of "Interplanetary Council" is doing what it can to halt the invasion of our planet and to correct the vast number of wrongs that have already been dealt to the human species.

A growing number of evangelical Christians are becoming convinced that Satan is behind the UFO mystery and that there is a conspiracy among the fallen angels to usher in the Antichrist in the guise of a benevolent Space Being. This false savior will perform miracles amid planetary Earth changes and chaos and ensnare millions of humans who will believe his lies. However, Christ and the Angelic Forces of Light will eventually prevail against the fallen angels and their perverse leader.

And so we are left with the argument that there are those angels or aliens who are genuinely concerned about our welfare and our spiritual and physical evolution, and there are those entities who seek to undermine and enslave us— or, at best, seem largely indifferent to our personal needs or our species' continued existence.

As for defining the difference between angels and aliens, it seems that we are once again caught in the corner of cultural perspective and spiritual biases. Until we somehow achieve definite proof of heavenly address or alien registration, all that remains are assumptions, opinions, and theories.

EVEN EXPERIENCERS OF ANGELIC AND ALIEN ACTIVITY HAVE A HARD TIME TELLING THEM APART

Of the more than 25,000 respondents to the *Steiger Questionnaire of Paranormal, Mystical, and UFO Experiences*, 89 percent are convinced that they have witnessed UFO activity. Of those approximately 22,000 people, 90 percent, or 20,000 individuals, state that they saw an entity of some sort associated with their UFO experience.

Thirty-four percent believed the being was an alien entity, either of extraterrestrial or multidimensional origin.

Twenty-four percent indicated that the being seemed to them more like an elf or some kind of magical creature.

Thirty-seven percent expressed their feelings that the entity was some kind of Light Being, similar to that of an angel or some higher intelligence.

In another section of the questionnaire, however, *38 percent* reported the visitation of an angel, *35 percent* felt that they had been blessed by the appearance of a holy figure, and *50 percent* are convinced that they have a personal guardian angel or spirit guide.

During the course of our research in the field, interviewing percipients of both angelic and alien experiences, and distributing the questionnaire on a global basis, we have found it increasingly difficult to differentiate between the two beings. Even when witnesses feel strongly that they have truly encountered an extraterrestrial intelligence or been blessed by a messenger from God, from our perspective the accounts sound nearly identical. To list only a few similarities:

- Both angels and aliens have been seen to descend from the sky, independent of any type of vehicle or craft.
- Witnesses have observed both types of entity arriving or descending on a shaft of light into their presence.
- Percipients have been awakened from their sleep by a sense of presence or by a touch and seen an angel or an alien at their bedside.
- A percipient may hear a voice that tells him or her to go to a certain place and do a certain thing. When the person does as the voice requests, the angel or the alien appears.
- Witnesses often report being awakened by the shining of a bright light in their bedroom. When they open their eyes, they perceive the angel or the alien.
- A cloud is seen moving toward a person. As it draws near, the form of an angel or an alien emerges. In other instances, the entities disappear into a cloud.

- A cloud or a mist forms within a room, and an angel or an alien manifests before a percipient.

- The angel or alien appears to several persons at the same time but is perceived differently by individuals in the group. By one, the entity manifests as a physical being; by another, as a ball or cloud of light; by the next, as an inner or external voice; and by yet another, as a threatening or frightening figure.

- The beings appear in what are regarded as paranormal dreams because of a miraculous healing or other special manifestation that occurs in connection with the dreams.

- Both angels and aliens have been said to disappear quickly—to fade gradually—to walk away and disappear in the distance—to pass through walls or doors that are closed—to ascend through ceilings—to ascend in a cloud or a glowing object.

- During an out-of-body experience, witnesses have claimed to have seen an angel or an alien that was invisible to them during their normal in-body condition.

- During out-of-body experiences, men and women have claimed to have visited the lower spirit worlds (hells) or the higher spirit worlds (heavens) and have reported seeing aliens and/or angels while on these otherworldly journeys.

- Men and women who have been restored to life after a near-death experience have stated that they have been in the company of aliens and/or angels.

Perhaps we humans waste a great deal of valuable time attempting to separate, identify, and catalogue such encounters with the unknown. It may be that angelic contact and alien contact are one and the same. But for those who are offended theologically or intellectually by such a statement, we'll reword it and say that it may well be that both aliens and angels have as one aspect of their respective missions the demonstration of the truth that we humans are an integral part of the universe and that the universe is a part of us. If our species can truly recognize and feel in touch with an intelligence and an energy source outside of ourselves, then we may soon come to feel a new power and awareness rising within our own being.

8

Superscientists
from the Stars

It is the thesis of many UFO researchers that extraterrestrial superscientists visited our planet in its prehistory and set about manipulating the DNA of the indigenous primate beings. Their goal was to "jump start" the human species and to accelerate the process of civilization and technological progress on Earth.

Once these extraterrestrial scientists had isolated the DNA fragment that they were seeking, they were able to clone that fragment and produce many identical copies. It was at that time that they began to shape the forerunners of the human species.

While many consider such a theory exceedingly far-out, perhaps even blasphemous, in 1982, the highly respected Dr. Francis Crick, codiscoverer of DNA, boldly suggested that the seeds of life on Earth may well have been sent here in a rocket launched from some faraway planet by "creatures like ourselves."

Science writer David Rorvik explored such a provocative theory, and other related subjects, in an interview with Dr. Crick that appeared in the March 1982 issue of *Omni* magazine. Dr. Crick told of a meeting in Soviet Armenia in 1971 where scientists discussed the idea that the uniformity of the genetic code made it appear as if life went through a "rather narrow bottleneck." In addition, he came to realize that sufficient time had elapsed for life to have evolved twice:

> That is, a civilization capable of sending out rockets could already have come into existence at the time the solar system and Earth got going. Leslie Orgel [a biochemist at the Salk Institute] and I . . . came up with the idea of a directed panspermia.

Panspermia is the theory that life may be distributed throughout the universe in the form of spores or germs that will develop in a propitious environment. When asked by Rorvik to comment on precisely which things made the theory of panspermia attractive to him, Dr. Crick replied:

> The easiest way to see that it's attractive is to realize that we might find ourselves doing the same thing a thousand or two thousand years from now, seeding life in the same way.

REPTILIAN SUPERSCIENTISTS SEEK TO REPLICATE THEIR OWN KIND

Some researchers feel that there is strong evidence to indicate that millions of years ago the extraterrestrial superscientists first attempted to accelerate our reptilian predecessors on this planet.

An archaeological enigma with which we dealt extensively in an earlier work has to do with what appear to be humanoid footprints that are found widely scattered around the planet—but especially in the southwestern United States—in geologic strata that suggest a time a *quarter of a billion* years ago.

This being left shoe prints, sandal prints, and barefoot prints on sands of time that have long since hardened into rock. This bipedal creature with a humanlike stride apparently vanished and left a baffling riddle that has had scientists scratching their heads for decades—for only four-legged, belly-sliding, tail-dragging amphibians were supposed to be around at that time.

Perhaps the reason why the most frequently reported UFOnauts resemble reptilian humanoids is that this is exactly what they are: highly evolved members of a serpentine species. Perhaps the Overlords themselves are reptilian or amphibian humanoids.

In most alien encounters, the UFO beings are described as standing about four and a half to five feet tall and being dressed in one-piece, tight-fitting jumpsuits. Their skin is most often characterized as hairless and gray or grayish green in color. Their faces are dominated by extremely large eyes, very often with snakelike, slit pupils. They are said to have no discernible lips, just "straight lines" for mouths. They seldom are described as having noses, just little stubs if anything at all. Most often the witnesses see only nostrils nearly flush against the UFOnauts' smooth, hairless faces. Sometimes a percipient mentions pointed ears, but on most occasions comments on the absence of noticeable ears on a large, round head. And repeatedly, witnesses describe an insignia of a flying serpent on an alien's shoulder patch, badge, medallion, or helmet.

There are two popular theories regarding the interaction of the reptilian Overlords.

1. Terrestrial amphibians evolved into a humanoid species that eventually developed a culture that ran its course— or was destroyed in an Atlantis-type catastrophe just after it began to explore extraterrestrial frontiers. Today's UFOnauts, then, may be the descendants of the survivors of that terrestrial amphibian culture returning from their space colony on some other world to monitor the present dominant species on the home planet.

2. The UFOnauts reported by contactees, abductees, and other witnesses may, in fact, be a highly advanced amphibian or reptilian culture from an extraterrestrial world, who evolved into the dominant species on their planet millions of years ago—and who have interacted in Earth's evolution as explorers, observers, caretakers, and genetic engineers.

   As early as 250 million years ago, these reptilian Star Gods visited our planet and began efforts to accelerate the evolution of certain terrestrial amphibians and reptiles in an attempt to replicate their own culture on Earth. When these experiments in genetic engineering failed, they made a decision to focus upon evolving mammals.

EARTH—A BIOLOGICAL LABORATORY
FOR THE CREATION OF HUMANS

According to the Overlord theorists, whether the extraterrestrial superscientists were reptilian, mammalian, or beyond our present awareness, when they came to this green oasis in space they viewed it as a great biological laboratory. And they must also have computed that it would take the slow process of evolution a hundred million years to alter a species or to develop a new one.

For whatever reason, they made a decision to accelerate the normal process of evolution and to fashion a rational creature before its time.

Fossils discovered in the Moroto site in Uganda in the 1960s and in 1994 and dated at 20.6 million years ago reveal a one-hundred-pound creature that, in addition to the ability to swing from trees, could stand upright. The date of the fossils, initially discovered by W. Bishop, pushes back the appearance of an apelike being by at least five million years.

Daniel Gebo, lead author of a report in *Science* magazine, stated that the find in Uganda represented "the earliest evidence for a significantly apelike body plan in the primate fossil record."

Before this history-making discovery of *Morotopithecus bishopi*, scientific consensus was that apes and humans evolved from a common ancestor and diverged into separate groups around six million years ago. The oldest fossils accepted as being of human origin after the split from apes are said to be three million to four million years old.

Most paleoanthropologists agree that our genus, *Homo,* appeared about two and a half million years ago and includes at least three species: *Homo habilis, Homo erectus,* and *Homo sapiens*.

One of the greatest mysteries confronting paleoanthropologists is when, where, and how *Homo* replaced *Australopithecus*, the genus that thrived in much of Africa beginning around four million years ago. Although *Australopithecus* had apelike bodies and much smaller brains than *Homo*, they had accomplished bipedalism.

"Lucy," the so-called mother of humankind, is a 3.18-million-year-old *Australopithecus afarensis* and was, before the recent discovery in Uganda, the oldest and most complete hominid known to science.

Charting the divergent branches of a family tree that spans nearly five million years has never been an easy task. And now that *Morotopithecus bishopi* is likely to add another five million years to the search, perhaps more scientists will be at least willing to consider the possibility that such an outside agency as the extraterrestrial Overlords lent an unrequested helping hand to the family *Homo*.

The puzzle of humankind's origins is difficult to solve perhaps because the genetic engineering efforts of the reptilian Overlords did not always achieve the exact results that they wanted.

Archaeological digs in the United States have discovered skeletal remains of primitive men and women more than seven feet tall; hominids with horns; giants with double rows of teeth; prehistoric peoples with sharply slanting foreheads and fanged jaws; pygmy cultures far smaller in height than any known groups.

As more and more such anomalous discoveries are unearthed in the geologic strata of our continent, it begins to seem as though North America in particular might have served as some vast living laboratory in genetic engineering. Perhaps all of these apparent stops and starts and dead-end spurts of the *Homo* family tree might really have been the failures and near successes of ancient extraterrestrial scientists. Even the monster-humans of mythology

might have been abortive genetic experiments that were
rejected by the Serpent People as they sought to achieve
Homo sapiens in the field laboratory of Terrestrial Biology 101.

AND THERE WERE GIANTS IN THE EARTH

Many serious-minded UFO researchers have suggested
that if we were to read the creation story in Genesis with
our current awareness of genetic engineering, the interaction between the sons of God and the fair daughters of
men assumes a rather different interpretation.

> And it came to pass, when men began to multiply on
> the face of the earth and daughters were born to them,
> that the sons of God saw the daughters of men were fair;
> so they took them wives of all whom they chose . . .
> There were giants in the earth in those days; and also
> after that, when the sons of God came in unto the daugh-
> ters of men, and they bore children to them, and they be-
> came giants who in the olden days were men of renown.
> [Genesis 6:1–4]

If those smitten sons of God were actually extraterrestrial scientists conducting experiments on female members of the developing strain of *Homo sapiens*, rather than
decadent heavenly beings sinning with Earth's daughters,
they might have been carrying out the directive of the
Overlords to provide nascent humankind with a genetic
boost.

It seems clear that the ancient Israelites thought the sons

of God were god-beings or angels, possessed of supernatural powers. Contemporary researchers believe that
these particular "sons of God" came from another world—
not a heaven, but an actual physical place. And that their
"coming in unto" the daughters of men to produce the "giants" quite likely refers to genetic manipulation, rather
than actual sexual intercourse.

Later, we learn that the Lord has grown dissatisfied with
the human experiment and is grieved in his heart that he
had even made man on the Earth (Genesis 6:5–6). Perhaps an assessment was made that the great majority of
the apelike beings were not progressing as hoped. Perhaps many of the creatures remained too close to the animal
level.

But certain of the Lord's "sons" were not ready to give
up on the experiment. They considered the offspring of the
daughters of men, the evolving product of their genetic
engineering, to be making satisfactory progress. They only
needed more time to eliminate some of the more negative
aspects of the primitive man-beings.

THE GREAT FLOOD, SYMBOL OF THE OVERLORDS' DISSATISFACTION WITH HUMANS

For those UFO researchers who espouse the theory that
Earth's humans may well be considered "property" by an
extraterrestrial species, the Great Flood becomes a symbol
of the time when certain of the Overlords coldly and dispassionately made the decision to eliminate great numbers of
those primitive offshoots of humans and to preserve only
the strain that would lead to *Homo sapiens*, modern man.

But the Book of Enoch suggests that Noah himself was a very unusual individual, far different in appearance from his brothers, sisters, and friends, describing him as a person with "a body white as snow, hair white as wool, and eyes that are like the rays of the sun." Passages in the Dead Sea Scrolls reveal that Noah's mother, Bat-Enosh, was suspected of infidelity when the strange baby was born.

In the Book of Enoch, however, Bat-Enosh tells her husband, Lamech, that the child is truly his son. "He is not the child of any stranger, nor of the watchers, nor of the sons of heaven," she insists. The Book of Enoch claimed that the "watchers" were two hundred fallen angels. Other apocryphal sources state that they were the Georgoroi, other visitors from the heavens.

SODOM AND GOMORRAH AND OTHER EVIDENCE OF PREHISTORIC NUCLEAR WAR

The Old Testament also lends credence to the theory that Star Gods from other worlds may have prompted the destruction of Sodom and Gomorrah. Russian scientist Matest M. Agrest has suggested that the cities were devastated by an ancient nuclear blast.

Moscow's *Literary Gazette* published an account of Dr. Agrest's theories as early as the 1960s, and we were privileged to hear him discuss the matter in person a few years ago. In his view, simply stated, the two cities were fused together under the searing heat of a prepaleolithic atomic explosion.

In Genesis 19:1–28, we are informed that Lot is waiting by the community gate of Sodom when two angels approach him. Some scholars conclude that Lot must have made prior arrangements to meet these heavenly beings. After their meeting, he escorts the entities to his home where they are fed and lodged.

Such researchers as Professor Agrest maintain that if these angels were wholly spiritual beings, they would not have been interested in an evening meal, nor in a bed for the night.

Later, when the coarse men of Sodom pound on Lot's door and demand to "know" his visitors sexually, the angels appear to employ some kind of unusual weapon that instantly blinds the Sodomites and blots out their lust.

When Lot is informed by the heavenly representatives that Sodom will soon be destroyed, he chooses to remain in the city. Neither Lot nor other members of his family seem to take the warning seriously.

However, when the morning sun rises, the angels urge Lot and his family to flee at once. Those who subscribe to Professor Agrest's theory believe that a nuclear device had been triggered and the "angels" had been assigned to lead Lot and his family away from the blast area.

Perhaps the Overlords had become concerned by the rampant sin and perversion being conducted by their human creations in those cities, and they utilized an atomic bomb as the fastest way of eliminating the transgressors from the "laboratory."

Sacred Hindu texts also tell of the wrath of the Overlords and clearly delineate flying machines, advanced technology, and awesome weapons wielded by supernatural beings in ancient times. The Hindu hymns, the *Rig-Veda*, constitute some of the oldest known religious documents, and tell of the achievements of the Hindu pantheon.

Indra, who became known as the "fort destroyer" because of his exploits in war, was said to travel through the skies in a flying machine, the *Vimana*. This craft was equipped with weapons capable of destroying a city. These weapons seem to have had an effect like that of laser beams or a nuclear device.

Another ancient Indian text, the *Mahabharata*, tells of an attack on an enemy army: "It was as if the elements had been unfurled. The sun spun around in the heavens. The world shuddered in fever, scorched by the terrible heat of this weapon. Elephants burst into flames . . . The rivers boiled. Animals crumpled to the ground and died . . . Forests collapsed in splintered rows. Horses and chariots were burned up . . . The corpses of the fallen were mutilated by the terrible heat so that they looked other than human."

There are many very old traditions that speak of a war between the forces of light and darkness that raged in humankind's prehistory. Perhaps there were rival extraterrestrial forces that fought for dominance over prehistoric Earth.

Throughout our world there are accounts of sand melted into glass in certain desert areas, of hill forts with vitrified portions of stone walls, of the remains of ancient cities destroyed by what appears to have been extreme heat—far beyond what could have been created by the torches of primitive human armies. Even conventionally trained archaeologists encountering such anomalous finds have admitted that none of these catastrophes could have been caused by volcanoes, lightning, crashing comets, or conflagrations set by prehistoric humankind.

GALACTIC AND CHEMICAL BEINGS
AND THE SERPENT PEOPLE

In his book *The Sky People*, British author Brinsley Le Poer Trench, the Earl of Clancarty and a member of the House of Lords, presents his theory that the biblical book of Genesis gives clear indication of two creation stories.

There is the creation of Man, Adam I, as related in 1:26–27: "Then God said, Let us make man in our image, in the image of God he created him; male and female he created them." And then there is the forming of Adam II, our traditional Adam, who is not fashioned until Genesis 2:7: "And the Lord God formed Adam out of the soil of the earth, and breathed into his nostrils the breath of life; and man became a living being."

In Trench's view, Adam II was not molded from the soil of planet Earth until long after God had already made male and female. Genesis 1:26–27 is an account of the *prior* creation of Galactic Man, whose fabled Garden of Eden was located on some extraterrestrial world, quite possibly Mars.

The British author argues that the Hebrew version of the Old Testament employs the word "Elohim" instead of "God" in Genesis because "Elohim" represents many gods rather than a single deity. "Let us make man in our image," the Elohim say in 1:26, "after our likeness."

Although conventional biblical scholars hold that "Elohim" is used to represent the many facets of God in his relationship to Earth as its Creator, Trench insists that one has missed the entire point if one considers the various names of Jehovah as simply representing different aspects of the same deity. In his view, the Jehovah are members of a family, or even a race of gods, much as the ancient Greek myths show the Olympians to be—or, an extraterrestrial race of beings thought by primitive humankind to be gods from the stars, "who deliberately created, by means of their genetic science, a race of hu-man beings peculiarly adapted to perform certain definite and predetermined functions."

Trench is quick to assure us that the existence of many deities (or extraterrestrial beings) need in no way alter one's belief in a single Universal Spirit, who set the cosmos into motion and who will continue to nourish life through eternity. He is merely theorizing that there may be many godlike beings in an ever-expanding scale of grandeur "on the stairway to the evolution to the stars."

However, Trench steadfastly argues that the Old Testament nowhere refers to Jehovah as the One Supreme God. Jehovah is but one of the Elohim. And it was the Jehovah—a powerful race of gods or extraterrestrial entities—that created Adam II, hu-man with his "earth-animal chemical body" (Genesis 2:7), ages after the creation of Galactic Man, Adam I.

The Galactic Race, Trench tells us, has been known since time immemorial as the Serpent People. The serpent is the symbol of the wave form of energy, a sperm-symbol representative of life. Nearly every known Earth culture has its legends of wise Serpent Kings who came from the sky to promulgate the beneficent and civilizing rule of the Sons of the Sun, or the Sons of Heaven, upon Earth. For example, Quetzalcoatl, the "feathered serpent," the culture-bearer of the Aztecs, was said to have descended from heaven in a silver egg.

Intruders in the Garden of Human Creation

In Trench's scenario, the extraterrestrial Serpent People became curious about the Jehovah's experiment with the hu-mans, and certain of them began to enter the garden in which the most creative member of the Elohim had sheltered his new Adams.

True to their instructions from the Jehovah to guard the boundaries of their pleasant laboratory paradise, the Adam II men drove the Serpent People out of the garden. The new women, however, were less hesitant about fraternizing with the sophisticated trespassers.

The race of hu-mans was not intended to reproduce, and their sterility was assured by carefully restricting their diet. When the Serpent People began to fraternize with the women of Earth-animal Chemical Man, they told the curious females that the so-called forbidden fruit was not inherently deadly.

The Jehovah had lied to the hu-mans, the Serpent People explained. Such food would actually prolong the life of Chemical Man and allow the hu-man males and females to reproduce. Assured that the Serpent People spoke the truth, the women of Adam II gathered the forbidden fruit and took it home to serve to their men.

When the Jehovah learned of the manner in which the Serpent People, Galactic Man, had interfered with their experiment with Chemical Man, they pronounced the curse that is given in Genesis 3:14–17: "Because thou hast done this, thou art cursed above . . . every beast of the field, upon thy belly shalt thou go, and dust shalt thou eat all the days of thy life."

Trench envisions the Jehovah as among the more irascible and violent-tempered of the Elohim. But since the

Jehovah did not truly represent the Supreme Being, their malediction did not really set the Serpent People to crawling on their bellies. And in spite of the Jehovah's vigilance and extensive safeguards, Galactic Man and Chemical Man began to mix blood.

Cross-Man Builds Mighty Atlantis

To complicate matters, the humans turned out to be a prolific species that seemed to take special delight in reproducing. The "giants in the Earth in those days" were the progeny of Galactic Man and the daughters of Chemical Man.

And it was these "giants," Cross-Men, who established the great kingdom of Atlantis. With the technological aid of the Serpent People, Cross-Man sought to recreate the glory that his progenitors had known in the extraterrestrial Garden of Eden and Noah's Ark may have been a great space transport.

The might of Atlantis grew steadily, and the image of Atlas, the giant who supported Earth on his shoulders, became the symbol of its great strength. Atlantean missionaries and technicians touched every corner of the globe, which, Trench observes, is why the many linguistic, ethnological, theological, and archaeological similarities on both sides of the Atlantic indicate one common heritage.

Great and mighty Atlantis destroyed itself, and the Cross-Men, members of *Homo sapiens* who survived the cataclysm have as a race suffered from a kind of collective amnesia, their true origins forgotten. Occasional flashes of memory have been clouded with myth—although every now and then when archaeological excavations yield some strange anomalous artifact, contemporary humans are forced to remember an antediluvian time before the present epoch.

WE ARE SLOWLY REGAINING THE WONDERS
OF PREHISTORIC SUPERSCIENCE

In Trench's assessment, Cross-Man is a secondary type of humankind, one that has been slowly regaining the technology that its prehistoric ancestors possessed.

Although the majority of UFO investigators who scour the scriptures of the world's religions for clues to the flying saucer enigma and for evidence of prehistoric genetic engineering would be unlikely to put forth such an elaborate hypothesis as the one espoused by Brinsley Le Poer Trench, a number of researchers have become convinced that the Bible contains details of many accounts of UFOs transporting Old Testament prophets to another world or another dimension.

Those UFO researchers who have conducted a careful analysis of Biblical texts have found three types of cosmic conveyances employed as vehicles of transportation for celestial beings: (1) the wheel, or disk-shaped object described by Ezekiel; (2) the chariot of fire mentioned in the second book of Kings; and (3) the cloudy chariot found in the writings of Moses, Daniel, David, Matthew, Paul, and John.

Today, as Cross-Man in his evolutionary state as contemporary humankind, stands poised on the brink of space travel, it remains to be seen whether or not Galactic Man, the Serpent People, will remove the "quarantine" that was placed on Earth so many centuries ago and permit us to soar free of terrestrial bondage. Perhaps such physical and mental examinations as those allegedly conducted during the abductee experience are actually tests devised by the Serpent People to assess any notable improvements that have been effected within the human species.

9

Travelers through
Time and Space

The UFOnauts seem always to have an inordinate interest in our measurement of time, an element of the UFO mystery that has led a number of researchers to theorize that the alien beings might really be time travelers—perhaps even our descendants from the future.

"Time," Dr. Roger W. Wescott states in his paper, *Toward an Extraterrestrial Anthropology,* "as Western Man conceived it at least since the Renaissance Period, is single in dimension, uniform in pace, and irreversible in direction. If time should turn out to have more than one dimension, discontinuity of pace, or reversibility of direction—or if space should turn out to have more than three dimensions—then it would be quite possible for solidly and prosaically material beings from the 'real' world to pass through our illusively constricted space-time continuum as a needle passes through a piece of cloth."

If such interdimensional traffic should exist, Dr. Wescott suggests we might consider such beings to be fantastic because from our perspective they would seem inexplicably to materialize and vanish. We might, in fact, dismiss them from our reality as hallucinations or hoaxes.

"Rather than existing in space and/or time in the conventional sense of these terms," Dr. Wescott offers, "our planet may exist in 'hyperspace' and/or 'hypertime,' where hyperspace is understood to mean space with four or more dimensions and hypertime to mean time which permits events and processes to occur in other than an irreversible linear and unidirectional manner."

On such a "hyperhistorical" sphere—or, alternatively, such a historical "hypersphere"—Dr. Wescott says, "all the supernatural beings and all the miraculous occurrences known to us from religion and folklore would become explicable as intrusions from the larger earth of reality into the smaller earth of our self-habituation."

There is no question that extraordinary beings have been intruding upon our planet and shocking its inhabitants for many, many time periods.

About the middle of November 1837, the lanes and commons of Middlesex, England, suddenly became places of dread. A bizarre figure said to be possessed of supernatural powers was stalking the frightened villagers by night and effortlessly avoided capture by the police. Because of this creature's ability to leap over tall hedges and walls from a standing jump, he was given the appellation of "Springheel Jack."

Whoever this being was, those witnesses who encountered him face-to-face described him as being tall, thin, and powerful. A prominent nose stuck out of his pinched physiognomy and his ears were pointed like those of an animal. His long, bony fingers were said to resemble claws.

The remarkably agile Springheel Jack wore a long, flowing cape over his slender shoulders, and he affected a tall, metallic helmet on his head. Numerous witnesses testified that the mysterious intruder wore what appeared to be metal mesh under his cloak and that he had a strange kind of lamp strapped to his chest.

Springheel Jack had the residents of Middlesex so unsettled by his nocturnal forays that the Lord Mayor approved the forming of a vigilante committee to hunt down the interloper. A reward was posted for Springheel Jack's capture, and even the old Duke of Wellington put on a brace of pistols and rode out at night along with the magistrates, army officers, and police.

It proved impossible to capture Springheel Jack. Townspeople saw him leap eight-foot walls and covered wagons as he worked his way upstream to the west, passing from village to village. Later, it was determined that Springheel Jack stayed primarily in private parks during the day, coming out at night to knock at certain doors, as if he were seeking some particularly hospitable host. As far as it is known, the mysterious stranger never found anyone who invited him in for a visit. Most people reacted in the same manner as Jane Alsop.

Miss Alsop, a young woman of eighteen, lived at Bear Bine Cottage in the village of Old Ford. When she went to answer the knocking at the door, she assumed that she was opening the door to a top-hatted, cloaked member of the horse patrol. But the "most hideous appearance" of Springheel Jack caused her to scream for help.

The monster's eyes, she later testified, were glowing red balls of fire. Before she could flee, he seized her in the powerful grip of his clawlike fingers and projected balls of fire that rendered both Jane and her sister unconscious.

When the report of the Alsop sisters' encounter reached the press, it came to light that a Miss Scales had survived a similar encounter with Springheel Jack as she walked through Green Dragon Alley. Before she could scream for help, he spurted a blue flame into her face, thereby dropping her to the ground in a swoon.

Springheel Jack conducted himself in such a manner for three months: He hid away during the day, then he ventured out at night to rap on a villager's door, as if seeking sanctuary.

According to the old records, Springheel Jack knocked on his last door on February 27, 1838, when he visited the house of one Mr. Ashworth. The servant who opened the door took a good look at the bizarre inquirer, then set Springheel Jack to running with his screams for help.

Inspector Hemer of the Liverpool police may have had the last mortal glimpse of the strange visitor when he was patrolling the long boundary of Toxteth Park one night in July. A sudden and vivid flash of what the inspector assumed to be lightning seized his attention and caused him to notice a large fiery globe hovering motionless over a nearby field. The object remained stationary for about two more minutes, then, amid showers of sparks, lowered itself closer to the ground to receive the same strangely costumed character that all of England had been seeking. Inspector Hemer decided not to become the hero who captured Springheel Jack, and he wheeled his horse away from the scene. When he looked back over his shoulder, the great ball of fire had disappeared.

Some students of weird phenomena, searching old records, have found indications that another Springheel Jack–type entity was seen at Aldershot, Hampshire, in 1877. This being also had the ability to soar over the heads of his pursuers and to stupefy them with a burst of his mysterious blue flames.

THE ASTRAL WORLD OF ILLUSION

In a speech to British UFOlogists in May 1969, Sir Victor Goddard, air marshal in the Royal Air Force, made the following provocative observation concerning such mysterious visitors as Springheel Jack and their place of origin:

> The astral world of illusion which (on physical evidence) is greatly inhabited by illusion-prone spirits, is well-known for its multifarious imaginative activities and exhortations. Seemingly some of its denizens are eager to exemplify "principalities and powers." Others pronounce upon morality, spirituality, deity, etc. All of these astral exponents who invoke human consciousness may be sincere but many of their theses may be framed to propagate some special phantasm . . . or to indulge an inveterate and continuing technological urge towards materialistic progress or simply to astonish and disturb the gullible "for the devil of it."[1]

That inveterate collector of damned and bizarre phenomena, Charles Fort, might have adjudged Springheel Jack and all of his assorted cousins as occult mischiefmakers from the "astral world of illusion . . . inhabited by illusion-prone spirits" to which Sir Victor Goddard referred. Such beings may come from an astral world that coexists with our own on reconnaissance missions—or they may have walked through some invisible door that separates the dimensions for the pure devil of it. Fort theorized that ravagers and mischiefmakers from this astral world might be prepared to present themselves as angels, demons, spacemen, or whatever served their purpose in order to divert suspicion from themselves, because they may be "exploiting life upon this earth in ways more subtle, and in orderly or disorganized fashion."

THE WORLD THAT EXISTS OUTSIDE
OUR OWN SPACE-TIME CONTINUUM

In his *Strange Creatures from Time and Space*, John A. Keel theorizes that "another world exists outside our space-time continuum and that these myriad objects and creatures have found doors from their world to ours." Keel suggests that such dimensional interpenetration may occur in certain "window" areas or when certain magnetic conditions prevail.

"They are paraphysical," Keel states, referring to the denizens of this astral world of illusion, "and they can assume the forms of one-eyed giants stepping out of magnificent flying machines or long-fingered [Men in Black] driving around in black Cadillacs which can melt into air. Their shenanigans over the past several thousand years have spawned many of our religious and occult beliefs. In trying to record their activities, we have built up a literature based upon nonsensical manipulations and induced hallucinations."

It is Keel's contention that an invisible phenomenon "is always stalking us and manipulating our beliefs. We see only what it chooses to let us see, and we usually react in exactly the way it might expect us to react. Every culture on earth has legends and stories about the same thing."[2]

VISITORS FROM THE FOURTH DIMENSION

Meade Layne, director of Borderland Science Research Associates in San Diego, California, has long been one of the leading advocates of a "fourth-dimensional" explanation for UFOs. In various of his writings and newsletters, Layne has stated that "aeroforms" (UFOs) should be considered "emergents," because they are objects emerging onto our plane of perception from a space-time frame of reference that is different from ours. The process by which the aeroforms enter our dimension may also be described as a conversion of energy and a change of vibratory rates. He states in one of his newsletters:

> When this conversion takes place, the aeroform becomes visible and tangible. It appears to be, and definitely is, what we call solid substance, and so remains until the vibratory rate is again converted. The *steel* of a landed disk is *etheric steel* and its copper *etheric copper*. This change amounts to a process of . . . materialization and dematerialization.
>
> Just as there is a spectrum of sound and color, so there is also a spectrum of tangibility, ending in forms of matter which are too dense to be touched. The ordinary matter of our plane is rarefaction: the interspaces between the nucleus and electrons are relatively enormous. This extremely dense matter of the ether passes through earth substance much as wind or water would flow through a screen with meshes a mile wide. But if the vibratory rate of an etheric object is slowed down, it becomes less dense and enters our field of perception.

Oops, The Invisibility Screen Needs Repairs

From time to time, UFO witnesses have perceived aero-forms from other dimensions whose vibratory rates have slowed down long enough to have allowed an Earthling a peek into their craft.

On a clear January afternoon in 1969, a UFO witness in Pennsylvania was driving home from work when he sighted a saucer-shaped object hovering over a pond about a hundred yards away. He stopped his car and rolled down a window for a clearer look at the UFO, which was at eye level.

The front of the craft was transparent, and the interior was clearly visible to the motorist. The two beings that he could see moving around inside wore coverall-style cloth-ing and seemed to be making repairs. Their backs were toward the witness, until one of the UFO occupants turned to pick up a tool and spotted the human onlooker.

With the knowledge that they were visible to the mo-torist, the two beings returned to their task with added vigor.

According to the witness, one of the beings nodded his head "and the other ran over and pulled two levers . . . and they disappeared just like that! Everything! Nothing left!"

Sometimes Aliens Just Seem to
Stumble into Our Dimension

The elderly woman dressed in black was first noticed when she crossed the E. Tyler Avenue intersection in Fresno, California. Passersby saw that she was moving slowly, with apparent difficulty, as if her legs were not functioning properly.

Assuming that the lady must be ill, seventeen-year-old

Carmen Chaney and her aunt Frankie ran out into the street to help her.

When the old lady saw the two solicitous women approaching her, her reaction was far from one of relief. In fact, she reacted with panic, as if she didn't want anyone to approach her.

As Carmen and Frankie drew nearer, they became fascinated by the woman's "large, blazing eyes, set deep in a chalk-white face, the skin of which appeared to be stretched tightly over her skull. She was about four feet, ten inches tall, thin and scrawny; snow white hair showed in wisps under her large black hat; she wore a high-necked, long-sleeved dress and high button shoes of a decade gone by. Her black hat, which was pulled down low over her face, as well as her dress, were old to the point of decay . . . she carried no bag or purse. Altogether she was a pathetic figure."[3]

Within a short time a number of people were watching the strange old woman retreating from the two well-meaning young women. The old lady hobbled into an alley, then looked around helplessly, as she realized that more than thirty people were intently observing her bizarre behavior.

She stopped for a brief moment—then she vanished. As Carmen Chaney said later, "She disappeared in the blink of an eyelash!"

The many witnesses to the fantastic disappearance of the elderly woman excitedly exchanged opinions and speculations. Police officers who were summoned to the scene chose to believe that the old lady had been ill and had simply stumbled out of sight of her observers. But an extensive search of the area produced no sign of the mysterious woman.

She Got Off at the Wrong Floor and Stepped into Another Dimension

Miriam Golding and her fiancé were riding a crowded elevator in a Chicago music store when she inadvertently got off at the wrong floor and found it impossible to push her way back into the jammed car.

Miriam sighed, prepared to await the elevator's return. When she looked around her, however, she was astonished to see that she was not in a downtown office building at all, but a large railroad station. She watched crowds of travelers hurrying about. Announcers gave times of departures and arrivals. Passengers bought tickets, grabbed sandwiches and snacks from lunch counters, idled impatiently in waiting rooms.

Miriam approached the information booth, but stalked away indignantly when the woman seemed to ignore her repeated inquiries.

At last she noticed a TO THE STREET sign and followed its directions into the open air. It was a beautiful, mid-summer afternoon. Crowds of people jostled by on the streets, but everyone ignored Miriam and her requests for someone to tell her where she was.

She wandered aimlessly for several minutes until she noticed a teenage boy standing near the center of the sidewalk, staring in all directions. At about the same time, he spotted her. "I guess they let you off at the wrong stop, too!" he said with a broad smile.

The teenager explained that he had been playing tennis in Lincoln, Nebraska. He had gone into the locker room to change his shoes, and when he came back out into the courts, he found himself in that same railroad depot that had replaced the music store that Miriam had visited. Whatever incredible thing had occurred, it had somehow happened to both of them.

Within a brief period of time, the crowded streets had changed into the open country where, amazingly, Miriam saw her fiancé's sister on a sandbar with a number of other girls. To Miriam's great relief, they saw her, too; and they began to call her name and wave at her.

The teenager became very excited, suggesting that somehow the girls formed some kind of connection between dimensions. He slipped out of his trousers and shirt until he stood there only in his tennis shorts. It did not seem far to the sandbar. He felt certain that he could swim to the girls in a few minutes.

Even though the teenager was a strong swimmer, he could not get anywhere near the girls and their hoped-for link between worlds. Exhausted, he returned at last to shore and fell to the sand in complete discouragement. When they looked again toward the sandbar, it had disappeared.

Miriam felt despondent. Would she be forever trapped in this other plane of existence? Then she was suddenly enveloped in darkness, and she felt as if she were floating through space.

With a jolt she found herself on a stool in the music store. A clock signaled closing time, and the clerks were directing impatient glances her way. Miriam looked about in vain for her fiancé. She decided to leave the store and go directly to his home—but this time she would take the stairs and avoid the elevator.

When her fiancé opened the door, he looked greatly relieved, saying that he had somehow lost her on the elevator and had been unable to find her anywhere in the music store. He had waited awhile, then decided to go home.

Miriam entered the house and was surprised to see her fiancé's sister with the same friends she had been with on the sandbar. The sister smiled and teased her that they had seen her in town, but she and her fiancé had been so engrossed in one another that they had not even noticed them.[4]

Where had Miriam Golding been during those strange hours? What remarkable distortion of time and space made downtown Chicago appear to be a river and a sandbar? And how had the girls been able to serve as a kind of link between dimensions, so that at least some kind of communication, even though false—they saw Miriam with her fiancé rather than a blond teenage boy; she saw them on a sandbar rather than a crowded Chicago street—had been established? Or was it all some kind of illusion prompted by unknown elements or intelligences working upon the human brain?

For Two Hundred Years, the Bridegroom Had Tried to Get to the Church on Time

Just before midnight one evening in 1933, Father Litvinov opened the door of the church to admit a young man in ornate knee breeches and a look of complete horror on his face. Once the priest managed to calm his strange visitor, he heard a most incredible story.

The young man gave the priest the name of Dmitri Girshkov, and he claimed that he was to have been married that day. On his way to the church, he had stopped by the cemetery to visit the grave of his boyhood friend. As he stood there paying his respects, he was startled to see an image of his friend, who had been dead for more than a year.

The next thing he knew, he told Father Litvinov, it was

evening—and as he made his way back to the church, he was frightened to find nearly everything changed in the small Siberian village.

Although Father Litvinov tried his best to comfort Dmitri, the young man shouted in anguish that he must find his bride, his family, his friends. As Dmitri began to run from the church, the priest noticed a strange light materializing and a gray mist forming around the younger man. In the blink of an eye, the curiously dressed young man had vanished.

Greatly intrigued by the provocative and eerie experience, Father Litvinov went back through old parish records. To his astonishment he at last found the name of Dmitri Girshkov and the records of a young man who had stopped by a friend's grave on his wedding day in 1746 and who then disappeared, never to be seen again. Father Litvinov also discovered that in the intervening 187 years, two other priests and a schoolmaster had seen the young man who stepped out of the past (or who stepped into the future, depending upon one's point of view).[5]

He Disappeared from an Airliner in Midflight

On June 29, 1968, Jerrold L. Potter, a fifty-four-year-old businessman, and his wife, Carrie, were flying from Kankakee, Illinois, to Dallas, Texas. The Potters had been looking forward to attending the Lion's Club convention in Dallas, and Jerrold was in especially affable spirits. He was also in very good health and financially secure.

As the DC-3 was flying north of Rolla, Missouri, approaching the Ft. Leonard Camp area, Potter got up to go to the lavatory. His wife watched him start toward the compartment in the tail end of the airplane. Several of his friends exchanged brief comments with him as he walked down the aisleway.

Then the DC-3 gave a peculiar and unaccountable jolt, as if it somehow had struck an object in its flight path. The plane seemed to quiver a bit, then recovered almost at once. The passengers remained unconcerned by the slight bump.

After a few minutes, Carrie Potter glanced down the aisle to see if her husband was returning to his seat. She became uneasy when he was nowhere in sight, and she expressed her discomfort to a flight attendant, who checked the lavatory and found it empty.

Copilot Roy Bacus answered the attendant's signal and was stunned to hear her report that a passenger was missing in midflight. He investigated the area near the rear lavatory and found that the boarding door was slightly ajar.

Bacus rushed forward to the pilot, Captain Miguel Cabeza, with a small section of safety chain from the exit door. Cabeza radioed that he was changing course, indicated the nature of the emergency, then headed for Springfield, Missouri, the nearest airport.

Investigating authorities found it difficult to accept the theory that Potter had mistakenly opened the exit door instead of the lavatory door. According to airline regulations, the exit door bore a warning inscription in large white letters on a red background. The exit door was hinged at the top and was secured by a safety chain and a heavy handle that could only be released by turning it 180 degrees to free two thick plunger bolts.

Grove Webster, the president of Purdue Aviation Corporation, commented:

It would take a concentrated effort to open the door during the flight. The door was locked securely on take-off. You can stand in the doorway of a DC-3 in flight and not be sucked out. The plane is not pressurized. And to open the door takes a lot of effort. Crews close the door for our stewardesses and open it. And it is harder to open and close in flight than on the ground.[6]

There were twenty-two passengers and two flight attendants in the cabin when Jerrold Potter disappeared, yet no one saw the businessman force open the exit door and plummet to his death. In fact, no one could recall seeing him after the DC-3 hit that "bump" in midair.

Could Potter have been in precisely the proper position for an undesired entrance into a hole in space and time? Or could he have been the victim of other-dimensional kidnappers? No trace of the unfortunate man has ever been found on this plane of reality.

ALIEN INTELLIGENCES ADVISE THAT HUMANKIND MUST INCREASE ITS VIBRATORY RATE

A recurrent theme among the messages that UFO contactees claim to receive from alleged extraterrestrial beings is that a New Age will soon be upon humankind and all humans must learn how to increase their "vibratory rate" so they may be translated into a higher dimension of being.

A space entity calling itself OX-HO told Robin McPherson, a channeler from British Columbia, that there was a whole new world awaiting the people of Earth in the fourth dimension:

The very earth on which you stand will be stepped up in frequency to match this dimensional vibration and each form of life will take on new shades of being. There are seven dimensions of being. Each planet understands one dimension at a time, but as we aid your evolution, your Earth will be stepped up in frequency and vibration to the next level . . .

People of Earth, you are becoming fourth dimensional whether you are ready or not. Leave the old to those who cling to the old. Don't let the New Age leave you behind.[7]

Aleuti Francesca, "telethought channeler" of the Solar Light Center in Oregon, received the following message from a space being known as Voltra:

The transition of matter into a finer, more etherialized matter will take place. You will still be yourselves; you will still function as human beings . . . but you will be of a more rarefied construction. Transition from physical to fourth etheric substance will take place.

[Space Beings] lower the frequency rate of our bodies to become visible to the physical retina of your eyes. We are *physical-etheric*, whereas you are *physical-dense* . . . The composition of all matter on your planet is rapidly reaching a point wherein it will either become of a finer etherealized structure or it will disintegrate . . .

We once more stress that you will not become discarnate beings: you merely step up one level and gain so much by so doing. Your sense perceptions, rather than being eliminated, will only become heightened and an awareness of all that which is of beauty, of love, of eternal nature, will become as one with you.[8]

ARE THE UFO INTELLIGENCES EXPERIMENTING
WITH OUR TIME SEQUENCES?

In 1972, Michel C. of Montreal was vacationing in a remote area of Quebec's Laurentian Mountains when he sighted three bright white objects moving through the sky very slowly. At the same time, he encountered a strange man sitting on a rock.

Michel emphasized that he was high up in the mountains, and yet there, suddenly, was a man in gray jumpsuit staring at him intently. Michel returned the stare until he began to feel very uneasy. "The stranger didn't move at all, but I ran away," he said.

Shortly after the mysterious mountain encounter, Michel began to experience recurring dreams in which he was always seated in a reclining chair in some sort of flying machine. At his left side was a blond woman who held his hand and kept checking with him to see if he was all right. Michel could look out a window to his right, but all he could see were eerie, swirling colors.

"The craft was round, somewhat small, and had four pods equidistant to each other which were linked to the main body by some kind of struts all made of the same seamless, dull gray metal," Michel said.

"There were no true edges to the roundish vehicle, and it seemed to be moving among these swirling colors as if through an ocean of sunlight. The dream would always stop with no apparent logical ending."

In 1986, Michel was awakened in his home in Montreal by peculiar beeping sounds, followed by a sequence of numbers and the words "symbiosis link." His attention was next drawn to two greenish lights moving outside his window.

A loud, electronic gong resounded in the air and a very loud, computerized voice said, "Universal Time, 1812."

Suddenly everything around him appeared very strange. It was as if everything had slowed down. Even the shadows in his room were wrong.

His digital clock indicated 3 A.M., but when he looked out his window, the park outside his house was fully illuminated and filled with people walking and talking.

How could the park be open and packed with people at three in the morning? There were even women pushing baby carriages.

Michel tried to fall back asleep, but he was too troubled by the bizarre events.

"I hadn't lain in bed for more than two or three minutes when I got up and walked back to the window for another look at the strange scene in the park," he said. "But now the place was completely dark and deserted. There was not a single person to be seen."

Michel knew that it would be impossible to disperse such a crowd of people in three minutes.

"There were no people in sight," he said, "but on the sidewalk on the other side of the street I saw a strange concentration of grayish mist advancing slowly through the air."

After relating a number of similar tricks with time, Michel asked, "Could some intelligence be experimenting with time and other kinds of strange phenomena? And if so, what do these weird experiments mean?"

THE UFONAUTS MAY BE TIME TRAVELERS
FROM OUR FUTURE

Whether there may exist entities from other planes of being who are experimenting with our time sequences, whether swirling vortexes may snatch people and send them spinning into another space-time continuum, and whether there may be uniquely talented human beings who can will themselves into other dimensions must at this time be considered viable hypotheses for examination. For the purpose of this book, however, we must now turn our attention to the theories of those UFO researchers who believe that our visitors may be time travelers from our own future, rather than aliens from another world.

In his *Visitors from Time: The Secret of the UFOs*, Marc Davenport writes that many of the UFOs are not space-ships "in the common sense of the word, but vehicles designed to travel through time . . . Many are not from other planets, but from a future Earth":

These time machines are peopled by a complex mixture of human beings, evolved forms of human beings, genetically engineered life forms, androids, robots and/or alien life-forms. These occupants make use of advanced technology based on principles that will be discovered at some point in our near future to produce fields around their craft that warp space-time. By manipulating those fields, they are able to traverse what we think of as space and time almost at will.[9]

THE UFO ABDUCTORS ARE TIME TRAVELERS

While Dr. Bruce Goldberg does not deny the possibility that some abductions of humans have been conducted by extraterrestrials, he believes the great majority of abductions are the work of time travelers who have the ultimate goal of assisting us in our spiritual growth. In the guise of UFOnauts, they may accomplish healings of a wide variety of diseases and physical problems. Some of the "chrononauts" could even function as guardian angels to certain humans with particular missions to accomplish.

In his research, Dr. Goldberg has isolated four groups of time travelers: (1) the Grays, the ubiquitous insectlike aliens with the large black eyes; (2) the Hybrids, a genetic mixture of humans and beings from other planets; (3) the Pure Humans, between six and seven feet tall, blond, blue-eyed, dressed in white robes; and (4) the Reptilians, extraterrestrials who have little interest in promoting the general welfare of humans.

Among the abilities that Dr. Goldberg credits to the time travelers are the following:

- They can show us our past and future by way of holograms.
- Telepathy is their basic means of communication, although they can speak.
- A state of suspended animation can be instantly induced in anyone they choose.
- They have mastered hyperspace travel between dimensions and can move through walls and solid objects.
- By existing in the fifth dimension, they can observe us and remain invisible.
- Genetic manipulation of our chromosomes is a routine

procedure for them. They have greatly accelerated our rate of evolution.

- The less advanced groups make many errors with experiments, but the more advanced ones manipulate time and space with proficiency.[10]

Dr. Goldberg has based his conclusions on thousands of future life progressions conducted with subjects under hypnosis. Among the many illustrations that he selects from his files is one about a former gang member who, at the age of eighteen, was involved in a fight between rival gangs and was facing a gun in the hand of a punk who was about to pull the trigger.

Before the gun could go off, however, a blue and lavender swirling cloud surrounded the young hoodlum with the gun in his hand. "A luminous figure of a human time traveler in a white robe stood between the gunman and my young patient," Dr. Goldberg says. "The gun went off, but the bullets seemed to enter the chrononaut's body and disappear from sight. While all this was going on, everyone else was placed in a state of suspended animation. When the swirling cloud evaporated, the time traveler was gone and every gang member regained consciousness. They just dispersed.

"The following day," Dr. Goldberg continued, "my patient resigned from the gang and his whole life changed. He began working to help support his poor family, and he became far more spiritual than he ever demonstrated before."

Out of the nearly one hundred abductees on whom Dr. Goldberg has conducted hypnotic regressions over two decades, he has determined that the great majority interacted with time travelers from between one thousand and three thousand years in our future. He is now of the opinion that our history has been manipulated by these chrononauts and that they have been responsible for the quantum leaps in our technology during this century.

His clinical experience since 1974 in working with UFO abductees has suggested such data as the following:

- Abductions begin at ages four to seven and persist to around the age of forty.
- Although reproductive experiments are conducted (eggs and sperm samples are taken), the main purpose of these tempnauts is to monitor our *spiritual growth*.
- These time travelers function as our "guardian angels" by placing attackers in states of suspended animation to allow our escape and so on. They can manipulate our physical laws to assist us in time of need.
- These chrononauts follow us from lifetime to lifetime. They trace our souls back to our previous lives and monitor our spiritual unfoldment.
- There are possible parallel universes in the future with many wars, emotional problems, pollution, and so on that can be averted if the time travelers assist us now in our spiritual progress.

In Dr. Goldberg's opinion, the basic message of the time travelers throughout history is that "each of us is unique and possesses infinite potential for spiritual, as well as technological, growth. We are each, as individuals, responsible for this growth. By establishing and maintaining a connection with our Higher Self, we can be more in harmony with a larger, whole, infinity."[11]

TIME TRAVELERS OR TIME INTRUDERS?

Author-researcher John A. Keel concedes that there have been indications in some cases that certain UFOs could be time travelers, but he thinks it is more likely that the same object could intrude into our reality in different time periods. The same UFO could move in and out of our time dimension—appearing, perhaps, in the days of the Roman Empire—slip out again, then move into our reality again in 1999.

And that could be why so many UFOnauts ask contactees and abductees what time it is. They might be referring to the year, rather than the hour.

"According to those who have held dialogues with the UFO entities, the beings don't really seem to know who or what they are, but they know that they have turned up in other periods of time, that they have been reconstructed generation after generation," Keel said. "They seem to be timeless in that sense."

Continuing with this line of thought, Keel commented that the UFO being who might have appeared before Julius Caesar might also have appeared before Adolf Hitler:

> To us there would be an enormous gap of thousands of years. To the entity, there would hardly have been any interim period at all. UFO entities become confused when they talk to us about time. They have been unable to convey to us truly accurate information about the cosmic structure. What they have given us is their version of the cosmos, which doesn't apply to us at all.[12]

In the next chapter, we shall encounter a force that is very much a part of our own planet and that applies to each one of us.

10

UFO Energy and Our Planet's Mysterious X-Force

In his book *Consilience* Edward O. Wilson, the Pelligrino University research professor and honorary curator in entomology at Harvard University, tells of his lifelong desire to establish that all knowledge and understanding is bound together by some as yet unknown common theory. Like other scholars who have embarked on a similar quest, Wilson is convinced that there must exist one grand scheme to explain and unite all that humankind knows and can know.

Only eighteen when he was captured by the dream of unified learning, Wilson borrows from physicist and historian Gerald Hoton the expression "Ionian Enchantment" as a name for his belief in the unity of the sciences. The conviction that the world is orderly and can be explained by a small number of natural laws, Wilson explains, goes back to Thales of Miletus in Ionia in the sixth century B.C. Albert Einstein, with his own quest for a unified field theory, was, according to Wilson, "the architect of grand unification in physics . . . Ionian to the core."

We, too, have undertaken a similar quest in the field of UFO research. We, too, have sought a means of discovering a unified theory of UFOs, an explanation that will unite all that we know and can know about the perplexing mystery.

Although the single hypothesis still eludes us, our UFO odyssey has awakened within us an awareness that there exists one central, unifying energy on this planet that has the potential to transform our entire species—and it may well be the same energy that draws extraterrestrial or multi-dimensional intelligences to manifest on Earth.

THE TRANSFORMATIVE POWER OF THE X-FORCE

All cultures at one time or another have sensed an un-known energy that underlies all paranormal and mystical phenomena and that is an essential part of all life on this planet. The Hindus call it *prana*, the Chinese name it *chi*, the Japanese *ki*, the Kahuna *mana*, the old Norse *wodan*; the Native American Plains tribes chant its name as *wakan*, the Hebrew tradition knows it as *ruach ha-kodesh*, and Christians welcome it as the *Holy Spirit*. We shall refer to this unknown energy as the X-Force.

Throughout history, thousands and thousands of men and women who attained certain levels of awareness and self-mastery have perceived that the conduit for the X-Force is the human psyche. Feats of mind over matter, psychokinesis, clairvoyance, telepathy, materialization and dematerialization, extraordinary acts of healing have all been achieved by a conscious or unconscious control of the X-Force.

Whether spontaneously or through disciplined training, contemporary psychic sensitives, mystics, and shamans have learned to control the same unknown energy that certain masters and adepts were aware of thousands of years ago. The Algonquins' *Manitou*, the Sufis' *Baraka*, Plato's *Nous*, and Aristotle's *Formative Cause* all epitomize humankind's persistent attempts to identify and define the energy that the more sensitive of the species have always known existed around them.

Down through the ages, mystics have intuitively apprehended consciousness as a nonphysical, but very real, quality, and they have understood that physical reality is connected to consciousness by means of a single physically fundamental element: the X-Force.

Science long ago discovered that everything, no matter how solid it may appear to the physical senses, is vibrating at its own particular frequency. Every human being, every animal, every band of metal transmits short waves of different lengths. What is more, these personal wavelengths are as individual as fingerprints.

Within every living organism there exists an energy that, however weak, however unpredictable, can be refracted, polarized, focused, and combined with other energies.

Sometimes it appears as though this energy has effects similar to those of magnetism, electricity, heat, and luminous radiation—yet it truly appears to be none of these things. Paradoxically, while the X-Force is often observed in the operation of heat, light, electricity, magnetism, and chemical reactions, it is somehow different from all of these.

The X-Force appears to fill all of space, penetrating and permeating everything. It seems likely that the great French Magus Eliphas Levi was thinking of the X-Force when he wrote the following: "There exists an agent which is natural and divine, material and spiritual, a universal plastic mediator, a common receptacle of the vibrations and the motions and the images of form, a fluid and a force, which may be called in some way the *Imagination of Nature*. The existence of this force is the Great Arcanum of Practical Magick."

The X-Force is basically synergetic; that is, it is a very cooperative energy, one that blends well with other energies. It is so cooperative that things with which it might come into contact do not disintegrate or disorganize the way they normally would. Therefore, it might be said that the X-Force has a basic "negentropic" effect, which makes it the opposite of entropy, the expected disintegration and disorganization of matter.

If an intelligent group of beings from another world or dimension had long ago mastered techniques through which they became one with the X-Force, they would truly have become masters of the universe. They could control matter, materialize and dematerialize, and teleport themselves almost instantly across the reaches of space— perhaps even time.

One would hope that such beings would be of the requisite spiritual awareness so they might practice benevolence and compassion toward entities on lower levels of consciousness, entities who were still stumbling around in the darkness of ignorance or who were confined by their own self-limiting and materialistic boundaries of time and space.

Proper application of the X-Force depends upon the spiritual status and intention of the practitioner, so that the unknown energy is used only for good. But as long as we exist on the Earth plane in a three-dimensional world, we must recognize that the X-Force may be used for both positive and negative accomplishments.

As an example, let us say that a yoga master used his disciplined mind to channel the X-Force into the creation of a *tulpa*, a thought-form that can appear to assume life independent of the psyche. The proper channeling of the X-Force would literally feed the *tulpa* and enable it to accumulate power and strength. Yogis claim that they are able to carry on intelligent conversations with these creations of their own minds, and in certain cases, they may send the *tulpa* on errands of mercy or utilize them as instructors for advanced students. The duration of a *tulpa*'s life and vitality are in direct proportion to the energy expended in its creation.

A negative application of the X-Force in a similar act of creation might be the materialization of a threatening entity, a Man in Black, a Brother of the Shadow figure, to harass or to frighten others.

The effort of an untrained, undisciplined psyche would probably result in unrestrained poltergeistic activity, such as the destruction of furniture, the smashing of crockery, and the materialization of grotesque entities.

Of itself, the X-Force is neither good nor evil, just as electricity in itself is neither good nor evil. We all know, however, that just as electricity can be used to warm our breakfast toast, heat our homes, and light up our cities, it can also be used to project violent and pornographic films, broadcast the destructive propaganda of prejudice, and electrocute someone. So it is with the X-Force.

MOBILIZING CONSCIOUSNESS

Consciousness is more than a biochemical phenomenon confined to our bodies. It is also a force or energy that partakes of a nonphysical realm unbounded by the constraints of linear time and three-dimensional space.

George Wald of Harvard University, winner of the 1967 Nobel Prize for physiology or medicine, agrees that consciousness lies outside the parameters of space and time and, believing in its importance, has tried to put consciousness and cosmology together. Perhaps, he has mused, consciousness, rather than being a late evolutionary development, was there all the time. Consciousness may have formed the material universe and brought out life and overt forms of consciousness.

The act of mobilizing our consciousness becomes an act of psychic functioning that may impinge directly upon the cosmos along the entire continuum of reality—from consciousness to energy to matter. Thus, anyone who is capable of directing his or her consciousness with intense focus and concentration may be capable of significant psychic functioning and have the ability to summon—or create—benevolent angelic aliens or destructive, Asmitor-like demonic aliens. That is why those who do not take the potential hazards of psychic development or UFO contact seriously can find themselves in serious difficulties.

Plants, animals, humans, and crystals contain a series of geometrical points in which the energy of the X-Force can become highly concentrated. Such points seem to respond to the chakras, of which the yogis speak; in humans they are located at the top of the head, between the eyebrows, the throat, the heart, the spleen, the solar plexus, the base of the spine, and the genitals. Since these are the same regions that UFO contactees and abductees so often mention are stimulated in one way or another by the alien "doctors," one may wonder if those men and women allegedly taken on board spacecraft were given physical examinations or chakra alignments.

A GLIMPSE INSIDE A UFO WINDOW AREA

There are dozens of small towns and villages throughout the United States—from Massachusetts to Wisconsin, from Arizona to Oregon—where UFO activity has become so frequent that every single member of the community has experienced a sighting of mysterious bobbing or zigzagging lights in the sky. In addition to the rather conventional UFO overflights, these communities have also been visited with a wide range of associated phenomena, such as the appearance of bizarre monsters, supposed extraterrestrial humanoids, and eerie ghost and poltergeist manifestations. This is the story of three scientists who set out to investigate such a UFO "window area." Their names have been changed to preserve their anonymity.

Dr. Henry Lazarus, a physics professor from a small midwestern college, took a lot of teasing from his colleagues about his interest in such weird and far-out matters as alternative medicine, radionics, ESP, and UFOs. When a member of a national UFO research group told him about a small town that regularly claimed UFO and creature sightings, Lazarus wanted to investigate such claims firsthand.

Lazarus had told Dr. Benjamin Chiang, a fellow physics professor, about his safari to the UFO hunting grounds, and asked Chiang to accompany him. Although basically a skeptic, Chiang maintained an open-minded attitude of scientific inquiry.

While Lazarus and Chiang were discussing their preparations for the weekend road trip over coffee in the faculty lounge, Dr. Philip Reisman, a very skeptical, hard-nosed professor of biology, overheard their plans and insisted on inviting himself along "to be a voice of sanity in the midst of madness." In true scientific spirit, Lazarus welcomed Reisman to the expedition. The biologist's closed mind would serve as a kind of control.

A few days later, on a crisp October afternoon, the three scientists arrived at their UFO harbor. Henry Lazarus had been told there was a woman at the local newspaper who had become an authority on the UFO and creature sightings that had been made in the area over the past thirty years. He had called her earlier in the week and made an appointment for that Saturday. She was waiting for them in the coffee shop three doors down from the newspaper office.

Mary Higgins was a jolly, round-faced woman in her mid-fifties, who seemed only mildly impressed by their academic and professional credentials. She told them that the UFOs often left scorched circles in farmers' fields, and a couple of dairy farmers claimed that prize milk cows had been mutilated by aliens. Over the years, at least a dozen townsfolk insisted that they had been taken on board the spaceships, and they all described the UFOnauts as being little folks, no more than four and a half to five feet tall, with oversized heads, big eyes with catlike pupils, hardly any noses to speak of, just a couple of slits for mouths, and pointed ears.

A couple of times, Henry Lazarus had to quiet Philip Reisman, who persisted in interrupting Mary's narrative flow with cynical questions and comments. Silenced by Benjamin Chiang's stern glare, Reisman then limited his scientific comments to smirks and sighs.

Mary Higgins's anecdotal accounts of the phenomena that had occurred in her town seemed to add up to a cauldron of mysterious occurrences that never stopped boiling. For at least the last thirty years—and before that if the old-timers could be believed—there had been regular manifestations of UFOs, UFOnauts, Big Foot, Cat People, Giant Birdmen, ghosts, phantoms, and poltergeists.

Mary herself favored the theory that throughout the world, scattered here and there, there were "window areas," openings between dimensions of reality—places where, in what seemed to be cyclical patterns, mysterious phenomena appeared, then disappeared. According to one aspect of this theory, the UFOnauts made use of such window areas in order to enter and leave our space-time continuum.

Philip Reisman shook his head and said that it all sounded dangerously akin to madness.

But that night, at the very stroke of midnight, a glowing UFO appeared above the clump of trees before which Henry Lazarus had parked his car.

Lazarus said later that he felt fully alive for the first time in his life. Benjamin Chiang gasped with excitement. Mary Higgins stared smugly at Philip Reisman, who said absolutely nothing, seemingly transfixed by the sight before him.

The car could not contain Lazarus and Chiang. Within moments they were racing across the open meadow that lay before the grove in which the illuminated UFO appeared to have settled.

"Don't rush it, boys," Mary Higgins warned them. "Don't get too close. Give it a minute or two."

Reisman shouted at them to come back, to be careful.

When they were about halfway across the meadow, two balls of greenish light moved out from the grove and came toward Lazarus and Chiang. The two physicists slowed their pace and looked curiously at the lights hovering above them.

Mary Higgins stepped out of the car and yelled at them that they were being monitored.

As Lazarus and Chiang stood there, not wanting to transgress any alien rules that they could not hope to comprehend, they heard the footsteps of unseen entities crushing the fallen autumn leaves in the grove ahead of them.

To their right, they heard what seemed to be heavy breathing. To their left, the mumble of hollow alien voices.

The only source of illumination emanated from the UFO, which somehow managed to fill the grove and meadow with a soft, greenish light that cast eerie shadows along the branches and tree trunks.

Lazarus lifted his arms and shouted into the darkness that he was a man of goodwill and peace. Motivated by his friend's example, Chiang did the same. Through the mist that clouded the grove before them, they could see the dark figures of smallish, large-headed beings moving cautiously toward them.

"Good lord," Chiang said in a hoarse whisper. "There, look! Henry, I see three, no, four figures moving toward us. Do you see them?"

Lazarus's brain seemed about to explode with sensory overload. *They were about to make contact!*

At that moment, the harsh, discordant sound of the car horn shattered the reverential attitude that the two scientists held toward the promise that lay just beyond them in the grove of trees.

From the very first decibel of the metallic screech, every aspect of the UFO manifestation seemed to shrink back, as if the balls of light, the breathing, the voices, the smallish entities were but multiple probings of a single entity—an entity that had now begun to retreat, to withdraw, like a wild thing startled by the blare of a hunter's trumpet.

In the matter of a very few blurred seconds, all facets of the phenomenon had been pulled back into the grove, and Lazarus and Chiang stood in the center of the meadow. They watched in anguish as the UFO rose into the night sky at a rate of speed that they could not comprehend in terms of the science that they understood. They felt alone, disappointed, like two small children who had only been able to catch a glimpse of Santa's boot as he disappeared up the chimney without leaving any toys.

When they returned to the car, they angrily demanded to know why Reisman had pressed on the horn. His reply was barely distinguishable through his chattering teeth, but it had something to do with having saved them from being abducted and sexually molested by aliens.

Mary Higgins's face in the light from the dashboard bore an expression of equal parts of contempt and pity for the biologist. "He scared it away," she told Lazarus and Chiang. "You boys might as well call it a night. It's not gonna come back tonight."

They drove Mary back into town and thanked her for her graciousness and her tolerance. Her smile seemed forced; her words of farewell insincere. It was doubtful that she would ever again take the time to guide them to a UFO landing site.

Reisman insisted that they not look for a motel, that they drive home that night in spite of the lateness of the hour. Lazarus and Chiang acquiesced, since another day spent with the man would have been intolerable to both of them.

They were not five miles out of town when Reisman, who was sitting in the backseat, began to shout that they were being followed by two glowing green lights.

When Chiang glanced in the rearview mirror, he was excited to see that Reisman was correct. He clutched at Lazarus's shoulder, and both wished aloud that they might have another opportunity to interact with the UFO occupants.

But the lights whooshed by them, one on either side, and vanished into the darkness. To their great disappointment, they did not appear again during the three-hour drive home.

By the time Lazarus and Chiang dropped Reisman off at his apartment, the man was clearly disoriented. On the drive back he had screamed a dozen times at imagined monsters at the side of the highway.

When Lazarus joined Chiang in his apartment for a nightcap and to discuss the incredible events of the day, the telephone was ringing. It was Reisman, babbling into the receiver about something pounding at his walls.

Chiang was about to tell him to take some tranquilizers and to go to sleep when a remarkable thing occurred. A mysterious pounding began on the walls of his own apartment.

At this point, Reisman screamed that a dark, hooded figure had appeared in a corner of his apartment.

Almost as soon as Chiang repeated for Lazarus's benefit what their colleague had said, the two of them were blinking in disbelief at the materialization of a dark, hooded figure in a corner of Chiang's living room.

Before either of them could assimilate that phenomenon, the radio unit in the stereo console clicked on, and some unseen agency moved the dial from station to station. Three books flew from the shelf where they had rested. The refrigerator door popped open. All the water faucets in the kitchen and bathroom were turned to full stream.

The weird, pointless manifestations disrupted both apartments until dawn, about two hours after they had begun.

The three scientists had undergone an initiation of sorts that night, and the phenomena continued intermittently for several weeks. Benjamin Chiang would be speaking to Henry Lazarus in their respective homes at night, and he would say, "Oh, good grief, there's that dark hooded entity standing in the corner again," and Henry would turn to see a similar figure standing inside a closet door or in a corner of a room. Since Lazarus was married with two small children, the materialization was especially disconcerting to his family.

Philip Reisman became dependent on tranquilizers and alcohol and resigned his position with the college so that he might enter a detoxification program. The last thing Chiang and Lazarus heard of him, he was considering entering the ministry.

Drawing upon his knowledge of the UFO enigma and his exploration of the X-Force, Lazarus made some interesting comments about their experience with UFO energy:

"I feel that there had been a *genuine* UFO landing near that small town at some undetermined time in the past," he said. "It was quite likely witnessed by one or more townspeople. This incident became so important to the psyches of the men and women in that rather remote area that their collective energy began to affect the X-Force in such a way that a phantom was created by the conduit of the group mind. The more energy they invested in the archetype of the UFO experience, the more solid and material it became. The more material it became, the more people who witnessed it coming back into being, the stronger the phantom of the real UFO experience became."

Lazarus's research has convinced him that there is a reflexive, imitative aspect of the X-Force. "That is why the initiate who seeks to manipulate the energy must always strive for balance. If you are at the level of awareness that envisions monsters, you may quite likely fashion them."

In his opinion, Reisman's fearful response triggered certain negative patterns into which the X-Force could flow and express itself.

Remember that with the Unknown Energy, the pattern is everything. So once he became spooked, he set a whole ghostly repertoire into action—the poundings on the wall, the hooded figure, the poltergeist activity. And he transmitted those images to us according to the same law of patterns which exists in the X-Force. That is why we must seek to make ourselves pure sending and receiving sets for the energy. We must not permit ourselves to become negative.

"Philip Reisman's rigidly closed mind did not serve him well," Dr. Lazarus concluded. "It is best to be at least somewhat open to all aspects of existence so that when you come face to face with something that has not previously been a part of your reality, you can deal with it without shattering into mental and emotional fragments."

11

The UFO Experience
as Initiation to
Higher Consciousness

At some level of the universe, the X-Force blends and interconnects each of us to the other—and to all other living things. On some level of consciousness, every living cell is in communication with every other living cell. The UFO experience may be yet another method the universe has devised to get humankind in touch with aspects of self and other life-forms in the cosmos.

In recent years the hologram has been found to be a workable analogy to illustrate the concept of the oneness of things. What is most remarkable about a hologram is that every single part of it contains all the information about the whole, just as the DNA in each cell of the body contains the blueprint for the entire physical structure. Split a hologram in half, shine a laser through it, and the whole object is reconstituted in three dimensions.

It has been postulated by some that the entire universe may be a single hologram. It may well be that information about all of the cosmos is encapsulated in each part of it—and that includes each of us human beings. We may all be unfolded images of aspects which exist in a higher reality.

In his book *Wholeness and the Implicate Order*, physicist David Bohm of the University of London urges contemporary men and women to become aware that the modern view of the world has become fragmented, especially in the sciences, but also in our daily lives. In science's efforts to divide our universe into stars and atoms, it separated us from nature. In humankind's penchant for dividing itself into races, nations, ethnic groups, political parties, and economic classes, we have fragmented ourselves and obscured our underlying wholeness.

Perhaps all along there has been a Higher Intelligence that has been striving to bring our species into the Wholeness, the Oneness. Perhaps the circular shape of the UFO is a symbol of the wholeness of life in the universe.

ATTUNING ONESELF TO INNER GUIDANCE

Since the most ancient of times, tribal elders, priest-crafts, and religious orders have worked to develop spiritual traditions to provide inspiration for life's challenges. Rituals and rites were designed to reveal certain truths, explain various mysteries, and present a process by which initiation into a higher awareness might be achieved. Spiritually, the significance of initiation lies in the death of the egoistic, physical self and its rebirth in the divine, transcendental order.

In some sacred traditions, such special knowledge and power was kept secret and reserved exclusively for the initiated. Other great master teachers focused their energies on arousing the sleeping spiritual senses of their students, thereby bringing about enlightenment through the personal mystical experience. These wise masters were aware that the individual mystical experience was the catalyst that awakened the initiate to the Inner Voice that speaks of a sense of Oneness with All That Is and the wisdom that the Great Mystery dwells within each soul.

"Attune yourself to the active inner guidance," the great yogi Lahiri Mayasaya said. "The Divine Inner Voice has the answer to every dilemma of life."

And his most famous student, Paramahansa Yogananda, agreed that to develop intuition is to receive soul guidance. "The goal of yoga is to calm the mind so that without distortion it may hear the infallible counsel of the Inner Voice."

THE TRANSFORMATIVE POWER OF UFO ENERGY

Many great spiritual teachers have declared that initiation may be bestowed upon the sincere seeker by entities that exist on higher planes of being. Consider the following as evidence of the ancient, the modern, the timeless energy of revelation and initiation:

Blinded by a Light from Above

Saul, a young firebrand, a member of the Sanhedrin who were dedicated to halting the Apostles' preaching of Christ, was struck blind on the road to Damascus. When he recovered his sight by heeding instructions given to him in a vision, he not only changed his name, his religion, and his life's work, but in many ways he altered the course of history.

In like manner, a salesman in South Dakota, a businessman in New Jersey, and a policeman in Nebraska were temporarily blinded by a strange and powerful light from a UFO that appeared above them as they traveled lonely highways. When they recovered their sight, they changed their names, their occupations, and began to devote their lives to the preaching of peace, love, brotherhood, and a coming time of transition for all of humanity.

A Summons from an Unseen Being

The boy Samuel heard his name being called at night. When no earthly voice could be found responsible, Eli, the priest whom Samuel would one day succeed, told the lad that it must be the Lord calling. Samuel was told to lie down and say, "Speak, Lord; for thy servant heareth." When Samuel did this, the Lord came and stood before him. Samuel became the last of the judges, the first of the prophets, and as founder of the monarchy, the sole ruler between Eli and Saul, whose principal mission was to organize the Kingdom of Israel.

In like manner did a housewife in Colorado hear her name being called at night. When no earthly voice could be found responsible, she opened herself to the Lord. Now, a few months later, she is practicing touch healing, speaking in a tongue that confounds academic linguists, providing spiritual lessons to an ever-growing flock, and prophesying on both an international and personal level.

Angels from a Wheel within a Wheel

Ezekiel saw a wheel within a wheel land before him. He watched four angelic occupants emerge, and he felt the Spirit enter him when one of the beings spoke to him. From that day on, Ezekiel had the gift of prophecy and the ability to work miracles.

In like manner, a television copywriter in California, an Air Force pilot in Florida, and a female college student in Washington observed the landing of unknown aerial vehicles. They communicated with the occupants, felt the

Spirit enter them, and later discovered that they had remarkable precognitive and clairvoyant abilities.

A Voice Speaking from a Glowing Orb

Moses spoke to the Angel of the Lord as it appeared in a pillar of flame near a wilderness bush. The voice from the fire assured Moses of divine aid and the power to work miracles.

In like manner, a voice from a glowing orb spoke to an artist from England, a clergyman from Illinois, and a sailor from Kentucky and promised them paranormal abilities. All have since forsaken their former callings and have devoted their lives to cleansing the Earth for the coming New Age.

UFOS APPEAR ABOVE ANCIENT SACRED SITES

Such contemporary revelatory experiences with UFO intelligences are currently taking place around the world. Interestingly, as many spiritual seekers conduct pilgrimages to ancient sites, they return reporting sightings of UFOs hovering above the sacred areas. And a good many of these pilgrims claim that they established contact with UFO intelligences at these holy places.

We ourselves have personally witnessed UFO activity at the following sacred sites and shrines:

Petra, the ancient Nabatean city in Jordan; **Machu Picchu**, the Incan metropolis located high in the Andes; the **Great Pyramid of Giza**; the **Sphinx**; the mystical city of **Luxor** in Egypt; **Masada**, the hilltop fortress at the edge of the Judean Desert; the remains of the Essene community at **Qumran**; the transformational vortex areas of

Sedona, Arizona; the powerful **Kahuna** shrines of Hawaii; the **Temple of the Sun** in Cuzco, Peru; **Mt. Nebo,** the legendary burial place of Moses; the ancient Incan healing springs at **Tambo Machay**; the gigantic, sprawling mystery lines in the **Nasca Desert**; the sacred Peruvian city of **Ollantaytambo**; tribal medicine power places in **Santa Fe** and the **Four Corners** area of the Southwest; and an ancient pre-Navajo monastery recently discovered on private property outside of Sedona.

COMBINING ANCIENT SYMBOLS OF INITIATION WITH THE SPACE AGE

In *Healing States* by Alberto Villoldo and Stanley Krippner, the shaman Don Eduardo speaks of the true meaning of initiation. He says initiation:

- represents a readiness to assume responsibility for the planet and for serving humanity.
- helps one to forge a link between oneself and an ancient lineage of knowledge.
- is not graduation. It is only the beginning of the great work that lies ahead of the initiate.
- is a salute to the spirit of a person whose consciousness has been awakened.

And, as Don Eduardo emphasizes, initiations are taking place all the time: "Initiations can occur on the way to the supermarket or on top of the Himalayas. And the most powerful initiations . . . are bestowed from the hands of the masters who work directly from the 'overworld.' These initiations may occur in our dreams or during meditation or may take us by surprise . . . when we least expect them. But in the final analysis we make the choice to be initiated ourselves."

To many UFO experiencers, the contact that they received during an encounter with alien beings was translated by their human psyches to be an initiation into greater awareness by "masters from the overworld." Their interaction with an intelligence that had previously existed far beyond their normal mundane world of ordinary expectations served as an impetus to awaken their consciousness to consider undreamed-of facets of the universe.

Ancient symbols that initiate those who have been touched by the UFO experience into higher levels of awareness include the following.

The Sphinx

The Sphinx, created by the oldest human priesthood, represents in its majestic combination of human head, bull's body, lion's paws, and eagle's wings the living unity of nature's kingdoms. These same four animal representations also manifest in the otherworldly entities in Ezekiel's vision; they are also the four constituent elements of microcosm and macrocosm—water, earth, air, and fire, the foundations of esoteric science.

The answer to the ancient riddle of the Sphinx (What first walks on four legs, then two, then three?) is the human being, the divine agent that includes within itself all the elements and forces of nature. Achieving higher awareness with the Sphinx teaches the experiencer how human nature evolves from animal nature and develops "eagle wings" to travel to other worlds.

The Great Pyramid

Many spiritual teachers believe that the Great Pyramid was a holy place in which sacred initiations were conducted (rather than a tomb for Egyptian royalty) and that the sarcophagus in the King's Chamber was an agent of the initiate's resurrection into the Light.

In recent years, dozens of UFO conferences have been held near the Great Pyramid and thousands of UFO experiencers have lain in the ancient sarcophagus to make contact with the essence of the alien beings that they believe actually constructed the pyramid as a kind of cosmic educational toy to stimulate the nascent human thinking process.

Elijah, Messenger of God

The mysterious figure of the prophet Elijah, who had no known parents, who came from nowhere to challenge the forces of darkness, and who returned to heaven in a fiery chariot, has come to represent to UFO experiencers the very pinnacle of otherworldly wisdom and resolve. For many UFO contactees, Elijah has become their spiritual mentor, or, in some cases, his essence serves as the conduit that will connect them with their own personal spiritual guide.

Melchizedek

Melchizedek, King of Salem, priest of Elohim, initiated Father Abraham with wine served in a golden chalice. Jesus of Nazareth was also a priest of the Order of Melchizedek.

Many UFO experiencers have expressed their belief that the beings they have encountered came to Earth to perpetuate the Order of Melchizedek. These beings, many believe, hold the golden chalice of Melchizedek, a symbol of supreme spiritual transformation and divine inspiration, and give assurance that the Divine Being that exists above the soul dwells in each of us.

The Wisdom of the Serpent

Since ancient times, the image of a serpent gripping its tail in its mouth and becoming a living circle has represented the ineluctable cycle of universal life. The fact that so many UFO experiencers state that their contact was with reptilian entities is not surprising. Throughout human history, they point out, the serpent has represented wisdom, and vast numbers of early culture bearers were described as being reptilian in appearance. From these serpentine alien intelligences, UFO experiencers say that they have been able to envision the universe as a living whole, endowed with intelligence, soul, and will. The universe is but the reflection of an invisible order of cosmogenic forces and spiritual kingdoms, classes, and species that through their perpetual involution into matter produced the evolution of life.

Child of Man, Child of God, Cross of Stars

A great number of UFO experiencers insist that the alien intelligences with whom they have been in contact revere the sign of the cross and that the cross is a symbol of profound universal teachings. The ancient Doctrine of the Divine Word taught by Krishna in India, by the priests of Osiris in Egypt, by Pythagoras in Greece, and by the prophets of Israel reveals the great mystery of the Child of Man and the Child of God.

In Hindu, Egyptian, and Greek initiations, the term "Child of God" meant a consciousness identified with Divine Truth and a will capable of manifesting it. The universal sign of the Child of Man is that of four stars in the form of a cross.

This sign of ancient spiritual transformation was familiar to the priests of Egypt, preserved by the Essenes, and worshipped by the sons of Japhet as the symbol of earthly and heavenly fire. Initiates from ancient Egyptians to Native American medicine practitioners have seen in the Cross of Stars the symbol of balance, the wholeness of the Great Mystery, the image of the Ineffable Being that reveals itself in the cosmos.

Achieving Starbirth on Other Worlds

The ancient masters predicted a time when the great mass of earthbound humanity would pass to another planet to begin a new cycle of evolution; as we have seen, one of the principal messages of the UFO contactees has to do with the graduation of *Homo sapiens* into a higher vibratory state and a higher dimension.

Both the ancient teachers of wisdom and the contemporary UFO experiencers state that in the series of cycles that constitute the planetary evolution of Earth, all humankind will one day develop the intellectual, spiritual, and transcendent principles that were previously manifested only in the great initiates. Such a development may require many more thousands of years and will likely bring about changes in the overall condition of humankind that are difficult to imagine.

Those UFO contactees who have received such messages from alien intelligences maintain that each successive evolution of humanity on its new planetary environment will become ever more ethereal, bringing humankind ever closer to the purely spiritual state.

The supreme goal of spiritual transformation is to reproduce divine perfection in the perfection of the soul. Only when spiritual seekers can say that they have acquired divine freedom and conquered Fate can they become true prophets, seers, healers, and initiators. Only those who control themselves through spiritual discipline can teach others. Only those who have set themselves free can set others free.

The final goal of humankind will have been attained when the soul has developed all of its spiritual faculties and decisively conquered matter. At that time, physical incarnations will no longer be necessary and the soul will enter the divine state through a complete union with divine intelligence. It will become supremely creative and totally one with the Ineffable Light whose immensity is the Great Mystery.

12

Encountering Phantoms between Past and Future

On his wide-ranging travels from London to Damascus, British author Thurston Hopkins apparently had a predisposition for encountering the supernatural in its many guises. In addition to spirits of the deceased, Hopkins came to recognize another kind of phantom that appeared to occupy a kind of spiritual "no-man's land" between the past and the future. "I refer," he wrote, "to those phantoms who are not fully quick, nor fully dead."

Hopkins went on to comment that one need not be living in a world of witches and goblins to perceive that there are beings in this world who may mimic us and pretend to be as we are, but are not of us. "They are creatures who have strayed away from some unknown region of haunted woods and perilous wilds. They dress like us; pretend that they belong to mankind and profess to keep our laws and code of morals. But in their presence we are always aware that they are phantoms and that all their ideas and actions are out of key with the general pitch and tone of normal life."

Researchers who are not extremely cautious in the pursuit of the UFO mystery may soon find themselves and all their ideas and actions woefully "out of key with the general pitch and tone of normal life." Those investigators who do not maintain a disciplined mental and physical balance in their attitude toward the multilayered puzzle of the UFO enigma may soon find themselves mentally and physically unbalanced.

Throughout the course of our more than forty years of investigating the mysteries of the paranormal and the UFO, we have encountered the gamut of eerie phenomena. Hooded beings and greenish balls of light have invaded our bedrooms; poltergeistic energy has tossed books from our shelves; UFOs have manifested seemingly on demand on a couple of occasions to quiet skeptics; an angry unseen force once smashed down a door and hoisted us and several witnesses in the air to prove its existence; disconnected telephones have rung in our presence; and on numerous occasions our lives have been saved by the intervention of benevolent beings.

There have been experiences that have been frightening, such as having entities materialize before us in dark and lonely places. There have been instances that have been unsettling, such as selecting a motel late at night completely at random and discovering that our names have already been registered. Others are strangely amusing, such as the time a talk-show host in a major Texas city challenged us to produce an alien on the spot and a greenish ball of light materialized and completely blew out every electrical apparatus in the television station, from cameras, lights, and transmitters right down to soda machines, typewriters, and computers.

You can say that as investigators of the paranormal and the UFO enigma we have chosen to be challenged by such experiences with the so-called supernatural and it is up to us to be prepared for such encounters, whether they be awesome or awful. That is true. And that is why we have such sympathy for those who are unprepared by their conventional worldview to deal with such extraordinary encounters with the unknown.

THE ORDEAL OF A MINNESOTA FARM FAMILY

A Minnesota farmer named Gary Jensen saw a UFO one night as he was working late in the field during spring plowing. The next morning over breakfast, he learned that his wife, Melanie, fourteen-year-old Jake, and twelve-year-old Lisa had also seen the bright object as the kids were getting ready for bed.

That day at school, a man who claimed to be from the state board of education asked to see Jake. The principal of the junior high school was told that the boy had attracted attention because of his high scores in the state tests and had been selected to enter a special educational project.

The principal called Jake into his office and allowed the man to speak to him in a private room, but he had become suspicious of the man's motives. He was aware that Jake was an above-average student, but he knew that the boy's test scores were hardly exceptional enough to warrant a special visit from a representative of the state board. A call to the state office revealed that they had no one on their staff by the man's name, and they had no special project for junior high students in progress.

When the principal entered the private room to confront the man, he found a puzzled Jake sitting alone. The teenager could only shrug that the special state project must be about space travel, for all the man asked him were questions about UFOs, aliens, and life on other planets. Jake had glanced away from his interrogator for just a moment, and when he looked back at him, he seemed to have vanished.

That same day, Lisa's teacher called the police when she noticed a man and a woman dressed in black trying to pull the child into a dark-colored van. The distraught girl told officers that the couple had approached her on the playground during recess and asked her to come with them to see some toy UFOs and alien dolls that they had in their van. When Lisa resisted, the woman had grabbed her arm and started to pull her toward the vehicle.

The couple were complete strangers to Lisa and her friends on the playground. Although one of her alert classmates copied down the license plate of the van, the police and the highway patrol said that such a plate number did not exist in any files of vehicle registration.

While their children were being harassed by mysterious strangers in their school environments, out on the Jensen farm, Gary and Melanie received a visit from two men dressed in black while they were eating lunch. The men identified themselves as agents of a special government task force investigating UFOs, and said they had learned that the Jensen family had sighted a bright object in the sky on the previous evening.

Melanie and Gary were puzzled, since they had not had the opportunity to tell anyone of their sighting. The "government agents" then adopted a threatening manner and demanded that they turn over any photographs they may have taken of the UFO.

The Jensens said that they had taken no photographs,

but the two agents refused to accept their denials. "You had better cooperate if you know what's good for you," the taller of the two men said. "We can make it really tough on you."

"You must cooperate," the other said, "for your own good, the good of your country, the good of your world."

At that point, one of the agents began to choke and seem to have difficulty breathing. Without another word, the two men quickly left the farmhouse and drove off in their car, which Gary said later looked like a bizarre blending of three or four different makes of automobile.

Later that afternoon, Gary was certain that he saw the two men watching him from the shadows of his machine shed while he fed the cattle on the feedlot. Melanie answered the telephone on four occasions to hear nothing but a peculiar static. Finally, on the fifth ring, a voice in a strange accent told her to forget all she knew about UFOs or terrible things would happen to her entire family.

That night, shortly after the children went to bed, Lisa began screaming that some animal had crawled under her covers. When Gary and Melanie investigated, they found nothing, but then Jake yelled that his bed was jumping up and down. As they ran to his room, they could hear the thumping sounds of his bed lifting and slamming to the floor.

Such poltergeistic disturbances continued on a nightly basis for nearly a week before they dissipated. And during the day, all four members of the family felt that mysterious, shadowy figures were keeping a close watch on them—at school, out in the fields, and in their home.

The eerie harassment of the Jensen family continued intermittently for about a month, then finally ended with a most bizarre display of supernatural prowess. Although he hated to leave his family while such strange occurrences were taking place, Gary had to honor a prior commitment and go on an overnight business trip.

As he was about to board the plane in their small local airport, Gary saw the two "government agents" behind him, going through security. It was obvious that they were tailing him and that they would keep him under surveillance while he was away from home. In one sense, he was relieved that they would not remain to harass his family. On the other hand, what if they should arrest him while he was away? And in the worst case scenario, what if the two weird agents were really some freelance wackos who would take him out once they got him away from his own community?

Gary felt especially uneasy when the two Men in Black took seats directly behind him. One half of him wanted to turn and confront the men. The other half advised him to sit still and ignore them.

About halfway through the flight, one of the men leaned forward and whispered in Gary's ear: "Remember, in one way or another, we'll always be around to keep an eye on you."

Angrily, Gary turned around—to face empty seats. The two men had disappeared.

Gary felt dizzy, disoriented, nauseated. He heard several of the passengers near him complaining loudly to the flight attendants about a terrible smell. Some began to cough; others reached for vomit bags. All around them was the foul, suffocating odor of rotten eggs, or burning sulfur.

Several minutes later, after the wretched odor had dissipated, Gary asked one of the flight attendants what had

happened to the two passengers who had been sitting behind him. Neither she nor any of the other passengers remembered seeing anyone in the seats directly behind him.

Gary felt as if he were going insane. Perhaps the two
flight attendants and every one of the fifty-four passengers
on board were in on a plot to break him down or arrest
him—or assassinate him. Maybe he and all the other passengers were already dead and they were lost souls on the
way to hell.

Somehow he managed to control his frayed nerves until
the plane landed. Once he got up to walk the aisle and to
check the restrooms to see if the two men had hidden
themselves somewhere on board the airplane.

He waited in the airport for over an hour, watching the
grounded aircraft, monitoring the hallways, knowing without question that he really had seen the two strange men
enter the aircraft and take the seats directly behind him.
Finally, satisfied that the Men in Black had not hidden
somewhere on the airplane and were not going to exit sur-
reptitiously, Gary left the airport, sensing that his family's
ordeal had ended.

TWENTY-FIVE YEARS ON THE
RUN FROM UFO ENTITIES

On Halloween 1968, Martin Jacobs, a Protestant minister, had a conventional sighting of a UFO as he was
trick-or-treating with Sarah, his four-year-old daughter.
He happened to glance up and see a bright light moving in
a zigzag motion across the sky. Since the night was cloudy
with a light rain falling, he knew that he had not seen a star,

and because of the erratic motion of the object, he knew that he had not seen any kind of conventional aircraft.

He mentioned the sighting to his wife, Connie, and his nine-year-old son, Paul, that night around the dinner table, but after a few shared words of amazement, the matter was dropped. Later that evening, however, Martin had a vivid dream of a UFO entity who came to stand beside his bed and warn him not to tell anyone else about the sighting.

The next day, as he was going about his normal ministerial duties, Martin became aware of someone—or something—following him. Once when he turned around quickly at the sound of footsteps, he caught a glimpse of what appeared to be a tall thin man dressed completely in black ducking behind a parked truck. Another time, he blinked his eyes at what appeared to be some kind of large, reptilian gargoylelike being sitting on a high tree branch staring at him. An uneasy feeling told him that some form of intelligence related to the UFO sighting was stalking him.

That next Sunday in church, as Martin was in the midst of his sermon, the entire building seemed to be filled with the nauseating odor of rotting flesh. Several members of the congregation became ill and had to leave. Martin himself became so nauseated that he could barely continue.

Word soon spread that the building had been overrun by rats, and church attendance dropped so severely that the denomination's board of supervisors considered closing its doors. When exterminators were summoned, they stated that they could find no evidence of rats or any reason why the terrible stench remained in the church.

After three weeks, the awful smell seemed to lift of its own volition, and a few of the original congregation resumed worship in Martin's church. But on the very next

Sunday, nearly sixty blackbirds suddenly burst through a window in the midst of Martin's sermon and began swooping and pecking at the congregants. The next day, the church was officially closed until it could be learned what manner of devilish affliction was besetting its pastor.

Investigators from the denomination's home office arrived to record a virtual litany of incredible charges against the Reverend Martin Jacobs. Some members of his congregation swore that they saw two small demonic entities materialize behind him as he was administering the host during Holy Communion. Others said that they had seen Pastor Jacobs leering at them through their windows as they sat in their own homes. When they went outside to investigate, it was as if he vanished before their eyes.

As for Martin Jacobs himself, it seemed as though a bizarre series of happenings afflicted him wherever he went. When he and his wife went to a movie theater to attempt to get their minds off their troubles, they were accused of releasing a noxious odor and were asked to leave. A relaxing meal at a restaurant turned into a nightmare when Pastor Jacobs was accused of tripping a waiter and creating a disturbance. A drive in the country resulted in a minor accident and a traffic ticket when the automobile that the pastor had left in park with the emergency brake applied jumped the curb and smashed into five other parked cars before it came to a halt.

And always at night, the entire Jacobs family was haunted by dark, shadowy figures that lurked about their home and frightened the children in their beds.

By spring of 1970, Martin Jacobs found himself without a church. Although the church hierarchy admitted that it was no longer fashionable to speak of such things as demonic possession, they could think of no better explanation for the bizarre occurrences in Pastor Jacobs's church. He also found himself without a wife. Connie, his wife of fourteen years, was on the brink of a nervous breakdown. She said that she was truly sorry, but she felt that a divorce and her restored mental equilibrium would make her a better mother than institutionalization for insanity.

In utter confusion, Martin Jacobs formally resigned from his duties with the congregation, signed the divorce papers, and left for another city in another state.

For ten years, he worked as a counselor in a halfway house. He found it impossible to accept another parish ministry because of the ongoing series of weird events that continued to haunt his very existence.

On Halloween night in 1978, the tenth anniversary of his UFO sighting, to his complete and utter astonishment, the entities finally called on him in his own apartment. There were three of them, nondescript, smallish fellows that looked almost completely human—and yet, upon close scrutiny, there was some vague, undefinable difference that set them apart.

They explained that they hoped there were no hard feelings. He had just set some things in motion that could not be stopped once they had begun. To demonstrate their goodwill, they would now permit him to do what no human had ever been allowed to do: he could take their pictures as they demonstrated just a small portion of their repertoire of guises.

Within the next several hours, the frightened and astonished minister saw the three entities change shape, glow in the dark, materialize and dematerialize right in front of him. While he snapped away with his Polaroid, it became apparent that the beings could assume whatever physical form they chose. As he watched, they shifted forms from large-skulled, big-eyed Grays to winged angelic beings; from grotesque gargoyles to blond, blue-eyed Space Brothers.

The next day, feeling secure with his photographic evidence, Martin believed that he held some kind of cosmic trump card that would somehow keep the things away from him. Suffused also with feelings of vindication, he called his parents; his ex-wife Connie, who had since remarried; his son Paul, now a sophomore at a church college; and a half dozen of his friends in the ministry, and told them that he now had proof that he was not crazy and had not been making up paranoid stories for the past ten years.

Two days later, three friendly police officers appeared at Martin's apartment. With broad smiles they explained that they were sincere UFO buffs and had heard about his remarkable photographs of alien beings. Although the minister was surprised that the few people in whom he had confided had broadcast his coup of having obtained snapshots of otherworldly beings, these men, after all, were the police. And they weren't laughing at him.

The three men were very serious when they examined the dozens of photographs, and they were firm in their arguments that such solid proof of aliens among human society should be widely published in the media.

Martin was very reluctant. He had endured enough ridicule since his initial sighting a decade before.

The three police officers were extremely sympathetic when Martin told them a little about the ordeal that he had endured. They spoke in disgusted tones about the fickle nature of the average human in today's society. They shook their heads in disbelief that Martin's church had turned him out, rather than sticking by him. They were openly contemptuous of a wife who would leave a man when he most needed her support and love. Martin was long overdue for his day in court. It was time that he was vindicated.

The officers told him that they were extremely well informed about constructive public relations campaigns. They assured him that they would use their credentials to get the pictures published and to restore his credibility as a clergyman. Together, the four of them would prove to the world at large that such creatures were walking among humankind and that the UFO phenomenon was very real.

That night, for the first time in a decade, Martin Jacobs slept peacefully. At last he had the support of three fine men who would help him clear his name and restore his reputation as a minister.

However, when the officers arrived unannounced the following night, they threatened Martin, confiscated his photographs, taped his hands behind his back, pulled a stocking cap over his face, and tossed him roughly into the back of a van. After the policemen drove him around for a while, loudly debating whether or not they should kill him, they finally released him in a remote wooded area.

Although Martin Jacobs felt fortunate that he was still alive, he realized that his proof of the alien entities had been taken by the men who had been posing as police officers. A few days later, he began to notice strange physical effects on his body which he blamed on his close contact with the three policemen—who, he now understood, were actually the alien beings assuming yet another disguise. The upper portion of his torso became scaly. His vision became blurred, and from time to time he was temporarily blind for several days.

We learned of Martin Jacobs's plight six years ago when he was interviewed by an incredulous journalist, who was convinced by the minister's apparent sincerity, but completely unnerved by his incredible story. At that time, after twenty-five years of torment by alien beings, the beleaguered clergyman was receiving emotional support from other ministers and praying without ceasing that the UFO beings—the shape-changers, the angels, or the demons—had finally decided to leave him alone.

WHEN IT COMES TO NASTY UFO BEINGS, DON'T PLAY THEIR GAME

We have learned through firsthand investigations and personal experiences that such ordeals as those of the Jensen family and Martin Jacobs are very real and that the victims are not simply suffering from particularly eerie delusions. The phenomenon known euphemistically as the Men in Black or Brothers of the Shadow is very much like a macabre traveling repertory theater of terror that specializes in multilevel audience participation. Although the characters and stage settings differ in each of these bizarre psychodramas, the basic script remains unchanged.

The important thing to remember if you should be confronted by such entities is not to play their game—and especially do not cast them in the role of villains. If you permit hostility, then that is what you are likely to receive.

In our opinion, the Brothers of the Shadow phenomenon is the manifestation of a single source and is, of itself, neither good nor evil. How these ostensibly menacing figures conduct themselves depends in large part upon the behavior of the human percipient with whom they are interacting. Cry out in fear, and they'll give you good reason to fear them.

We have found ourselves in situations where we were seemingly under attack by bothersome entities that began pounding on the walls, scattering books from shelves, and emitting disgusting odors and irritating sounds. On more than one occasion when we have had enough of such shenanigans, we have commanded the energy to cease and gone back to work without taking further notice of the troublesome activity around us.

Every kind of intelligence, regardless of how high or how low, wants to be recognized. Nothing shuts up any sentient entity faster than being ignored. In each instance, we commanded the poltergeistic force to cease its disruptive activity, and then we refused to go along with its framework of reality, thereby breaking its hold on our own. As a final touch, our change of attitude from passive fear to annoyance to rage had apparently done the trick.

THE MEN IN BLACK AS TRICKSTERS

It may be that since ancient times the so-called Brothers of the Shadow have tried to teach those humans with the requisite awareness that it is possible to command other forces by a sheer effort of will.

Yes, they may threaten, but when confronted by a firm refusal, or—as in our case—defiance, they simply slink away. Sometimes it seems as if these entities are deliberately bullying us into revolt, using childish, annoying methods to get us to stand up and take charge of our own lives.

As we theorized in an earlier work, the Men in Black/Brothers of the Shadow are suggestive of the mythological figure common to all cultures and known generically to ethnologists and anthropologists as the Trickster. The Trickster plays pranks on hapless humans, but often at the same time he is instructing people or transforming aspects of the environment for the good of his human charges.

Most cultures view the Trickster as a supernatural being with the ability to change his shape at will. Although basically very clever and wily, he can at times behave in a very stupid, childish manner, and may often appear to end up as the one who is tricked. The Trickster does not hesitate to lie, cheat, and steal. Often he seems to be the very essence of amoral animalism.

The Trickster figure frequently manifests in the guise of a culture hero. To the Native Americans of the southwest, he appeared as the wily coyote. To the Norse and the Greeks, the Trickster manifested often in the role of a mischievous—but hardly demonic—god.

To our contemporary culture, the Trickster, who is ageless and as old as time, must draw upon the ancient myths and combine them with our emerging fascination with other worlds in order to fashion the figures of wily and amoral extraterrestrial aliens.

We have the ability, however, to exorcise the negative aspects of the Trickster by refusing to play its silly games, thereby allowing us to concentrate on the positive aspects that he can bring to us.

Fire existed before Prometheus brought it to humanity. It was simply the *knowledge* of fire that he offered us. We believe that the abilities of telekinesis, teleportation, and telepathy already exist within us. It is merely the *aware-*

ness of these abilities that the Tricksters are trying to impart by providing us with tantalizing fragments of knowledge. It is up to us to move the pieces around until a pattern begins to form and we can utilize the energy of the *ki*, *manna*, *Holy Spirit*, *X-Force* to make it work.

PARASITES OF THE SOUL

To relate the Men in Black phenomenon in the role of teaching Trickster is not to deny the existence of such truly negative entities as the Ahrimanes, the jinn, or hostile UFO intelligences. As we stated in chapter 2, our planet is under attack. In addition to the aggressive fallen angels listed above, we have found that a great number of alleged alien confrontations have actually been with those beings that we have come to call "spirit parasites": disembodied entities that can seize control of the host body and direct the enslaved human to perform horrible, atrocious deeds.

Dr. Wilson Van Dusen is a university professor who has come to believe that there are entities that can possess the mind and bodies of human beings. Dr. Van Dusen served as chief psychologist at Mendocino State Hospital and as professor of psychology at John F. Kennedy University, Orinda, California. He has published more than 150 scientific papers and several books on his research.

In a landmark research paper, the clinical psychologist noted the striking similarities between the hierarchy of the unseen world described by the Swedish inventor-mystic Emanuel Swedenborg and the alleged hallucinations of his patients in a state mental hospital. He began to seek out those from among the hundreds of chronic schizophrenics, alcoholics, and brain-damaged persons who could distinguish between their own thoughts and the products of their hallucinations.

Dr. Van Dusen would question these other entities directly and instruct the patients to give a word-for-word account of what the voices had said or what was seen. In this way, he could hold long dialogues with a patient's hallucinations and record both his questions and their answers.

On numerous occasions, Dr. Van Dusen found that he was engaged in dialogues with the hallucinations that were above the patient's comprehension. He found this to be especially true when he contacted the higher order of hallucinations, which he discovered to be "symbolically rich beyond the patient's understanding."

Dr. Van Dusen found that the "Other Order" of beings could take over a person's eyes, ears, and voice, just as traditional accounts of demonic possession stated. The entities had totally different personalities from his patients, which indicated to him that they were not simply products of his patients' minds. Some of the beings had ESP and could predict the future.

The demons were described in a variety of shapes and sizes, but most generally appeared in human form. Many of the demons pretended to be space aliens, but any of them could change form in an instant.

Dr. Van Dusen admitted that some of the entities knew far more than he did, even though he tried to test them by looking up obscure academic references. He made detailed studies of about fifteen cases of demonic possession, but he dealt with several thousand patients during his twenty years as a clinical psychologist. In his opinion, the entities were present in every single one of those thousands of patients.

Considering once again some of the implications of Swedenborg's work, Dr. Van Dusen commented (*Psychedelic Review*, Winter 1970–71): "It is curious to reflect that . . . our lives may be the little free space at the confluence of giant higher and lower spiritual hierarchies. There is some kind of lesson in this—man freely poised between good and evil, under the influence of cosmic forces he usually doesn't know exist. Man, thinking he chooses, may be the resultant of other forces."

OUR SYMBIOTIC RELATIONSHIP WITH UFO INTELLIGENCES

As we said earlier, we do not rule out the extraterrestrial hypothesis as an explanation for certain aspects of the UFO enigma, but for many years now, we have leaned toward the theory that the UFO intelligences may be our multidimensional neighbors right around the corner in another space-time continuum.

We also have come to speculate that on occasion those objects that we so blithely label "spaceships" may actually be multidimensional mechanisms employed by our paraphysical neighbors.

And it may not be totally preposterous to suggest that in some instances certain "spaceships" may have been the actual form of the intelligence, rather than vehicles transporting occupants.

We have also become convinced that there exists a subtle kind of symbiotic relationship between us and the paraphysical UFO entities. In some integral way that we have yet to determine, they need us as much as we need them. It may well be that the very physical and spiritual evolution of Earth depends upon our establishing some kind of equilibrium with our cosmic cousins. One of the principal messages relayed by some who state that they have communicated with UFO intelligences is that we must learn to manage our own affairs, discover how to walk in balance on the Earth, and assume responsibility for our species' trespasses before we can join that larger community of intelligences.

THE UFO MAY REFLECT OUR NEED FOR A COHESIVE MYTHIC STRUCTURE

Our late friend Michael Talbot, author of such excellent works as *The Holographic Universe*, once suggested that it was humanity's emotional need for a cohesive mythic structure that, in one sense, generated the UFO phenomenon. We may all be creating UFOs on a collective level in much the same manner as we create dreams on an individual level.

But, Michael warned us, "The belief that we generate UFOs still entails the categories of real and unreal. The belief that reality is plastic or ideational must necessarily transcend this notion as well. In considering UFOs with the idea that we generate *them*, it is implicit that *we* are somehow more real than they. Beyond this myth, beyond real and unreal, lies an absolute elsewhere that is presently being realized by the study of human behavior and quantum mechanic physics."

What Talbot was really telling us, therefore, is that consciousness and reality are a continuum, UFOs are part of our self-reference cosmology, and that all possibilities exist in an indefinite number of universes. The myth that

UFOs are generating us is most assuredly just as valid as the myth that we generate UFOs.

THE ANSWER TO THE UFO MAY BE FOUND IN OUR FUNDAMENTAL MYSTERIES

James W. Moseley founded the Saucer and Unexplained Celestial Events Research Society (S.A.U.C.E.R.S.) in July 1954. After more than forty years of exploring all aspects of the UFO field from "nuts and bolts" spacecraft to other dimensions of reality, Moseley recently stated in one of his newsletters that his current view of the UFO mystery is that it is just one of a vast spectrum of unexplained events that seem unsolvable, "but which should convince us that this Universe is a much more complex place than most people have ever imagined."

Completely abandoning the caustic wit for which he is generally noted, Moseley continued in a philosophical vein, stating that one reason he believes UFO researchers will never solve the mystery is that it is interrelated with the most fundamental mysteries of human life: Where did we come from? Why are we here? Where, if anywhere, do we go next?

Such questions, Moseley acknowledged, may be answered through religious faith, but such puzzlers seem to be well beyond present-day science.

In *Consilience*, Edward O. Wilson, a biologist and firm advocate of the scientific method of seeking knowledge, writes that even though he may have left behind him the rigid piety of his youth, he experienced no desire to purge himself of religious feelings. He recognizes that they "suffused the wellsprings of his creative life" and that humans are "obliged by the deepest drives of the human spirit to make ourselves more than animated dust" and to tell a story about "where we came from and why we are here."

In a later chapter, Wilson acknowledges that for centuries "the writ of empiricism has been spreading into the ancient domain of transcendentalist belief . . . The spirits our ancestors knew intimately fled first the rocks and trees and then the distant mountains. Now they are in the stars, where their final extinction is possible. *But we cannot live without them.* People need a sacred narrative. They must have a sense of larger purpose . . . They will refuse to yield to the despair of animal mortality . . . They will find a way to keep the ancestral spirits alive."

THE UFO EXPERIENCE AS INDIVIDUAL MYSTICAL EXPRESSION

As serious researchers of both paranormal and UFO mysteries, we often find ourselves wondering if sighting a spaceship, making contact with alien beings, and the communication or abduction scenario that often results might not really be a twenty-first century evolution of the individual mystical experience.

The January 12, 1994, issue of *USA Today* presents the results of a survey conducted by Jeffrey S. Levin, associate professor at Eastern Virginia Medical School, Norfolk, which states that more than two-thirds of the U.S. population has undergone at least one mystical experience. Furthermore, Levin notes that while only 5 percent of the populace have such experiences often, "they seem

to be getting more common with each successive generation." And interestingly, those individuals who are active
in church or synagogue report *fewer* mystical experiences
than those in the general population.

In November 1997, a team of neuroscientists from the
University of California at San Diego announced to the
media that they believed they had discovered a "God
module" in the human brain that could be responsible for
humankind's evolutionary instinct to believe in religious
concepts. Admitting that such conclusions are preliminary, the scientists said that their initial results suggest that
the phenomenon of religious belief is "hard-wired" into
the human brain.

Evolutionists have theorized that belief in God, a common trait found in human societies around the planet and
throughout history, may be built into the brain's complex
electrical circuitry as a Darwinian adaptation to encourage
cooperation between individuals. Dr. Vilayanur Ramachan-
dran, head of the research team, speculated that if the existence of a "God module" can be established, then it might
suggest that people who are atheists may have a differently
configured neural circuit.

In the *Journal of Nervous and Mental Disease*, psychia-
trists Colin Ross of Dallas and Shaun Joshi of Winnipeg af-
firm, "Paranormal experiences are so common in the general
population that no theory of normal psychology which does
not take them into account can be comprehensive."

It may well be that we are turning into a nation of
mystics.

Some years ago, we had the opportunity to ask the brilliant and insightful Dr. Walter Houston Clark, professor
emeritus of Andover Theological Seminary, why he felt that

the individual mystical experience was becoming more respectable in the United States.

"I think the best explanation is the obvious starvation of man's nonrational needs over many decades," Dr. Clark replied. "Materialism, competition, power politics, and human exploitation can be endured only so long before they begin to make nonsense to sensitive natures jaded by the persistent denial of their essential longing—the longing for a living God and a vital religious experience. Just as a spiritual and artistic awakening suddenly emerged out of darkness in the twelfth century, so is a similar awakening occurring today."

In Dr. Clark's opinion, mystical sensitivity leads to a greatly lessened emphasis on external and material values in exchange for a strengthened valuing of the nonrational and a heightened compassion with its concern for others and for nature.

"On the basis of the knowledge of, and respect for, the mystical consciousness, which has been growing on me now for fifty years," Dr. Clark said, "I fully agree with William James's statement in his *Varieties of Religious Experience* to the effect that personal religion has its origin in the mystical consciousness. Succinctly, James expressed my position for me when he wrote in a letter to a friend: 'The mother sea and fountainhead of all religions lie in the mystical experience of the individual, taking the word mystical in a very wide sense. All theologies and all ecclesiasticisms are secondary growths superimposed.' "

Are we, then, becoming a nation of mystics?

Are we seeing more UFOs and having more paranormal experiences in answer to some basic human need within us?

Did the UFO odyssey originate in the human psyche and return us to our genesis as a species?

"I believe that all people are potential mystics, just as each one of us is a potential poet, artist, or ecstatic," Dr. Clark told us. "This hunger for the expression of the non-rational is sleeping within all of us. It goes beyond those valid needs of food, clothing, and shelter that keep our bodies alive. Nonrational and intangible values keep us alive by giving meaning to life—and whether consciously or unconsciously and though suppressed by the priority of material needs in our society, a sensitivity to them always has the possibility of being awakened by the proper stimuli. The longer this sensitivity is neglected or starved, the more spontaneously and forcefully it is expressed when it surfaces."

As part of the transformative process now under way, certain ancient archetypes are being reactivated and new archetypes are emerging. Once, in a conversation, Dr. Jean Houston compared the situation with an image from William James: "James said we are like dogs and cats who inhabit our drawing rooms. You know, happy and thinking about the food and the nap and going bye-bye, but having no idea at all of the intricate and fascinating goings-on around the house or what's in the master's bookcases. I think that's our level of reality. We have a very, very tiny notion of what is reality."

To suggest, as we have, that the UFO is a living mythological symbol does not diminish its reality in an objective, physical sense. Indeed, the UFO and the intelligence it represents may ultimately be more real than the transitory realities of computers, the Internet, associations, political parties, trade balances, or industrial averages.

And one day, if we truly are developing heightened mystical awareness, we may be able to see the UFO intelligences

as they really are, free of all psychological mechanisms and
telepathic projections. It may be at that time that we will
discover that the goal of our collective odyssey has been to
regain our lost paradise as spiritual beings and to achieve
our destiny as a transitional species between ape and angel,
between earth and stars.

References and Resources

1. CHARTING THE UFO ODYSSEY

Books

Binder, Otto. *What We Really Know About Flying Saucers*. New York: Fawcett, 1967.

Edwards, Frank. *Flying Saucers—Serious Business*. New York: Lyle Stuart, 1966.

Fawcett, Lawrence, and Barry J. Greenwood. *Clear Intent: The Government Coverup of the UFO Experience*. Englewood Cliffs, N.J.: Prentice-Hall, 1984.

Randle, Kevin D. *The Randle Report: UFOs in the '90s*. New York: M. Evans and Company, 1997.

2. EARTH UNDER ATTACK

Notes

1. Rense, Jeff. "The Battle of Los Angeles." Posted on *Sightings* website.
2. Manchester, New Hampshire, *Sunday News*. January 24, 1965.
3. Ibid.

4. Steiger, Brad, ed. *Project Bluebook*. New York: Con-Fucian Press/Ballantine, 1976.

5. Timmerman, John. J. Allen Hynek Center for UFO Studies. CNI News. Posted on *Sightings* website, November 5, 1997.

6. *News Europa*. January 1, 1959.

7. Filer, George A. MUFON *Skywatch* Investigations, "Filer's Files" #2–1998.

8. Steiger, Brad, and Joan Whritenour. *Flying Saucers Are Hostile!* New York/London: Award/Tandem, 1967.

9. Munoz, Carlos. *Agrupación de Investigaciones Onviologicas (AION)*. February 1997.

10. *La Razón,* Buenos Aires, June 3–4, 1968. See also *Flying Saucer Invasion: Target Earth* by Brad Steiger and Joan Whritenour, New York/London: Award/Tandem, 1969.

11. Swartz, Tim. "In Australia, Strange Things Are Happening." *UFO Universe* (Winter 1998).

Books

Condon, Edward U. (project director). *The Scientific Study of Unidentified Flying Objects*. New York: Bantam Books, 1969.

Erskine, Allen Louis. *Why Are They Watching Us?* New York: Tower, 1967.

Fuller, John. *Aliens in the Sky*. New York: Putnam/Berkley, 1969.

Good, Timothy. *Above Top Secret—The Worldwide UFO Coverup*. New York: William Morrow, 1988.

Hamilton, William F. *Cosmic Top Secret*. New Brunswick, N.J.: Inner Light, 1991.

Ruppelt, Edward J. *The Report on Unidentified Flying Objects*. New York: Doubleday, 1956.

Sagan, Carl, and Thorton Page. *UFOs—A Scientific Debate*. Ithaca/London: Cornell University Press, 1972.

Saunders, David R., and R. Roger Harkins. *UFOs? Yes! Where the Condon Committee Went Wrong*. New York: New American Library, 1958.

Steiger, Brad. *Strangers from the Skies*. New York: Award, 1966.

Periodicals

Beckley, Timothy Green, and Harold Salkin. "Apollo 12's Mysterious Encounters with Flying Saucers." *Saga* (May 1970).

Binder, Otto O. "Eleven Scientists Prove UFOs Are Real." *Saga* (May 1969).

Hewes, Hayden C. "UFOs After 30 Years." *New Realities* (June 1977).

Huneeus, Antonio. "An Alien–U.S. Government Liaison— A Matter Above Top Secret." *UFO Universe* (January 1990).

Keel, John A. "The Secret UFO-Astronaut War." *Men* (September 1968).

Steiger, Brad. "Flying Saucers on the Attack." *Saga* (September 1967).

3. THE CASE FOR EXTRATERRESTRIAL INVADERS

Notes

1. Posted in *UFO Roundup*, Vol. 3, No. 3., Joseph Trainor, editor, January 18, 1998. Credit: CNI news editor Michael Lindemann and contributor James Sutton.

2. Willms, Judith. "Close Encounters Update." *UFO Universe* (Fall 1992).

3. Ibid.

4. Friedman, Stanton T. *Top Secret/Majic*. New York: Marlowe and Company, 1996.

5. Randle, Kevin D., and Donald R. Schmitt. *The Truth About the UFO Crash at Roswell*. New York: M. Evans, 1994.

6. Randle, Kevin. "An Alien Survived the Roswell Crash." *UFO Universe* (Fall 1993).

7. Steiger, Brad, ed. *Project Bluebook*. New York: Con-Fucian Press/Ballantine, 1976.

8. Ibid.

9. Ibid.

10. Ibid.

11. "Eyewitness to the UFO Case More Substantial Than Roswell," *The Hierononymous & Co. Newsletter*, Issue 12–13 (1997).

12. Ibid.

13. The first account of this remarkable case was published in the Brazilian magazine *O Cruzeiro* in 1958. Dr. Olvao Fontes, one of the original investigators of the incident, later sent transcripts of the initial declaration made by Antonio Villas Boas on February 22, 1958, to Gorden Creighton, who translated the story for Great Britain's *Flying Saucer Review* in 1965. The case was also included in *The Humanoids*, Charles Bowen, editor (Chicago: Henry Regnery, 1969).

14. Pontillo, James. "Demons, Doctors, and Aliens." *INFO Occasional Paper #2* (March 1993).

Books

Bryant, Alice, and Linda Seeback. *Healing Shattered Reality—Understanding Contactee Trauma*. Tigard, Oreg. Wild Flower Press, 1991.

Corso, Col. Philip J. *The Day After Roswell.* New York: Pocket Books, 1997.

Craft, Michael. *Alien Impact.* New York: St. Martin's Press, 1996.

Crystal, Ellen. *Silent Invasion.* New York: Paragon House, 1991.

Hopkins, Budd. *Witnessed—The True Story of the Brooklyn Bridge UFO Abductions.* New York: Pocket Books, 1996.

Kanon, Gregory M. *The Great UFO Hoax.* Lakeville, Minn.: Galde Press, 1997.

Keyhoe, Donald E. *Flying Saucers from Outer Space.* New York: Henry Holt, 1953.

Palmer, Raymond A. *The Real UFO Invasion.* San Diego: Greenleaf, 1967.

Randle, Kevin D. *A History of UFO Crashes.* New York: Avon Books, 1995.

————. *Roswell Crash Update: Exposing the Military Coverup of the Century.* New Brunswick, N.J.: Global Communications, 1995.

————. *Conspiracy of Silence.* New York: Avon Books, 1997.

Steiger, Brad. *The Gods of Aquarius: UFOs and the Transformation of Man.* New York: Harcourt Brace Jovanovich, 1976.

Sutherly, Curt. *Strange Encounters.* St. Paul: Llewellyn Publications, 1996.

Warren, Larry, and Peter Robbins. *Left at East Gate.* New York: Marlowe & Co., 1996.

Periodicals
Binder, Otto O. "Flying Saucer Mother Ships." *Saga* (December 1968).

Bird, Elizabeth. "Invasions of the Mind Snatchers." *Psychology Today* (April 1989).

Hamilton, William. "Aliens in Dreamland." *UFO Universe* (July 1990).

Keel, John A. "UFOs and the Mysterious Wave of Worldwide Kidnappings." *Saga* (December 1970).

Loftus, Elizabeth F. "Creating False Memories." *Scientific American* (September 1997).

Sanderson, Ivan T. "Visitors from Outer Space." *Argosy* (February 1969).

Steiger, Brad, and Sherry Hansen Steiger. "UFOs: Friend or Foe?" *UFO Universe* (October/November 1991).

4. THE SORCERERS' TRIUMPH

Notes

1. Charles Mackay's *Extraordinary Popular Delusions and the Madness of Crowds*, originally published in 1852, includes the basis for this story in his section on "Alchymists." This book may be found in libraries or perhaps has been reprinted in a more contemporary edition.

2. *Republican,* Algona, Iowa, April 7, 1897.

3. *The Evening Times,* Pawtucket, Rhode Island, April 17, 1897.

4. *The Post,* Houston, Texas, April 22, 1897.

5. *Modern News,* Harrisburg, Arkansas, April 23, 1897.

6. *The Post,* Houston, Texas, April 24, 1897.

7. *The Mail,* Cardiff, Wales, May 18, 1909.

8. *The Gazette,* Little Rock, Arkansas, December 13, 1909.

For additional information about the work of Richard Hoagland, write to The Enterprise Mission, P. O. Box 1130, Placitas, NM 87043.

If you are interested in the latest word about global conspiracies from the evangelical Christian perspective, write for Texe Marrs's *Flashpoint*, Living Truth Ministries, 1708 Patterson Road, Austin, TX 78733.

Books

Anderson, Ken. *Hitler and the Occult.* Amherst, N.Y.: Prometheus Books, 1995.

Commander X. *The Ultimate Deception.* New Brunswick, N.J.: Inner Light, 1992.

Daraul, Arkon. *A History of Secret Societies.* New York: Citadel Press, 1962.

Hayakawa, Norio F. *UFOs—The Grand Deception and the Coming New World Order.* New Brunswick, N.J.: Civilian Intelligence Network/Inner Light, 1993.

Steiger, Brad. *Mysteries of Time and Space.* Englewood Cliffs, N.J.: Prentice-Hall, 1974.

Vallee, Jacques. *Messengers of Deception.* New York: Bantam Books, 1980.

Wilgus, Neal. *The Illuminoids.* New York: Pocket Books, 1978.

5. UFO MYSTERIES UNDERSEA AND UNDERGROUND

Notes
1. From a personal interview with Ray Palmer, January–February 1968.
2. Ibid.

3. Field, Ben. *UFO Updates.* Toronto, January 14, 1998. Posted on *Sightings* website.

4. Wilkins, Harold T. *Flying Saucers Uncensored.* New York: Citadel Press, 1955.

5. *News and Sun-Sentinel,* Ft. Lauderdale, Florida, January 20, 1969.

Books

Barker, Gray. *They Knew Too Much About Flying Saucers.* New Brunswick, N.J.: Inner Light, 1992.

Beckley, Timothy Green. *Subterranean Worlds.* New Brunswick, N.J.: Inner Light, 1992.

Commander X. *Underground Alien Bases.* New Brunswick, N.J.: Inner Light, 1991.

Evans, Hilary. *Visions, Apparitions, Alien Visitors.* Wellingborough, Northamptonshire: Aquarian Press, 1984.

Keel, John A. *Strange Creatures from Time and Space.* New York: Fawcett, 1970.

Roerich, Nicholas. *Shambala.* New York: Frederick A. Stokes Co., 1930.

Steiger, Brad. *Atlantis Rising.* New York: Dell, 1973.

Periodicals

Binder, Otto O., and Joan Whritenour. "Underground Network of UFO Bases." *Saga* (November 1969).

Imbrogno, Phil. "UFO Power Stations." *UFO Universe* (October/November 1991).

Keel, John A. "Secret UFO Bases Across the U.S." *Saga* (April 1968).

Sanderson, Ivan T. "Mysterious Salt Water Bases." *Saga* (June 1971).

6. MERRY PRANKSTERS FROM THE MAGIC THEATER

Books

Barclay, David. *Aliens—The Final Answer?* London: Blandford Books, 1995.

Beckley, Timothy Green. *The American Indian UFO-Starseed Connection.* New Brunswick, N.J.: Inner Light, 1992.

Clark, Jerome, and Loren Coleman. *The Unidentified.* New York: Warner Paperback Library, 1975.

Lorenzen, Coral and Jim. *Encounters with UFO Occupants.* New York: Berkley, 1976.

Steiger, Brad. *Alien Meetings.* New York: Grosset & Dunlap, 1978.

————. *The UFO Abductors.* New York: Berkley, 1988.

Streiber, Whitley. *Communion.* New York: Beech Tree/William Morrow, 1987.

7. FROM HEAVEN ABOVE TO EARTH BELOW

Notes

1. Porteous, Skip. *Freedom Writer Press Release.* Posted on the *Sightings* website.
2. From *The Steiger Questionnaire of Paranormal, Mystical, and UFO Experiences.*
3. Personal correspondence, June 1996.
4. Personal response to questionnaire.
5. Drake, Raymond. *Gods and Spacemen in Greece and Rome.* New York: Signet Books, 1976.
6. Personal correspondence.
7. Constable, Trevor James. *The Cosmic Pulse of Life.* Santa Ana, Calif.: Merlin Press, 1976.

8. Ibid.
9. Ibid.
10. Ibid.

Books

Adamski, George. *Behind the Flying Saucer Mystery (Flying Saucers Farewell)*. New York: Paperback Library, 1967.

Downing, Barry H. *The Bible and Flying Saucers*. New York: Avon, 1970.

Fry, Daniel. *To Men of Earth*. Elsinore, Calif.: El Cariso, 1973.

Menger, Howard. *From Outer Space to You*. New York: Pyramid, 1967.

Steiger, Brad. *The Fellowship*. New York: Doubleday, 1988; Ballantine, 1989.

Steiger, Brad, and Sherry Hansen Steiger. *Starborn*. New York: Berkley, 1992.

————. *Angels around the World*. New York: Fawcett Columbine, 1996.

8. SUPERSCIENTISTS FROM THE STARS

Books

Drake, W. Raymond. *Gods and Spacemen in the Ancient West*. New York: New American Library, 1974.

Ginsburgh, Irwin. *First Man, Then Adam!* New York: Pocket Books, 1978.

Gladden, Lee, and Vivianne Cervantes Gladden. *Heirs of the Gods*. New York: Rawson, Wade, 1978.

Greene, Vaughan M. *Astronauts of Ancient Japan*. Millbrae, Calif.: Merlin Engine Works, 1978.

Sitchin, Zecharia. *The 12th Planet*. New York: Avon, 1978.

Trench, Brinsley Le Poer. *The Flying Saucer Story*. New York: Ace, 1966.

9. TRAVELERS THROUGH TIME AND SPACE

Notes

1. Sir Victor Goddard, air marshal in the Royal Air Force, in a speech to British UFO researchers in May 1969.

2. Keel, John A. *Strange Creatures from Time and Space*. New York: Fawcett, 1970.

3. Kerska, Joseph. *Fate* (January 1961).

4. Golding, Miriam. "I Was Lost in the Fourth Dimension." *Fate* (September 1956).

5. Macklin, John. *Orbits of the Unknown*. New York: Ace, 1968.

6. Schurmacher, Emile. *More Strange Unsolved Mysteries*. New York: Ace, 1970.

7. Robin McPherson of Burnaby, British Columbia, was a popular channeler of material from the Space Brothers in the late 1960s.

8. Aleuti Francesca remains active on the lecture circuit. She may be contacted directly by writing to her at the Solar Light Center, 7700 Avenue of the Sun, White City, OR 97503.

9. Davenport, Marc. *Visitors from Time: The Secret of the UFOs*. Tuscaloosa, Ala.: Greenleaf Publications, 1992, 1994.

10. Goldberg, Bruce. *Time Travelers from Our Future: An Explanation for Alien Abductions*. St. Paul, Minn.: Llewellyn Publications, 1998.

11. Ibid.
12. Keel, op. cit.

Books

Beckley, Timothy Green. *The UFO Silencers*. New Brunswick, N.J.: Inner Light, 1990.

Keel, John A. *Our Haunted Planet*. New York: Fawcett, 1971.

————. *The Mothman Prophecies*. New York: Saturday Review Press, 1975.

FOR ADDITIONAL STUDY

Books

Asimov, Isaac. *Is Anyone There?* New York: Ace Books, 1967.

Binder, Otto O. *Flying Saucers Are Watching Us*. New York: Tower, 1968.

Clarke, Arthur C. *Voices from the Sky*. New York: Harper and Row, 1965.

Fry, Daniel. *The White Sands Incident*. Madison, Wis.: Horus House, 1992.

Fuller, John. *Incident at Exeter*. New York: G. P. Putnam, 1966.

Goldsen, Joseph M., ed. *Outer Space in World Politics*. New York: Frederick A. Praeger, 1963.

Good, Timothy. *The UFO Report*. New York: Avon, 1989.

Hynek, J. Allen, and Jacques Vallee. *The Edge of Reality*. Chicago: Henry Regnery, 1975.

Jung, C. G. *Flying Saucers: A Modern Myth of Things Seen in the Sky*. New York: New American Library, 1967.

Michel, Aime. *The Truth about Flying Saucers*. New York: Pyramid, 1967.

Rimmer, John. *The Evidence for Alien Abductions*. Wellingborough, Northamptonshire: Aquarian Press, 1984.

Shklovskii, I. S., and Carl Sagan. *Intelligent Life in the Universe*. New York: Dell, 1968.

Steiger, Brad, and Hayden Hewes. *Inside Heaven's Gate*. New York: Signet, 1997.

Velikovsky, Immanuel. *Worlds in Collision*. New York: Dell, 1967.

Walton, Travis. *The Walton Experience*. New York: Berkley, 1978.

Watkins, Leslie. *Alternative 3*. London: Sphere, 1978.

Woodrew, Greta. *On a Slide of Light*. New York: Macmillan, 1981.

Periodicals

Binder, Otto O. "Is Shooting Humanoids Murder?" *Saga* (September 1968).

Bulantsev, Sergei. "Russia's Most Bizarre Unsolved UFO Cases." *UFO Universe* (October/November 1991).

Gaddis, Vincent. "Are Flying Saucers Really Creatures That Live in Outer Space?" *True* (August 1967).

Huneeus, Antonio. "Spain's Non-Stop UFO Invasion Has Begun," *Unsolved UFO Sightings*, Vol. 1, No. 2 (1993).

Keel, John A. "UFO Agents of Terror." *Saga* (October 1967).

Lasco, Jack. "Has U.S. Captured a Flying Saucer?" *Saga* (April 1967).

Phelan, James S. "Looking for the Next World." *New York Times Magazine* (February 29, 1976).

Schurmacher, Emile G. "Mexico's Phantom Flying Saucers." *Saga* (November 1972).

Steiger, Brad. "Flying Saucers Scorch Iowa Farms." *Male* (April 1971).

Steiger, Brad, and Sherry Hansen Steiger. "Beware the Tricksters from Outer Space." *UFO Universe* (Fall 1993).

———. "The Incredible Ancient Astronauts of Peru," *Unsolved UFO Sightings,* Vol. 1, No. 2 (1993).

If you would like to receive a copy of *The Steiger Questionnaire of Paranormal, Mystical, and UFO Experiences,* send a stamped, self-addressed envelope to Timewalker Productions, P. O. Box 434, Forest City, IA 50436.

If you liked UFO Odyssey, *don't miss*
the exciting Alien Contact trilogy
by Jacques Vallee that begins with

Dimensions

A Casebook of Alien Contact

Throughout the modern UFO era, thousands of honest scientists and informed laymen have seen through the official denials, the suppressions, and the whitewash—and realized that, indeed, we are not alone.

To them author Jacques Vallee, the world's most renowned UFO expert, presents a tantalizing question: What if these alien visitors are not from other planets? What if they have always been among us, living on earth for centuries, perhaps from the beginning of time? What if they inhabit another dimension, a dimension startlingly different from our own?

Get a little closer to the unknown in the
thrilling sequel to the bestseller
Dimensions . . .

Confrontations

A Scientist's Search for Alien Contact

Dr. Jacques Vallee sweeps readers into the very real world of UFO sightings, contact, and in some instances abduction and human injury.

Going far beyond theoretical analysis, Dr. Vallee meticulously documents his own firsthand investigations into sightings around the world. *Confrontations* presents eyewitness accounts and case studies from the United States, Europe, and South America, where Dr. Vallee has personally investigated claims of UFO sightings and close, occasionally deadly, encounters. Complete with maps, sketches, diagrams, and on-the-spot photographs, this study serves up a riveting, spine-chilling view of the UFO phenomenon—a phenomenon that has been viewed for too long by too many as benign.

*Part scientific detective story,
part experiment in truth seeking,
here's Jacques Vallee's controversial finale
to his trilogy . . .*

Revelations

Alien Contact and Human Deception

Focusing in depth on cases reported in the United States and throughout the world, Dr. Vallee analyzes the full gamut of sensational UFO "incidents," from the alleged history of saucer "crashes" and the retrieval of aliens by the U.S. government to reports of a subterranean community of hostile humanoids in the American Southwest. In the process, he reveals that some of the most remarkable sightings are actually complex, carefully engineered hoaxes.

*The true story of a profound confrontation,
simultaneously as human and as unearthly
as one can conceive. . . .*

Intruders

The Incredible Visitations at Copley Woods
by Bud Hopkins

The UFO phenomenon is real. But no aspect is as
controversial—or as dramatic—as accounts of tem-
porary abduction of human beings onto UFOs.

The most important abduction in this long, bizarre
history took place during a dark summer night in
1983, in an ordinary rural area outside Indianapolis.
It began when Kathie Davis was floated out of her
room as she slept, then subjected to a physical examination inside a UFO.

Yet the ultimate meaning of that experience only came
to light months later when Kathie recalled—under
hypnosis, with solid corroboration by specialists and
by hundreds of other victims all over the country—
details of what followed the examination . . . .